The Norton Mix

COMPOSITION

W · W · NORTON & COMPANY · *New York · London*

The Norton Mix

COMPOSITION

A CUSTOM PUBLICATION

Food Writing

A Readymade Mix

W. W. Norton & Company has been independent since its founding in 1923, when William Warder Norton and Mary D. Herter Norton first published lectures delivered at the People's Institute, the adult education division of New York City's Cooper Union. The fi rm soon expanded its program beyond the Institute, publishing books by celebrated academics from America and abroad. By mid-century, the two major pillars of Norton's publishing program—trade books and college texts—were firmly established. In the 1950s, the Norton family transferred control of the company to its employees, and today—with a staff of four hundred and a comparable number of trade, college, and professional titles published each year— W. W. Norton & Company stands as the largest and oldest publishing house owned wholly by its employees.

Editor: Katie Hannah
Developmental editors: Mike Fleming, Erin Granville
Managing editor: Marian Johnson
Project editor: Melissa Atkin
Assistant editor: Erica Wnek
Editorial assistant: Sophie Hagen, Elizabeth Dana
Production managers: Eric Pier-Hocking, Ashley Horna, and Diana Spiegle
Permissions editor: Nancy Rodwan
Photo permissions editor: Trish Marx, Stephanie Romeo
Designer: Toni Krass
Cover designs: Debra Morton-Hoyt
Emedia editor: Eileen Connell
Marketing manager: Lib Triplett
Proofreaders: Paulette McGee, Ben Reynolds
Composition: LSC Communications, Inc.
Manufacturing: LSC Communications, Inc.

ISBN 978-0-393-65823-1

W. W. Norton & Company, Inc., 500 Fifth Avenue, New York, N.Y. 10110
www.wwnorton.com
W. W. Norton & Company Ltd., Castle House, 75/76 Wells Street, London W1T 3QT

GENERAL EDITORS

ELIZABETH RODRIGUEZ KESSLER
COORDINATING EDITOR
University of Houston

JEFFREY ANDELORA
Mesa Community College

MELISSA GOLDTHWAITE
St. Joseph's University

CHARLES HOOD
Antelope Valley College

KATHARINE N. INGS
Manchester College

ANGELA L. JONES
Western Kentucky University

CHRISTOPHER KELLER
University of Texas–Pan American

WITH CONTRIBUTIONS FROM

CEDRIC BURROWS
University of Kansas

LORI CHASTAINE
Boise State University

MICHELLE L. CHESTER
Towson University

DENNIS McGLOTHIN
*University of North Carolina
at Pembroke*

WANDA FRIES
Somerset Community College

HOLLY HASSEL
*University of Wisconsin–
Marathon County*

BETH DINATALE JOHNSON
Ursuline College

CONTENTS

MELISSA A. GOLDTHWAITE { *Food Writing*

WHAT IS FOOD WRITING?

MEMORY, AGRICULTURE, PLEASURE, INDUSTRY, HUNGER, advocacy, illness, culture, comfort, nutrition, economy—these are just a few of the topics associated with what has come to be known as "food writing," a descriptor applied to many kinds of writing about food. In the introduction to her anthology *American Food Writing*, Molly O'Neill observes that "a good piece of food writing is never just about the food; it is, among other things, about place and time, desire and satiety, the longing for home and the lure of the wider world" (xxi–xxii). O'Neill recognizes the tensions and conflicts seemingly inherent in food writing, explaining, "In a good piece of food writing, dozens of other tensions skittle just beneath the surface of these basic conflicts: the civilized competes with the wild, the idiosyncratic tugs at convention, self-control campaigns to squelch self-indulgence" (xxii). Food writing can be about humans, animals, land, work, or leisure. No matter what your experience—from taking photos of particular dishes to trying to avoid specific foods—you have some relationship to food and can write about it.

Like nature writing, sports writing, and travel writing, food writing is not limited to a specific genre; rather, it is topical. Food writing encompasses many forms and GENRES—cookbooks, MEMOIR, fiction, poetry, journalism, BLOGS, restaurant reviews, screenplays, and more. Even if you don't consider yourself a connoisseur of food writing, you're likely familiar with the names of television personalities and cookbook writers such as Julia Child, Anthony Bourdain, or Paula Deen; essayists such as M. F. K. Fisher or Laurie Colwin; or food journalists such as Michael Pollan or Mark Bittman. You may have read books or seen films that contain writing about food: *Heartburn*,

1

*Like Water for Chocolate, Fried Green Tomatoes, Big Night, Julie &
Julia*—to name just a few. Whether you look up recipes online, read a
blog about cheese, or check out restaurant reviews before you dine
out, food writing is likely already a part of your life.

READING ABOUT FOOD

Because everyone eats and most people spend at least part of every
day thinking about food—whether planning what or where to eat,
purchasing food, trying to avoid specific foods or savoring them—the
AUDIENCE for food writing is broad. Still, as you read, think about who
might be the target audience for particular pieces. Beyond the obvious (a vegan will likely not be a regular reader of a blog about bacon),
writers often provide subtle cues for who might be an ideal audience
for their work. For example, Michael Pollan gears his essay "An Animal's Place" not just to those trying to decide whether to eat meat but,
more broadly, to those willing to consider ethical practices related to
raising, killing, purchasing, and eating meat. That is, he does not want
his audience to stop at a simple "yes" or "no" answer to eating meat. At
times, the audience for a particular piece is not immediately obvious.
At first, Ann Hodgman's "No Wonder They Call Me a Bitch" might
seem to be addressed to dog owners, but anyone who is open to
considering the relationship between advertising and the reality of
taste and ingredients will find something of interest in this humorous
piece.

In addition to AUDIENCE, consider the writer's purpose while you are
reading. PURPOSE varies greatly in food writing—from informing readers about questionable practices common in the food industry, as Eric
Schlosser does in "Why McDonald's French Fries Taste So Good,"
to providing directions for how to make a particular dish, as Laurie
Colwin does in "How to Fry Chicken"; or from providing guidelines
for eating responsibly, as Wendell Berry does in "The Pleasures of
Eating," to showing the value of family traditions, as Teresa Lust
does in "The Same Old Stuffing."

A writer's sense of both audience and purpose often helps determine TONE and ETHOS. For example, if a writer's purpose is to enter-

2

tain readers and show the immediate pleasures of eating junk food—as Jill McCorkle does in "Her Chee-to Heart"—a lighthearted tone marked by RHETORICAL QUESTIONS, associational TRANSITIONS, and playful references to brand-name products works well. If, however, a writer wishes to persuade readers of the dangers of immigrants assimilating to certain food practices popular in America—as Juana Mora does in "Acculturation Is Bad for Our Health: Less Fast Food, More *Nopalitos*"—a more serious tone and the use of citations of scientific and sociological studies are appropriate.

As you are reading, also be attentive to any visual images that might be included. For example, food blogs almost always include photographs or other images. (Check out betterwithbutter.com for a good example of the importance of visuals.) Sometimes food writers use visuals such as photos or video clips—especially when sharing recipes—to illustrate different stages in the process of making a dish or to show what the final product should look like. Often, the images create an atmosphere—reinforcing the author's STYLE or TONE. Note the effect of particular images and how that effect is achieved. Are the images close-ups that show texture? Are they taken from a distance to show a particular environment—such as an elaborately set table, or perhaps an outdoor picnic table with a wooden fence in the background? To what is your eye drawn in the photograph? Are parts of the image blurred and other parts in focus? What colors and textures are prominent? Think about how the image supports the written word.

WRITING ABOUT FOOD

After reading different genres of food writing, you may feel inspired to write about food. Like the authors whose work you have read, you can combine different rhetorical methods of development. Some of the most popular methods of development in food writing include DESCRIPTION, NARRATIVE, ARGUMENT, COMPARISON AND CONTRAST, and PROCESS ANALYSIS. The methods of development you use depend largely on the GENRE you choose. If you are writing a food MEMOIR—like Marcus Samuelsson's "My African Mother"—you will likely use narrative, description, and REFLECTION. If you're sharing a recipe or teaching someone to prepare a particular dish or meal, you will likely use a mix of description and process analysis. If you are making an argument about the effects of eating certain foods, you will be attentive to CAUSE AND EFFECT and will include appropriate EVIDENCE to support your THESIS statement.

The best food writing contains sensory details: attention to smells, tastes, textures, colors, shapes, and sounds. Through IMAGES, this kind of writing allows readers to share the writer's experience imaginatively. Such writing does not always need to praise the food or show how good it is. For example, Ann Hodgman, in "No Wonder They Call Me a Bitch," uses sensory images to describe the differences between different types of Cycle dog food. The type for puppies is "wet and soyish," while the type for adult dogs "glistens nastily with fat" and is "a little like some canned Swedish meatballs" (3). Note the way Hodgman's words suggest texture and taste, even as she provides visual cues.

One of the hallmarks of bad food writing is the overuse of general adjectives such as "good," "bad," "delicious," "nice," "beautiful," "tasty," and "perfect." General adjectives, such as those listed above, do not give readers enough information. If you find yourself using general adjectives or abstractions, ask yourself what makes the food you are describing "delicious" or "perfect" or "unappetizing." In "Food Is Good," Anthony Bourdain describes his first experience eating vichyssoise, remembering "the way our waiter ladled it from a silver tureen into my bowl, the crunch of tiny chopped chives he spooned on as garnish, the rich, creamy taste of leek and potato, the pleasurable shock, the surprise that it was cold" (9–10). Note the way Bourdain describes the way the soup was served, the different textures of ingredients, and what surprised him (the temperature of the soup). METAPHORS and other forms of comparison can also help with specific description. In "How to Fry Chicken," Colwin describes the kind of fried chicken she does not like: "crisp little baby shoes or hockey pucks turned out by electric frying machines with names such as 'Little Fry Guy'" (29). As you read food writing you admire, try to figure out *why* and *how* it works so you can use similar strategies in your own writing.

Whether you are writing memoir, poetry, or arguments about food, never underestimate the importance of both experience and RESEARCH (reading books and doing interviews). If you are making an argument, sharing your personal experience can help establish your ethos. If you're writing about a dish you remember from your childhood, asking for the recipe is a form of research. Knowing the specific ingredients and how the dish was prepared will help you add detail to your writing.

Finally, images can add an extra and welcome dimension to food writing. Although some critics dismiss stylized photos that make food look particularly appetizing as "food porn," others recognize the ways images can draw readers in and support effective writing. If you do use images—ones you haven't taken or created yourself—be sure that you have permission to use such images and that you credit the creator, especially if you will be posting them online or in another public forum. Creativecommons.org provides guidelines and a search function so that you can find Creative Commons works to include without a fee.

WORKS CITED

Bourdain, Anthony. "Food Is Good." *Kitchen Confidential.* New York: Bloomsbury, 2000. Print.

Colwin, Laurie. "How to Fry Chicken." *Home Cooking: A Writer in the Kitchen.* New York: HarperCollins, 1988. 29–32. Print.

Hodgman, Ann. "No Wonder They Call Me a Bitch." *Spy* magazine, June 1989. 114–115. Print.

O'Neill, Molly. *American Food Writing.* New York: Library of America, 2007. Print.

Food and Ethics

RACHEL CARSON { *A Fable for Tomorrow*

RACHEL CARSON (1907–1964) was born in Springdale, Pennsylvania, where her mother instilled in her a love of nature. As a writer, she expressed this love first in works about the sea: *Under the Sea Wind* (1941), *The Sea Around Us* (1952), and *The Edge of the Sea* (1955). Turning her attention to the synthetic chemicals being produced by the government as well as by the chemical industry, she began investigating the use of agricultural pesticides. Her discoveries resulted in her seminal work, *Silent Spring* (1962), which challenged the short-sightedness of scientists and the government, and is widely acknowledged to have launched the contemporary environmental movement.

The selection reprinted here is the first chapter of *Silent Spring*, in which Carson describes a town suddenly made desolate by the mysterious loss of animals, birds, fish, and even humans. She captures the attention of the reader with this apocalyptic view of mysterious environmental degradation. However, rather than give the audience a quick solution to that mystery, she ends the first chapter with a rhetorical question to pull the reader into the text.

———

THERE WAS ONCE A TOWN in the heart of America where all life seemed to live in harmony with its surroundings. The town lay in the midst of a checkerboard of prosperous farms, with fields of grain and hillsides of orchards where, in spring, white clouds of bloom drifted above the green fields. In autumn, oak and maple and birch set up a blaze of color that flamed and flickered across a backdrop of pines.

Then foxes barked in the hills and deer silently crossed the fields, half hidden in the mists of the fall mornings.

Along the roads, laurel, viburnum and alder, great ferns and wild-flowers delighted the traveler's eye through much of the year. Even in winter the roadsides were places of beauty, where countless birds came to feed on the berries and on the seed heads of the dried weeds rising above the snow. The countryside was, in fact, famous for the abundance and variety of its bird life, and when the flood of migrants was pouring through in spring and fall people traveled from great distances to observe them. Others came to fish the streams, which flowed clear and cold out of the hills and contained shady pools where trout lay. So it had been from the days many years ago when the first settlers raised their houses, sank their wells, and built their barns.

Then a strange blight crept over the area and everything began to change. Some evil spell had settled on the community: mysterious maladies swept the flocks of chickens; the cattle and sheep sickened and died. Everywhere was a shadow of death. The farmers spoke of much illness among their families. In the town the doctors had become more and more puzzled by new kinds of sickness appearing among their patients. There had been several sudden and unexplained deaths, not only among adults but even among children, who would be stricken suddenly while at play and die within a few hours.

There was a strange stillness. The birds, for example—where had they gone? Many people spoke of them, puzzled and disturbed. The feeding stations in the backyards were deserted. The few birds seen anywhere were moribund; they trembled violently and could not fly. It was a spring without voices. On the mornings that had once throbbed with the dawn chorus of robins, catbirds, doves, jays, wrens, and scores of other bird voices there was now no sound; only silence lay over the fields and woods and marsh.

On the farms the hens brooded, but no chicks hatched. The farmers 5 complained that they were unable to raise any pigs—the litters were small and the young survived only a few days. The apple trees were coming into bloom but no bees droned among the blossoms, so there was no pollination and there would be no fruit.

The roadsides, once so attractive, were now lined with browned and withered vegetation as though swept by fire. These, too, were silent, deserted by all living things. Even the streams were now lifeless. Anglers no longer visited them, for all the fish had died.

In the gutters under the eaves and between the shingles of the roofs, a white granular powder still showed a few patches; some weeks before it had fallen like snow upon the roofs and the lawns, the fields and streams.

No witchcraft, no enemy action had silenced the rebirth of new life in this stricken world. The people had done it themselves.

• ○ •

This town does not actually exist, but it might easily have a thousand counterparts in America or elsewhere in the world. I know of no community that has experienced all the misfortunes I describe. Yet every one of these disasters has actually happened somewhere, and many real communities have already suffered a substantial number of them. A grim specter has crept upon us almost unnoticed, and this imagined tragedy may easily become a stark reality we all shall know.

What has already silenced the voices of spring in countless towns in America? 10

STUDY QUESTIONS

1. A FABLE tells a story with a lesson to be learned. What lesson is Carson attempting to teach?

2. Carson uses a RHETORICAL QUESTION at the end of the chapter to entice the AUDIENCE to continue reading. Has she already answered the question in the fable that precedes it? Explain.

3. DESCRIPTIONS of widespread death and destruction, as in "A Fable for Tomorrow," are used in countless stories to warn us that something about our way of life holds the seed of disaster. Consider a familiar story or film that uses such death and destruction to warn us of dangers, and analyze it. What is the writer's or filmmaker's intent? How persuasive do you find it, and why? Be sure to refer to and describe specific scenes.

4. *For Writing.* Go home when you finish classes today and look through your cabinets for all the chemical products in your house or apartment— chemicals to clean your toilet bowl, to wipe your counters, to dye your hair, to wash your clothes, and so forth. Find at least five different household products that you buy and use regularly. Read their labels for the ingredients they contain and the warnings they give. Do any of them warn that they might contain carcinogens? Might any of them harm the environment? Might any of them be dangerous on contact with your skin? Write a letter to the manufacturer of one of the more dangerous products that you use, taking a POSITION about the chemicals to which the manufacturer is exposing you and the environment.

MICHAEL POLLAN ⎰ *An Animal's Place*

MICHAEL POLLAN (b. 1955) is a journalist who has written extensively about the relationship among food, agriculture, and society in the United States. His numerous books include *The Omnivore's Dilemma: A Natural History of Four Meals* (2006) and *In Defense of Food: An Eater's Manifesto* (2008). Pollan's articles have appeared in the *New York Times Magazine*, where he is a contributing writer, as well as in *Mother Jones, Vogue*, and *Harper's*, where he was formerly the executive editor. Pollan directs the Knight Program in Science and Environmental Journalism at UC Berkeley's Graduate School of Journalism.

"An Animal's Place" first appeared in the *New York Times Magazine* in 2002; it served as the basis for *The Omnivore's Dilemma*. Here, Pollan weighs the standard arguments for and against animal rights before introducing a new perspective: that domesticated animals may be humanely raised for food. As you read, consider which perspective you think is the most convincing—and the most ethical.

THE FIRST TIME I OPENED Peter Singer's *Animal Liberation*, I was dining alone at the Palm, trying to enjoy a rib-eye steak cooked medium-rare. If this sounds like a good recipe for cognitive dissonance (if not indigestion), that was sort of the idea. Preposterous as it might seem, to supporters of animal rights, what I was doing was tantamount to reading *Uncle Tom's Cabin*[1] on a plantation in the Deep South in 1852.

Singer and the swelling ranks of his followers ask us to imagine a future in which people will look back on my meal, and this steak-

[1]Popular abolitionist novel by Harriet Beecher Stowe (1811–96).

house, as relics of an equally backward age. Eating animals, wearing animals, experimenting on animals, killing animals for sport: all these practices, so resolutely normal to us, will be seen as the barbarities they are, and we will come to view "speciesism"—a neologism I had encountered before only in jokes—as a form of discrimination as indefensible as racism or anti-Semitism.

Even in 1975, when *Animal Liberation* was first published, Singer, an Australian philosopher now teaching at Princeton, was confident that he had the wind of history at his back. The recent civil rights past was prologue, as one liberation movement followed on the heels of another. Slowly but surely, the white man's circle of moral consideration was expanded to admit first blacks, then women, then homosexuals. In each case, a group once thought to be so different from the prevailing "we" as to be undeserving of civil rights was, after a struggle, admitted to the club. Now it was animals' turn.

That animal liberation is the logical next step in the forward march of moral progress is no longer the fringe idea it was back in 1975. A growing and increasingly influential movement of philosophers, ethicists, law professors and activists are convinced that the great moral struggle of our time will be for the rights of animals.

So far the movement has scored some of its biggest victories in 5 Europe. Earlier this year, Germany became the first nation to grant animals a constitutional right: the words "and animals" were added to a provision obliging the state to respect and protect the dignity of human beings. The farming of animals for fur was recently banned in England. In several European nations, sows may no longer be confined to crates nor laying hens to "battery cages"—stacked wired cages so small the birds cannot stretch their wings. The Swiss are amending their laws to change the status of animals from "things" to "beings."

Though animals are still very much "things" in the eyes of American law, change is in the air. Thirty-seven states have recently passed laws making some forms of animal cruelty a crime, twenty-one of them by ballot initiative. Following protests by activists, McDonald's and Burger King forced significant improvements in the way the U.S. meat industry slaughters animals. Agribusiness and the cosmetics and apparel industries are all struggling to defuse mounting public concerns over animal welfare.

Once thought of as a left-wing concern, the movement now cuts across ideological lines. Perhaps the most eloquent recent plea on behalf of animals, a new book called *Dominion*, was written by a former speechwriter for President Bush.[2] And once outlandish ideas are finding their way into mainstream opinion. A recent Zogby poll found that 51 percent of Americans believe that primates are entitled to the same rights as human children.

What is going on here? A certain amount of cultural confusion, for one thing. For at the same time many people seem eager to extend the circle of our moral consideration to animals, in our factory farms and laboratories we are inflicting more suffering on more animals than at any time in history. One by one, science is dismantling our claims to uniqueness as a species, discovering that such things as culture, tool making, language, and even possibly self-consciousness are not the exclusive domain of Homo sapiens. Yet most of the animals we kill lead lives organized very much in the spirit of Descartes,[3] who famously claimed that animals were mere machines, incapable of thought or feeling. There's a schizoid quality to our relationship with animals, in which sentiment and brutality exist side by side. Half the dogs in America will receive Christmas presents this year, yet few of us pause to consider the miserable life of the pig—an animal easily as intelligent as a dog—that becomes the Christmas ham.

We tolerate this disconnect because the life of the pig has moved out of view. When's the last time you saw a pig? (Babe doesn't count.) Except for our pets, real animals—animals living and dying—no longer figure in our everyday lives. Meat comes from the grocery store, where it is cut and packaged to look as little like parts of animals as possible. The disappearance of animals from our lives has opened a space in which there's no reality check, either on the sentiment or the brutality. This is pretty much where we live now, with respect to animals, and it

[2]Matthew Scully (b. 1959).
[3]René Descartes (1596–1650), French philosopher.

POLLAN / *An Animal's Place*

is a space in which the Peter Singers and Frank Perdues[4] of the world
can evidently thrive equally well.

Several years ago, the English critic John Berger wrote an essay, 10
"Why Look at Animals?" in which he suggested that the loss of everyday contact between ourselves and animals—and specifically the loss
of eye contact—has left us deeply confused about the terms of our relationship to other species. That eye contact, always slightly uncanny,
had provided a vivid daily reminder that animals were at once crucially
like and unlike us; in their eyes we glimpsed something unmistak-
ably familiar (pain, fear, tenderness) and something irretrievably alien.
Upon this paradox people built a relationship in which they felt they
could both honor and eat animals without looking away. But that
accommodation has pretty much broken down; nowadays, it seems,
we either look away or become vegetarians. For my own part, neither
option seemed especially appetizing. Which might explain how I
found myself reading *Animal Liberation* in a steakhouse.

This is not something I'd recommend if you're determined to continue eating meat. Combining rigorous philosophical argument with
journalistic description, *Animal Liberation* is one of those rare books
that demand that you either defend the way you live or change it.
Because Singer is so skilled in argument, for many readers it is easier
to change. His book has converted countless thousands to vegetarianism, and it didn't take long for me to see why: within a few pages, he
had succeeded in throwing me on the defensive.

Singer's argument is disarmingly simple and, if you accept its premises, difficult to refute. Take the premise of equality, which most people readily accept. Yet what do we really mean by it? People are not, as
a matter of fact, equal at all—some are smarter than others, better looking, more gifted. "Equality is a moral idea," Singer points out, "not an
assertion of fact." The moral idea is that everyone's interests ought to
receive equal consideration, regardless of "what abilities they may possess." Fair enough; many philosophers have gone this far. But fewer
have taken the next logical step. "If possessing a higher degree of intel-

---

[4]Franklin Parsons Perdue (1920–2005), former president and CEO of Perdue Farms, a
major chicken producer in the United States.

ligence does not entitle one human to use another for his or her own ends, how can it entitle humans to exploit nonhumans for the same purpose?"

This is the nub of Singer's argument, and right around here I began scribbling objections in the margin. But humans differ from animals in morally significant ways. Yes they do, Singer acknowledges, which is why we shouldn't treat pigs and children alike. Equal consideration of interests is not the same as equal treatment, he points out: children have an interest in being educated; pigs, in rooting around in the dirt. But where their interests are the same, the principle of equality demands they receive the same consideration. And the one all-important interest that we share with pigs, as with all sentient creatures, is an interest in avoiding pain.

Here Singer quotes a famous passage from Jeremy Bentham, the eighteenth-century utilitarian philosopher,[5] that is the wellspring of the animal rights movement. Bentham was writing in 1789, soon after the French colonies freed black slaves, granting them fundamental rights. "The day may come," he speculates, "when the rest of the animal creation may acquire those rights." Bentham then asks what characteristic entitles any being to moral consideration. "Is it the faculty of reason or perhaps the faculty of discourse?" Obviously not, since "a full-grown horse or dog is beyond comparison a more rational, as well as a more conversable animal, than an infant." He concludes: "The question is not, Can they reason? nor, Can they talk? but, Can they suffer?"

Bentham here is playing a powerful card philosophers call the "argument from marginal cases," or A.M.C. for short. It goes like this: there are humans—infants, the severely retarded, the demented—whose mental function cannot match that of a chimpanzee. Even though these people cannot reciprocate our moral attentions, we nevertheless include them in the circle of our moral consideration. So on what basis do we exclude the chimpanzee?

Because he's a chimp, I furiously scribbled in the margin, and

15

---

[5]Utilitarian philosophy holds that morality should be determined by what produces the greatest good for the greatest number of people.

they're human! For Singer that's not good enough. To exclude the chimp from moral consideration simply because he's not human is no different from excluding the slave simply because he's not white. In the same way we'd call that exclusion racist, the animal rightist contends that it is speciesist to discriminate against the chimpanzee solely because he's not human.

But the differences between blacks and whites are trivial compared with the differences between my son and a chimp. Singer counters by asking us to imagine a hypothetical society that discriminates against people on the basis of something nontrivial—say, intelligence. If that scheme offends our sense of equality, then why is the fact that animals lack certain human characteristics any more just as a basis for discrimination? Either we do not owe any justice to the severely retarded, he concludes, or we do owe it to animals with higher capabilities.

This is where I put down my fork. If I believe in equality, and equality is based on interests rather than characteristics, then either I have to take the interests of the steer I'm eating into account or concede that I am a speciesist. For the time being, I decided to plead guilty as charged. I finished my steak.

But Singer had planted a troubling notion, and in the days afterward, it grew and grew, watered by the other animal rights thinkers I began reading: the philosophers Tom Regan and James Rachels; the legal theorist Steven M. Wise; the writers Joy Williams and Matthew Scully. I didn't think I minded being a speciesist, but could it be, as several of these writers suggest, that we will someday come to regard speciesism as an evil comparable to racism? Will history someday judge us as harshly as it judges the Germans who went about their ordinary lives in the shadow of Treblinka?[6] Precisely that question was recently posed by J. M. Coetzee, the South African novelist, in a lecture delivered at Princeton; he answered it in the affirmative. If animal rightists are right, "a crime of stupefying proportions" (in Coetzee's words) is going on all around us every day, just beneath our notice.

It's an idea almost impossible to entertain seriously, much less to 20 accept, and in the weeks following my restaurant face-off between

---

[6]German extermination camp located in Poland during World War II.

Singer and the steak, I found myself marshaling whatever mental power I could muster to try to refute it. Yet Singer and his allies managed to trump almost all my objections.

My first line of defense was obvious. Animals kill one another all the time. Why treat animals more ethically than they treat one another? (Ben Franklin tried this one long before me: during a fishing trip, he wondered, "If you eat one another, I don't see why we may not eat you." He admits, however, that the rationale didn't occur to him until the fish were in the frying pan, smelling "admirably well." The advantage of being a "reasonable creature," Franklin remarks, is that you can find a reason for whatever you want to do.) To the "they do it, too" defense, the animal rightist has a devastating reply: do you really want to base your morality on the natural order? Murder and rape are natural, too. Besides, humans don't need to kill other creatures in order to survive; animals do. (Though if my cat, Otis, is any guide, animals sometimes kill for sheer pleasure.)

This suggests another defense. Wouldn't life in the wild be worse for these farm animals? "Defenders of slavery imposed on black Africans often made a similar point," Singer retorts. "The life of freedom is to be preferred."

But domesticated animals can't survive in the wild; in fact, without us they wouldn't exist at all. Or as one nineteenth-century political philosopher put it, "The pig has a stronger interest than anyone in the demand for bacon. If all the world were Jewish, there would be no pigs at all." But it turns out that this would be fine by the animal rightists: for if pigs don't exist, they can't be wronged.

Animals on factory farms have never known any other life. Singer replies that "animals feel a need to exercise, stretch their limbs or wings, groom themselves and turn around, whether or not they have ever lived in conditions that permit this." The measure of their suffering is not their prior experiences but the unremitting daily frustration of their instincts.

O.K., the suffering of animals is a legitimate problem, but the world 25 is full of problems, and surely human problems must come first! Sounds good, and yet all the animal people are asking me to do is to stop eating meat and wearing animal furs and hides. There's no reason

I can't devote myself to solving humankind's problems while being a vegetarian who wears synthetics.

But doesn't the fact that we could choose to forgo meat for moral reasons point to a crucial moral difference between animals and humans? As Kant pointed out, the human being is the only moral animal, the only one even capable of entertaining a concept of "rights." What's wrong with reserving moral consideration for those able to reciprocate it? Right here is where you run smack into the A.M.C.: the moral status of the retarded, the insane, the infant and the Alzheimer's patient. Such "marginal cases," in the detestable argot of modern moral philosophy, cannot participate in moral decision making any more than a monkey can, yet we nevertheless grant them rights.

That's right, I respond, for the simple reason that they're one of us. And all of us have been, and will probably once again be, marginal cases ourselves. What's more, these people have fathers and mothers, daughters and sons, which makes our interest in their welfare deeper than our interest in the welfare of even the most brilliant ape.

Alas, none of these arguments evade the charge of speciesism; the racist, too, claims that it's natural to give special consideration to one's own kind. A utilitarian like Singer would agree, however, that the feelings of relatives do count for something. Yet the principle of equal consideration of interests demands that, given the choice between performing a painful medical experiment on a severely retarded orphan and on a normal ape, we must sacrifice the child. Why? Because the ape has a greater capacity for pain.

Here in a nutshell is the problem with the A.M.C.: it can be used to help the animals, but just as often it winds up hurting the marginal cases. Giving up our speciesism will bring us to a moral cliff from which we may not be prepared to jump, even when logic is pushing us.

And yet this isn't the moral choice I am being asked to make. (Too 30 bad; it would be so much easier!) In everyday life, the choice is not between babies and chimps but between the pork and the tofu. Even if we reject the "hard utilitarianism" of a Peter Singer, there remains the question of whether we owe animals that can feel pain any moral consideration, and this seems impossible to deny. And if we do owe them moral consideration, how can we justify eating them?

This is why killing animals for meat (and clothing) poses the most difficult animal rights challenge. In the case of animal testing, all but the most radical animal rightists are willing to balance the human benefit against the cost to the animals. That's because the unique qualities of human consciousness carry weight in the utilitarian calculus: human pain counts for more than that of a mouse, since our pain is amplified by emotions like dread; similarly, our deaths are worse than an animal's because we understand what death is in a way they don't. So the argument over animal testing is really in the details: is this particular procedure or test really necessary to save human lives? (Very often it's not, in which case we probably shouldn't do it.) But if humans no longer need to eat meat or wear skins, then what exactly are we putting on the human side of the scale to outweigh the interests of the animal?

I suspect that this is finally why the animal people managed to throw me on the defensive. It's one thing to choose between the chimp and the retarded child or to accept the sacrifice of all those pigs surgeons practiced on to develop heart-bypass surgery. But what happens when the choice is between "a lifetime of suffering for a nonhuman animal and the gastronomic preference of a human being?" You look away— or you stop eating animals. And if you don't want to do either? Then you have to try to determine if the animals you're eating have really endured "a lifetime of suffering."

Whether our interest in eating animals outweighs their interest in not being eaten (assuming for the moment that is their interest) turns on the vexed question of animal suffering. Vexed, because it is impossible to know what really goes on in the mind of a cow or a pig or even an ape. Strictly speaking, this is true of other humans, too, but since humans are all basically wired the same way, we have excellent reason to assume that other people's experience of pain feels much like our own. Can we say that about animals? Yes and no.

I have yet to find anyone who still subscribes to Descartes's belief that animals cannot feel pain because they lack a soul. The general consensus among scientists and philosophers is that when it comes to pain, the higher animals are wired much like we are for the same evolutionary reasons, so we should take the writhings of the kicked dog at face value. Indeed, the very premise of a great deal of animal testing—

the reason it has value—is that animals' experience of physical and even some psychological pain closely resembles our own. Otherwise, why would cosmetics testers drip chemicals into the eyes of rabbits to see if they sting? Why would researchers study head trauma by traumatizing chimpanzee heads? Why would psychologists attempt to induce depression and "learned helplessness" in dogs by exposing them to ceaseless random patterns of electrical shock?

That said, it can be argued that human pain differs from animal pain 35 by an order of magnitude. This qualitative difference is largely the result of our possession of language and, by virtue of language, an ability to have thoughts about thoughts and to imagine alternatives to our current reality. The philosopher Daniel C. Dennett suggests that we would do well to draw a distinction between pain, which a great many animals experience, and suffering, which depends on a degree of self-consciousness only a few animals appear to command. Suffering in this view is not just lots of pain but pain intensified by human emotions like loss, sadness, worry, regret, self-pity, shame, humiliation and dread.

Consider castration. No one would deny the procedure is painful to animals, yet animals appear to get over it in a way humans do not. (Some rhesus monkeys competing for mates will bite off a rival's testicle; the very next day the victim may be observed mating, seemingly little the worse for wear.) Surely the suffering of a man able to comprehend the full implications of castration, to anticipate the event and contemplate its aftermath, represents an agony of another order.

By the same token, however, language and all that comes with it can also make certain kinds of pain more bearable. A trip to the dentist would be a torment for an ape that couldn't be made to understand the purpose and duration of the procedure.

As humans contemplating the pain and suffering of animals, we do need to guard against projecting on to them what the same experience would feel like to us. Watching a steer force-marched up the ramp to the kill-floor door, as I have done, I need to remind myself that this is not Sean Penn in *Dead Man Walking*,[7] that in a bovine brain the con-

---

[7]Academy Award-winning film (1995) based on the 1993 nonfiction book of the same title by Sister Helen Prejean (b. 1939), who advocates abolishing the death penalty.

cept of nonexistence is blissfully absent. "If we fail to find suffering in the [animal] lives we can see," Dennett writes in *Kinds of Minds*, "we can rest assured there is no invisible suffering somewhere in their brains. If we find suffering, we will recognize it without difficulty."

Which brings us—reluctantly, necessarily—to the American factory farm, the place where all such distinctions turn to dust. It's not easy to draw lines between pain and suffering in a modern egg or confinement hog operation. These are places where the subtleties of moral philosophy and animal cognition mean less than nothing, where everything we've learned about animals at least since Darwin has been simply . . . set aside. To visit a modern CAFO (Confined Animal Feeding Operation) is to enter a world that, for all its technological sophistication, is still designed according to Cartesian principles: animals are machines incapable of feeling pain. Since no thinking person can possibly believe this anymore, industrial animal agriculture depends on a suspension of disbelief on the part of the people who operate it and a willingness to avert your eyes on the part of everyone else.

From everything I've read, egg and hog operations are the worst. 40 Beef cattle in America at least still live outdoors, albeit standing ankle deep in their own waste eating a diet that makes them sick. And broiler chickens, although they do get their beaks snipped off with a hot knife to keep them from cannibalizing one another under the stress of their confinement, at least don't spend their eight-week lives in cages too small to ever stretch a wing. That fate is reserved for the American laying hen, who passes her brief span piled together with a half-dozen other hens in a wire cage whose floor a single page of this magazine[8] could carpet. Every natural instinct of this animal is thwarted, leading to a range of behavioral "vices" that can include cannibalizing her cage-mates and rubbing her body against the wire mesh until it is featherless and bleeding. Pain? Suffering? Madness? The operative suspension of disbelief depends on more neutral descriptors, like "vices" and "stress." Whatever you want to call what's going on in those cages, the 10 percent or so of hens that can't bear it and simply die is built into the cost of production. And when the output of the others begins to

[8]That is, approximately 9½ × 11½ inches.

21

ebb, the hens will be "force-molted"—starved of food and water and light for several days in order to stimulate a final bout of egg laying before their life's work is done.

Simply reciting these facts, most of which are drawn from poultry-trade magazines, makes me sound like one of those animal people, doesn't it? I don't mean to, but this is what can happen when . . . you look. It certainly wasn't my intention to ruin anyone's breakfast. But now that I probably have spoiled the eggs, I do want to say one thing about the bacon, mention a single practice (by no means the worst) in modern hog production that points to the compound madness of an impeccable industrial logic.

Piglets in confinement operations are weaned from their mothers 10 days after birth (compared with 13 weeks in nature) because they gain weight faster on their hormone- and antibiotic-fortified feed. This premature weaning leaves the pigs with a lifelong craving to suck and chew, a desire they gratify in confinement by biting the tail of the animal in front of them. A normal pig would fight off his molester, but a demoralized pig has stopped caring. "Learned helplessness" is the psychological term, and it's not uncommon in confinement operations, where tens of thousands of hogs spend their entire lives ignorant of sunshine or earth or straw, crowded together beneath a metal roof upon metal slats suspended over a manure pit. So it's not surprising that an animal as sensitive and intelligent as a pig would get depressed, and a depressed pig will allow his tail to be chewed on to the point of infection. Sick pigs, being underperforming "production units," are clubbed to death on the spot. The U.S.D.A.'s[7] recommended solution to the problem is called "tail docking." Using a pair of pliers (and no anesthetic), most but not all of the tail is snipped off. Why the little stump? Because the whole point of the exercise is not to remove the object of tail-biting so much as to render it more sensitive. Now, a bite on the tail is so painful that even the most demoralized pig will mount a struggle to avoid it.

Much of this description is drawn from *Dominion*, Matthew Scully's recent book in which he offers a harrowing description of a North

[7] That is, the United States Department of Agriculture.

Carolina hog operation. Scully, a Christian conservative, has no patience for lefty rights talk, arguing instead that while God did give man "dominion" over animals ("Every moving thing that liveth shall be meat for you"), he also admonished us to show them mercy. "We are called to treat them with kindness, not because they have rights or power or some claim to equality but . . . because they stand unequal and powerless before us."

Scully calls the contemporary factory farm "our own worst nightmare" and, to his credit, doesn't shrink from naming the root cause of this evil: unfettered capitalism. (Perhaps this explains why he resigned from the Bush administration just before his book's publication.) A tension has always existed between the capitalist imperative to maximize efficiency and the moral imperatives of religion or community, which have historically served as a counterweight to the moral blindness of the market. This is one of "the cultural contradictions of capitalism"—the tendency of the economic impulse to erode the moral underpinnings of society. Mercy toward animals is one such casualty.

More than any other institution, the American industrial animal farm offers a nightmarish glimpse of what capitalism can look like in the absence of moral or regulatory constraint. Here in these places life itself is redefined—as protein production—and with it suffering. That venerable word becomes "stress," an economic problem in search of a cost-effective solution, like tail-docking or beak-clipping or, in the industry's latest plan, by simply engineering the "stress gene" out of pigs and chickens. "Our own worst nightmare" such a place may well be; it is also real life for the billions of animals unlucky enough to have been born beneath these grim steel roofs, into the brief, pitiless life of a "production unit" in the days before the suffering gene was found. 45

Vegetarianism doesn't seem an unreasonable response to such an evil. Who would want to be made complicit in the agony of these animals by eating them? You want to throw something against the walls of those infernal sheds, whether it's the Bible, a new constitutional right or a whole platoon of animal rightists bent on breaking in and liberating the inmates. In the shadow of these factory farms, Coetzee's notion of a "stupefying crime" doesn't seem far-fetched at all.

But before you swear off meat entirely, let me describe a very different sort of animal farm. It is typical of nothing, and yet its very existence puts the whole moral question of animal agriculture in a different light. Polyface Farm occupies 550 acres of rolling grassland and forest in the Shenandoah Valley of Virginia. Here, Joel Salatin and his family raise six different food animals—cattle, pigs, chickens, rabbits, turkeys and sheep—in an intricate dance of symbiosis designed to allow each species, in Salatin's words, "to fully express its physiological distinctiveness."

What this means in practice is that Salatin's chickens live like chickens; his cows, like cows; pigs, pigs. As in nature, where birds tend to follow herbivores, once Salatin's cows have finished grazing a pasture, he moves them out and tows in his "eggmobile," a portable chicken coop that houses several hundred laying hens—roughly the natural size of a flock. The hens fan out over the pasture, eating the short grass and picking insect larvae out of the cowpats—all the while spreading the cow manure and eliminating the farm's parasite problem. A diet of grubs and grass makes for exceptionally tasty eggs and contented chickens, and their nitrogenous manure feeds the pasture. A few weeks later, the chickens move out, and the sheep come in, dining on the lush new growth, as well as on the weed species (nettles, nightshade) that the cattle and chickens won't touch.

Meanwhile, the pigs are in the barn turning the compost. All winter long, while the cattle were indoors, Salatin layered their manure with straw, wood chips—and corn. By March, this steaming compost layer cake stands three feet high, and the pigs, whose powerful snouts can sniff out and retrieve the fermented corn at the bottom, get to spend a few happy weeks rooting through the pile, aerating it as they work. All you can see of these pigs, intently nosing out the tasty alcoholic morsels, are their upturned pink hams and corkscrew tails churning the air. The finished compost will go to feed the grass; the grass, the cattle; the cattle, the chickens; and eventually all of these animals will feed us.

I thought a lot about vegetarianism and animal rights during the day I 50 spent on Joel Salatin's extraordinary farm. So much of what I'd read, so much of what I'd accepted, looked very different from here. To many animal rightists, even Polyface Farm is a death camp. But to look at these animals is to see this for the sentimental conceit it is. In the same way that we can probably recognize animal suffering when we see it, animal happiness is unmistakable, too, and here I was seeing it in abundance.

For any animal, happiness seems to consist in the opportunity to express its creaturely character—its essential pigness or wolfness or chickenness. Aristotle speaks of each creature's "characteristic form of life." For domesticated species, the good life, if we can call it that, cannot be achieved apart from humans—apart from our farms and, therefore, our meat eating. This, it seems to me, is where animal rightists betray a profound ignorance about the workings of nature. To think of domestication as a form of enslavement or even exploitation is to misconstrue the whole relationship, to project a human idea of power onto what is, in fact, an instance of mutualism between species. Domestication is an evolutionary, rather than a political, development. It is certainly not a regime humans imposed on animals some 10,000 years ago.

Rather, domestication happened when a small handful of especially opportunistic species discovered through Darwinian trial and error that they were more likely to survive and prosper in an alliance with humans than on their own. Humans provided the animals with food and protection, in exchange for which the animals provided the humans their milk and eggs and—yes—their flesh. Both parties were transformed by the relationship: animals grew tame and lost their ability to fend for themselves (evolution tends to edit out unneeded traits), and the humans gave up their hunter-gatherer ways for the settled life of agriculturists. (Humans changed biologically, too, evolving such new traits as a tolerance for lactose as adults.)

From the animals' point of view, the bargain with humanity has been a great success, at least until our own time. Cows, pigs, dogs, cats and chickens have thrived, while their wild ancestors have languished. (There are 10,000 wolves in North America, 50,000,000 dogs.) Nor does their loss of autonomy seem to trouble these creatures. It is wrong, the rightists say, to treat animals as "means" rather than "ends," yet the happiness of a working animal like the dog consists precisely in serving as a "means." Liberation is the last thing such a creature wants. To say of one of Joel Salatin's caged chickens that "the life of freedom is to be preferred" betrays an ignorance about chicken preferences—

which on this farm are heavily focused on not getting their heads bitten off by weasels.

But haven't these chickens simply traded one predator for another—weasels for humans? True enough, and for the chickens this is probably not a bad deal. For brief as it is, the life expectancy of a farm animal would be considerably briefer in the world beyond the pasture fence or chicken coop. A sheep farmer told me that a bear will eat a lactating ewe alive, starting with her udders. "As a rule," he explained, "animals don't get 'good deaths' surrounded by their loved ones."

The very existence of predation—animals eating animals—is the 55 cause of much anguished hand-wringing in animal rights circles. "It must be admitted," Singer writes, "that the existence of carnivorous animals does pose one problem for the ethics of Animal Liberation, and that is whether we should do anything about it." Some animal rightists train their dogs and cats to become vegetarians. (Note: cats will require nutritional supplements to stay healthy.) Matthew Scully calls predation "the intrinsic evil in nature's design . . . among the hardest of all things to fathom." Really? A deep Puritan streak pervades animal rights activists, an abiding discomfort not only with our animality, but with the animals' animality too.

However it may appear to us, predation is not a matter of morality or politics; it, also, is a matter of symbiosis. Hard as the wolf may be on the deer he eats, the herd depends on him for its well-being; without predators to cull the herd, deer overrun their habitat and starve. In many places, human hunters have taken over the predator's ecological role. Chickens also depend for their continued well-being on their human predators—not individual chickens, but chickens as a species. The surest way to achieve the extinction of the chicken would be to grant chickens a "right to life."

Yet here's the rub: the animal rightist is not concerned with species, only individuals. Tom Regan, author of *The Case for Animal Rights*, bluntly asserts that because "species are not individuals . . . the rights view does not recognize the moral rights of species to anything, including survival." Singer concurs, insisting that only sentient individuals have interests. But surely a species can have interests—in its survival, say—just as a nation or community or a corporation can. The animal rights movement's exclusive concern with individual animals makes perfect sense given its roots in a culture of liberal individualism, but does it make any sense in nature?

In 1611 Juan da Goma (aka Juan the Disoriented) made accidental landfall on Wrightson Island, a six-square-mile rock in the Indian Ocean. The island's sole distinction is as the only known home of the Arcania tree and the bird that nests in it, the Wrightson giant sea sparrow. Da Goma and his crew stayed a week, much of that time spent in a failed bid to recapture the ship's escaped goat—who happened to be pregnant. Nearly four centuries later, Wrightson Island is home to 380 goats that have consumed virtually every scrap of vegetation in their reach. The youngest Arcania tree on the island is more than 300 years old, and only 52 sea sparrows remain. In the animal rights view, any one of those goats have at least as much right to life as the last Wrightson sparrow on earth, and the trees, because they are not sentient, warrant no moral consideration whatsoever. (In the mid-'80s a British environmental group set out to shoot the goats, but was forced to cancel the expedition after the Mammal Liberation Front bombed its offices.)

The story of Wrightson Island (recounted by the biologist David Ehrenfeld in *Beginning Again*)[8] suggests at the very least that a human morality based on individual rights makes for an awkward fit when applied to the natural world. This should come as no surprise: morality is an artifact of human culture, devised to help us negotiate social relations. It's very good for that. But just as we recognize that nature doesn't provide an adequate guide for human social conduct, isn't it anthropocentric to assume that our moral system offers an adequate guide for nature? We may require a different set of ethics to guide our dealings with the natural world, one as well suited to the particu-

---

[8]The *New York Times* later printed the following correction: "An article on Nov. 10 about animal rights referred erroneously to an island in the Indian Ocean and to events there involving goats and endangered giant sea sparrows that could possibly lead to the killing of goats by environmental groups. Wrightson Island does not exist; both the island and the vents are hypothetical figments from a book (also mentioned in the article), *Beginning Again*, by David Ehrenfeld. No giant sea sparrow is known to be endangered by the eating habits of goats."

lar needs of plants and animals and habitats (where sentience counts for little) as rights suit us humans today.

To contemplate such questions from the vantage of a farm is to 60 appreciate just how parochial and urban an ideology animal rights really is. It could thrive only in a world where people have lost contact with the natural world, where animals no longer pose a threat to us and human mastery of nature seems absolute. "In our normal life," Singer writes, "there is no serious clash of interests between human and non-human animals." Such a statement assumes a decidedly urbanized "normal life," one that certainly no farmer would recognize.

The farmer would point out that even vegans have a "serious clash of interests" with other animals. The grain that the vegan eats is harvested with a combine that shreds field mice, while the farmer's tractor crushes woodchucks in their burrows, and his pesticides drop song-birds from the sky. Steve Davis, an animal scientist at Oregon State University, has estimated that if America were to adopt a strictly vege-tarian diet, the total number of animals killed every year would actually increase, as animal pasture gave way to row crops. Davis contends that if our goal is to kill as few animals as possible, then people should eat the largest possible animal that can live on the least intensively culti-vated land: grass-fed beef for everybody. It would appear that killing animals is unavoidable no matter what we choose to eat.

When I talked to Joel Salatin about the vegetarian utopia, he pointed out that it would also condemn him and his neighbors to importing their food from distant places, since the Shenandoah Valley receives too little rainfall to grow many row crops. Much the same would hold true where I live, in New England. We get plenty of rain, but the hilliness of the land has dictated an agriculture based on animals since the time of the Pilgrims. The world is full of places where the best, if not the only, way to obtain food from the land is by grazing animals on it—especially ruminants, which alone can transform grass into protein and whose presence can actually improve the health of the land.

The vegetarian utopia would make us even more dependent than we already are on an industrialized national food chain. That food chain would in turn be even more dependent than it already is on fossil fuels and chemical fertilizer, since food would need to travel farther and manure would be in short supply. Indeed, it is doubtful that you can build a more sustainable agriculture without animals to cycle nutrients and support local food production. If our concern is for the health of nature—rather than, say, the internal consistency of our moral code or the condition of our souls—then eating animals may sometimes be the most ethical thing to do.

There is, too, the fact that we humans have been eating animals as long as we have lived on this earth. Humans may not need to eat meat in order to survive, yet doing so is part of our evolutionary heritage, reflected in the design of our teeth and the structure of our digestion. Eating meat helped make us what we are, in a social and biological sense. Under the pressure of the hunt, the human brain grew in size and complexity, and around the fire where the meat was cooked, human culture first flourished. Granting rights to animals may lift us up from the brutal world of predation, but it will entail the sacrifice of part of our identity—our own animality.

Surely this is one of the odder paradoxes of animal rights doctrine. 65 It asks us to recognize all that we share with animals and then demands that we act toward them in a most unanimalistic way. Whether or not this is a good idea, we should at least acknowledge that our desire to eat meat is not a trivial matter, no mere "gastronomic preference." We might as well call sex—also now technically unnecessary—a mere "recreational preference." Whatever else it is, our meat eating is something very deep indeed.

Are any of these good enough reasons to eat animals? I'm mindful of Ben Franklin's definition of the reasonable creature as one who can come up with reasons for whatever he wants to do. So I decided I would track down Peter Singer and ask him what he thought. In an e-mail message, I described Polyface and asked him about the implications for his position of the Good Farm—one where animals got to live according to their nature and to all appearances did not suffer.

"I agree with you that it is better for these animals to have lived and died than not to have lived at all," Singer wrote back. Since the utilitarian is concerned exclusively with the sum of happiness and suffering and the slaughter of an animal that doesn't comprehend that death need not involve suffering, the Good Farm adds to the total of animal happiness, provided you replace the slaughtered animal with a new one. However, he added, this line of thinking doesn't obviate the wrongness of killing an animal that "has a sense of its own existence over time and can have preferences for its own future." In other words, it's O.K. to eat the chicken, but he's not so sure about the pig. Yet, he wrote, "I would not be sufficiently confident of my arguments to condemn someone who purchased meat from one of these farms."

Singer went on to express serious doubts that such farms could be practical on a large scale, since the pressures of the marketplace will lead their owners to cut costs and corners at the expense of the animals. He suggested, too, that killing animals is not conducive to treating them with respect. Also, since humanely raised food will be more expensive, only the well-to-do can afford morally defensible animal protein. These are important considerations, but they don't alter my essential point: what's wrong with animal agriculture—with eating animals—is the practice, not the principle.

What this suggests to me is that people who care should be working not for animal rights but animal welfare—to ensure that farm animals don't suffer and that their deaths are swift and painless. In fact, the decent-life-merciful-death line is how Jeremy Bentham justified his own meat eating. Yes, the philosophical father of animal rights was himself a carnivore. In a passage rather less frequently quoted by animal rightists, Bentham defended eating animals on the grounds that "we are the better for it, and they are never the worse. . . . The death they suffer in our hands commonly is, and always may be, a speedier and, by that means, a less painful one than that which would await them in the inevitable course of nature."

My guess is that Bentham never looked too closely at what happens 70 in a slaughterhouse, but the argument suggests that, in theory at least, a utilitarian can justify the killing of humanely treated animals—for meat or, presumably, for clothing. (Though leather and fur pose distinct moral problems. Leather is a byproduct of raising domestic animals for food, which can be done humanely. However, furs are usually made from wild animals that die brutal deaths—usually in leg-hold traps—and since most fur species aren't domesticated, raising them on farms isn't necessarily more humane.) But whether the issue is food or fur or hunting, what should concern us is the suffering, not the killing. All of which I was feeling pretty good about—until I remembered that utilitarians can also justify killing retarded orphans. Killing just isn't the problem for them that it is for other people, including me.

During my visit to Polyface Farm, I asked Salatin where his animals were slaughtered. He does the chickens and rabbits right on the farm, and would do the cattle, pigs, and sheep there too if only the U.S.D.A. would let him. Salatin showed me the open-air abattoir he built behind the farmhouse—a sort of outdoor kitchen on a concrete slab, with stainless-steel sinks, scalding tanks, a feather-plucking machine and metal cones to hold the birds upside down while they're being bled. Processing chickens is not a pleasant job, but Salatin insists on doing it himself because he's convinced he can do it more humanely and cleanly than any processing plant. He slaughters every other Saturday through the summer. Anyone's welcome to watch.

I asked Salatin how he could bring himself to kill a chicken.

"People have a soul; animals don't," he said. "It's a bedrock belief of mine." Salatin is a devout Christian. "Unlike us, animals are not created in God's image, so when they die, they just die."

The notion that only in modern times have people grown uneasy about killing animals is a flattering conceit. Taking a life is momentous, and people have been working to justify the slaughter of animals for thousands of years. Religion and especially ritual has played a crucial part in helping us reckon the moral costs. Native Americans and other hunter-gathers would give thanks to their prey for giving up its life so the eater might live (sort of like saying grace). Many cultures have offered sacrificial animals to the gods, perhaps as a way to convince themselves that it was the gods' desires that demanded the slaughter, not their own. In ancient Greece, the priests responsible for the slaughter (priests!—now we entrust the job to minimum-wage workers) would sprinkle holy water on the sacrificial animal's brow. The beast would promptly shake its head, and this was taken as a sign of assent. Slaughter doesn't necessarily preclude respect. For all these people, it was the ceremony that allowed them to look, then to eat.

Apart from a few surviving religious practices, we no longer have 75 any rituals governing the slaughter or eating of animals, which perhaps helps to explain why we find ourselves where we do, feeling that our only choice is to either look away or give up meat. Frank Perdue is happy to serve the first customer; Peter Singer, the second.

Until my visit to Polyface Farm, I had assumed these were the only two options. But on Salatin's farm, the eye contact between people and animals whose loss John Berger mourned is still a fact of life—and of death, for neither the lives nor the deaths of these animals have been secreted behind steel walls. "Food with a face," Salatin likes to call what he's selling, a slogan that probably scares off some customers. People see very different things when they look into the eyes of a pig or a chicken or a steer—a being without a soul, a "subject of a life" entitled to rights, a link in a food chain, a vessel for pain and pleasure, a tasty lunch. But figuring out what we do think, and what we can eat, might begin with the looking.

We certainly won't philosophize our way to an answer. Salatin told me the story of a man who showed up at the farm one Saturday morning. When Salatin noticed a PETA[8] bumper sticker on the man's car, he figured he was in for it. But the man had a different agenda. He explained that after sixteen years as a vegetarian, he had decided that the only way he could ever eat meat again was if he killed the animal himself. He had come to look.

"Ten minutes later we were in the processing shed with a chicken," Salatin recalled. "He slit the bird's throat and watched it die. He saw that the animal did not look at him accusingly, didn't do a Disney double take. The animal had been treated with respect when it was alive, and he saw that it could also have a respectful death—that it wasn't being treated as a pile of protoplasm."

Salatin's open-air abattoir is a morally powerful idea. Someone slaughtering a chicken in a place where he can be watched is apt to do it scrupulously, with consideration for the animal as well as for the eater. This is going to sound quixotic, but maybe all we need to do to redeem industrial animal agriculture in this country is to pass a law requiring that the steel and concrete walls of the CAFO's and slaugh-

[9]People for the Ethical Treatment of Animals, an animal-rights organization.

terhouses be replaced with . . . glass. If there's any new "right" we need to establish, maybe it's this one: the right to look.

No doubt the sight of some of these places would turn many people 80 into vegetarians. Many others would look elsewhere for their meat, to farmers like Salatin. There are more of them than I would have imagined. Despite the relentless consolidation of the American meat industry, there has been a revival of small farms where animals still live their "characteristic form of life." I'm thinking of the ranches where cattle still spend their lives on grass, the poultry farms where chickens still go outside and the hog farms where pigs live as they did fifty years ago— in contact with the sun, the earth and the gaze of a farmer.

For my own part, I've discovered that if you're willing to make the effort, it's entirely possible to limit the meat you eat to nonindustrial animals. I'm tempted to think that we need a new dietary category, to go with the vegan and lactovegetarian and pescatarian. I don't have a catchy name for it yet (humanocarnivore?), but this is the only sort of meat eating I feel comfortable with these days. I've become the sort of shopper who looks for labels indicating that his meat and eggs have been humanely grown (the American Humane Association's new "Free Farmed" label seems to be catching on), who visits the farms where his chicken and pork come from and who asks kinky-sounding questions about touring slaughterhouses. I've actually found a couple of small processing plants willing to let a customer onto the kill floor, including one, in Cannon Falls, Minnesota, with a glass abattoir.

The industrialization—and dehumanization—of American animal farming is a relatively new, evitable and local phenomenon: no other country raises and slaughters its food animals quite as intensively or as brutally as we do. Were the walls of our meat industry to become transparent, literally or even figuratively, we would not long continue to do it this way. Tail-docking and sow crates and beak-clipping would disappear overnight, and the days of slaughtering 400 head of cattle an hour would come to an end. For who could stand the sight? Yes, meat would get more expensive. We'd probably eat less of it, too, but maybe when we did eat animals, we'd eat them with the consciousness, ceremony and respect they deserve.

STUDY QUESTIONS

1. What REASONS does Pollan present to support and refute "animal liberation"?

2. Refer to the beginning of Pollan's essay, where he ANALYZES Peter Singer's ARGUMENT in *Animal Liberation*. How does Pollan RESPOND to Singer's arguments? To the COUNTERARGUMENTS Singer anticipates? What is the effect of this analysis on the development of the essay?

3. When Pollan analyzes the process of raising animals for food, he concludes that animals' rights can be honored while preparing them to be eaten as meat. How does he arrive at this conclusion? What EVIDENCE does he present to support this POSITION? Do you find it convincing?

4. *For Writing.* What do you think "an animal's place" should be? Drawing on your own experiences, write an essay that confirms or challenges one of the perspectives that Pollan offers.

JONATHAN SWIFT { *A Modest Proposal*

JONATHAN SWIFT (1667–1745) was born in Dublin, Ireland, to an Irish father and an English mother. He graduated from Dublin University in 1686 and was working on his MA in 1688 when England's Glorious Revolution saw King James II deposed and William of Orange installed as king. Swift fled to England to escape the ensuing political upheaval in Ireland. After taking a position as secretary and assistant to English diplomat Sir William Temple, Swift completed his MA in 1692 and became a priest in the Established Church of Ireland. After some professional difficulty in securing a new position after Temple's death, Swift earned his Doctor of Divinity in 1702 from Trinity College, Dublin, and returned to London, where he published his satirical play *A Tale of a Tub* (1704). During the early 1700s he became involved with the Tory government, and when that rule fell he returned to Ireland and began writing political pamphlets, including *A Modest Proposal* (1729). He may be best known for his satirical novel *Gulliver's Travels* (1726).

In *A Modest Proposal*, a classic example of satire, Swift's speaker presents an apparently logical plan to eliminate poverty and hunger in Ireland. Swift employs a carefully crafted argument that seems to insist on one solution while actually arguing for a different one. Take note of how Swift's ethos and his use of logos and pathos make his audience receptive to his proposal, repel his readers when they find out what that proposal entails, and finally make them think about the underlying causes of the poverty and hunger that Swift proposes to end.

*A Modest Proposal for Preventing the Children of Poor People
in Ireland from Being a Burden to Their Parents or
Country, and for Making Them Beneficial to the Public*

IT IS A MELANCHOLY OBJECT to those who walk through this great town[1] or travel in the country, when they see the streets, the roads, and cabin doors, crowded with beggars of the female-sex, followed by three, four, or six children, all in rags and importuning every passenger for an alms. These mothers, instead of being able to work for their honest livelihood, are forced to employ all their time in strolling to beg sustenance for their helpless infants, who, as they grow up, either turn thieves for want of work, or leave their dear native country to fight for the Pretender[2] in Spain, or sell themselves to the Barbadoes.

I think it is agreed by all parties that this prodigious number of children in the arms, or on the backs, or at the heels of their mothers, and frequently of their fathers, is in the present deplorable state of the kingdom a very great additional grievance; and therefore whoever could find out a fair, cheap, and easy method of making these children sound, useful members of the commonwealth would deserve so well of the public as to have his statue set up for a preserver of the nation.

But my intention is very far from being confined to provide only for the children of professed beggars; it is of a much greater extent, and shall take in the whole number of infants at a certain age who are born of parents in effect as little able to support them as those who demand our charity in the streets.

As to my own part, having turned my thoughts for many years upon this important subject, and maturely weighed the several schemes of other projectors,[3] I have always found them grossly mistaken in their computation. It is true, a child just dropped from its dam may be supported by her milk for a solar year, with little other nourishment; at most not above the value of two shillings, which the

---

[1] Dublin.

[2] After King James II lost the English throne in the Glorious Revolution of 1688, his son, James Francis Edward, known as "the Pretender," in exile on the European continent, tried several times to retake the English throne.

[3] Schemers.

mother may certainly get, or the value in scraps, by her lawful occupation of begging; and it is exactly at one year old that I propose to provide for them in such a manner as instead of being a charge upon their parents or the parish, or wanting food and raiment for the rest of their lives, they shall on the contrary contribute to the feeding, and partly to the clothing, of many thousands.

There is likewise another great advantage in my scheme, that it will 5 prevent those voluntary abortions, and that horrid practice of women murdering their bastard children, alas, too frequent among us, sacrificing the poor innocent babes, I doubt, more to avoid the expense than the shame, which would move tears and pity in the most savage and inhuman breast.

The number of souls in this kingdom being usually reckoned one million and a half, of these I calculate there may be about two hundred thousand couple whose wives are breeders; from which number I subtract thirty thousand couples who are able to maintain their own children, although I apprehend there cannot be so many under the present distresses of the kingdom; but this being granted, there will remain an hundred and seventy thousand breeders. I again subtract fifty thousand for those women who miscarry, or whose children die by accident or disease within the year. There only remain an hundred and twenty thousand children of poor parents annually born. The question therefore is, how this number shall be reared and provided for, which, as I have already said, under the present situation of affairs, is utterly impossible by all the methods hitherto proposed. For we can neither employ them in handicraft or agriculture; we neither build houses (I mean in the country) nor cultivate land. They can very seldom pick up a livelihood by stealing till they arrive at six years old, except where they are of towardly parts;[4] although I confess they learn the rudiments much earlier, during which time they can however be looked upon only as probationers, as I have been informed by a principal gentleman in the county of Cavan, who protested to me that he never knew above one or two instances under the age of six, even in a part of the kingdom so renowned for the quickest proficiency in that art.

[4] Promising abilities.

I am assured by our merchants that a boy or a girl before twelve years old is no salable commodity; and even when they come to this age they will not yield above three pounds, or three pounds and half a crown at most on the Exchange; which cannot turn to account either to the parents or the kingdom, the charge of nutriment and rags having been at least four times that value.

I shall now therefore humbly propose my own thoughts, which I hope will not be liable to the least objection.

I have been assured by a very knowing American of my acquaintance in London, that a young healthy child well nursed is at a year old a most delicious, nourishing, and wholesome food, whether stewed, roasted, baked, or boiled; and I make no doubt that it will equally serve in a fricassee or a ragout.

I do therefore humbly offer it to public consideration that of the 10 hundred and twenty thousand children, already computed, twenty thousand may be reserved for breed, whereof only one fourth part to be males, which is more than we allow to sheep, black cattle, or swine; and my reason is that these children are seldom the fruits of marriage, a circumstance not much regarded by our savages, therefore one male will be sufficient to serve four females. That the remaining hundred thousand may at a year old be offered in sale to the persons of quality and fortune through the kingdom, always advising the mother to let them suck plentifully in the last month, so as to render them plump and fat for a good table. A child will make two dishes at an entertainment for friends; and when the family dines alone, the fore or hind quarter will make a reasonable dish, and seasoned with a little pepper or salt will be very good boiled on the fourth day, especially in winter.

I have reckoned upon a medium that a child just born will weigh twelve pounds, and in a solar year if tolerably nursed increaseth to twenty-eight pounds.

I grant this food will be somewhat dear, and therefore very proper for landlords, who, as they have already devoured most of the parents, seem to have the best title to the children.

Infant's flesh will be in season throughout the year, but more plentiful in March, and a little before and after. For we are told by a grave author, an eminent French physician,[5] that fish being a prolific diet, there are more children born in Roman Catholic countries about nine months after Lent than at any other season; therefore, reckoning a year after Lent, the markets will be more glutted than usual, because the number of popish infants is at least three to one in this kingdom; and therefore it will have one other collateral advantages, by lessening the number of Papists among us.

I have already computed the charge of nursing a beggar's child (in which list I reckon all cottagers, laborers, and four fifths of the farmers) to be about two shillings per annum, rags included; and I believe no gentleman would repine to give ten shillings for the carcass of a good fat child, which, as I have said, will make four dishes of excellent nutritive meat, when he hath only some particular friend or his own family to dine with him. Thus the squire will learn to be a good landlord, and grow popular among the tenants; the mother will have eight shillings net profit, and be fit for work till she produces another child.

Those who are more thrifty (as I must confess the times require) 15 may flay the carcass; the skin of which artificially[6] dressed will make admirable gloves for ladies, and summer boots for fine gentlemen.

As to our city of Dublin, shambles[7] may be appointed for this purpose in the most convenient parts of it, and butchers we may be assured will not be wanting; although I rather recommend buying the children alive, and dressing them hot from the knife as we do roasting pigs.

A very worthy person, a true lover of his country, and whose virtues I highly esteem, was lately pleased in discoursing on this matter to offer a refinement upon my scheme. He said that many gentlemen of this kingdom, having of late destroyed their deer, he conceived that the want of venison might be well supplied by the bodies of young lads and maidens, not exceeding fourteen years of age nor under twelve, so great a number of both sexes in every county being now ready to starve for want of work and service; and these to be disposed of by their parents, if alive, or otherwise by their nearest relations. But with

[5] François Rabelais (1483–1553).
[6] Skillfully.
[7] Slaughterhouses.

due deference to so excellent a friend and so deserving a patriot, I cannot be altogether in his sentiments; for as to the males, my American acquaintance assured me from frequent experience that their flesh was generally tough and lean, like that of our schoolboys, by continual exercise, and their taste disagreeable; and to fatten them would not answer the charge. Then as to the females, it would, I think with humble submission, be a loss to the public, because they soon would become breeders themselves: and besides, it is not improbable that some scrupulous people might be apt to censure such a practice (although indeed very unjustly) as a little bordering upon cruelty; which, I confess, hath always been with me the strongest objection against any project, how well soever intended.

But in order to justify my friend, he confessed that this expedient was put into his head by the famous Psalmanazar, a native of the island Formosa,[8] who came from thence to London above twenty years ago, and in conversation told my friend that in his country when any young person happened to be put to death, the executioner sold the carcass to persons of quality as a prime dainty; and that in his time the body of a plump girl of fifteen, who was crucified for an attempt to poison the emperor, was sold to his Imperial Majesty's prime minister of state, and other great mandarins of the court, in joints from the gibbet, at four hundred crowns. Neither indeed can I deny that if the same use were made of several plump young girls in this town, who without one single groat to their fortunes cannot stir abroad without a chair,[9] and appear at the playhouse and assemblies in foreign fineries which they never will pay for, the kingdom would not be the worse.

Some persons of a desponding spirit are in great concern about that vast number of poor people who are aged, diseased, or maimed, and I have been desired to employ my thoughts what course may be taken to ease the nation of so grievous an encumbrance. But I am not in the least pain upon that matter, because it is very well known that they are every day dying and rotting by cold and famine, and filth and vermin,

---

[8] George Psalmanazar, a Frenchman, masqueraded as a traveler from Formosa (Taiwan) and wrote a fictitious account of that country, including accounts of cannibalism.
[9] A sedan chair.

as fast as can be reasonably expected. And as to the younger laborers, they are now in almost as hopeful a condition. They cannot get work, and consequently pine away for want of nourishment to a degree that if at any time they are accidentally hired to common labor, they have not strength to perform it; and thus the country and themselves are happily delivered from the evils to come.

I have too long digressed, and therefore shall return to my subject. 20
I think the advantages by the proposal which I have made are obvious and many, as well as of the highest importance.

For first, as I have already observed, it would greatly lessen the number of Papists, with whom we are yearly overrun, being the principal breeders of the nation as well as our most dangerous enemies; and who stay at home on purpose to deliver the kingdom to the Pretender, hoping to take their advantage by the absence of so many good Protestants, who have chosen rather to leave their country than to stay at home and pay tithes against their conscience to an Episcopal curate.

Secondly, the poorer tenants will have something valuable of their own, which by law may be made liable to distress,[10] and help to pay their landlord's rent, their corn and cattle being already seized and money a thing unknown.

Thirdly, whereas the maintenance of an hundred thousand children, from two years old and upwards, cannot be computed at less than ten shillings a piece per annum, the nation's stock will be thereby increased fifty thousand pounds per annum, besides the profit of a new dish introduced to the tables of all gentlemen of fortune in the kingdom who have any refinement in taste. And the money will circulate among ourselves, the goods being entirely of our own growth and manufacture.

Fourthly, the constant breeders, besides the gain of eight shillings sterling per annum by the sale of their children, will be rid of the charge of maintaining them after the first year.

Fifthly, this food would likewise bring great custom to taverns, 25
where the vintners will certainly be so prudent as to procure the best receipts[11] for dressing it to perfection, and consequently have their

---

[1] Seizure for the payment of debts.
[2] Recipes. *Custom*: commerce.

houses frequented by all the fine gentlemen, who justly value themselves upon their knowledge in good eating; and a skillful cook, who understands how to oblige his guests, will contrive to make it as expensive as they please.

Sixthly, this would be a great inducement to marriage, which all wise nations have either encouraged by rewards or enforced by laws and penalties. It would increase the care and tenderness of mothers toward their children, when they were sure of a settlement for life to the poor babes, provided in some sort by the public, to their annual profit instead of expense. We should see an honest emulation among the married women, which of them could bring the fattest child to the market. Men would become as fond of their wives during the time of their pregnancy as they are now of their mares in foal, their cows in calf, or sows when they are ready to farrow; nor offer to beat or kick them (as is too frequent a practice) for fear of a miscarriage.

Many other advantages might be enumerated. For instance, the addition of some thousand carcasses in our exportation of barreled beef, the propagation of swine's flesh, and improvement in the art of making good bacon, so much wanted among us by the great destruction of pigs, too frequent at our tables, which are no way comparable in taste or magnificence to a well-grown, fat, yearling child, which roasted whole will make a considerable figure at a lord mayor's feast or any other public entertainment. But this and many others I omit, being studious of brevity.

Supposing that one thousand families in this city would be constant customers for infants' flesh, besides others who might have it at merry meetings, particularly weddings and christenings, I compute that Dublin would take off annually about twenty thousand carcasses, and the rest of the kingdom (where probably they will be sold somewhat cheaper) the remaining eighty thousand.

I can think of no one objection that will possibly be raised against this proposal, unless it should be urged that the number of people will be thereby much lessened in the kingdom. This I freely own, and it was indeed one principal design in offering it to the world. I desire the reader will observe, that I calculate my remedy for this one individual kingdom of Ireland and for no other that ever was, is, or I think ever can be upon earth. Therefore let no man talk to me of other expedients: of taxing our absentees at five shillings a pound: of using neither clothes nor household furniture except what is of our own growth and manufacture: of utterly rejecting the materials and instruments that promote foreign luxury: of curing the expensiveness of pride, vanity, idleness, and gaming in our women: of introducing a vein of parsimony, prudence, and temperance: of learning to love our country, in the want of which we differ even from Laplanders and the inhabitants of Topinamboo:[12] of quitting our animosities and factions, nor acting any longer like the Jews, who were murdering one another at the very moment their city was taken: of being a little cautious not to sell our country and conscience for nothing: of teaching landlords to have at least one degree of mercy toward their tenants: lastly, of putting a spirit of honesty, industry, and skill into our shopkeepers; who, if a resolution could now be taken to buy only our native goods, would immediately unite to cheat and exact upon us in the price, the measure, and the goodness, nor could ever yet be brought to make one fair proposal of just dealing, though often and earnestly invited to it.

Therefore I repeat, let no man talk to me of these and the like expedients, till he hath at least some glimpse of hope that there will ever be some hearty and sincere attempt to put them in practice. 30

But as to myself, having been wearied out for many years with offering vain, idle, visionary thoughts, and at length utterly despairing of success, I fortunately fell upon this proposal, which, as it is wholly new, so it hath something solid and real, of no expense and little trouble, full in our own power, and whereby we can incur no danger in disobliging England. For this kind of commodity will not bear exportation, the flesh being of too tender a consistence to admit a long continuance in salt, although perhaps I could name a country which would be glad to eat up our whole nation without it.

After all, I am not so violently bent upon my own opinion as to reject any offer proposed by wise men, which shall be found equally innocent, cheap, easy, and effectual. But before something of that kind

---

[3] That is, the people of the extremely cold regions of northern Europe and the people of the jungles of Brazil.

shall be advanced in contradiction to my scheme, and offering a better, I desire the author or authors will be pleased maturely to consider two points. First, as things now stand, how they will be able to find food and raiment for an hundred thousand useless mouths and backs. And secondly, there being a round million of creatures in human figure throughout this kingdom, whose sole subsistence put into a common stock would leave them in debt two millions of pounds sterling, adding those who are beggars by profession to the bulk of farmers, cottagers, and laborers, with their wives and children who are beggars in effect; I desire those politicians who dislike my overture, and may perhaps be so bold to attempt an answer, that they will first ask the parents of these mortals whether they would not at this day think it a great happiness to have been sold for food at a year old in the manner I prescribe, and thereby have avoided such a perpetual scene of misfortunes as they have since gone through by the oppression of landlords, the impossibility of paying rent without money or trade, the want of common sustenance, with neither house nor clothes to cover them from the inclemencies of the weather, and the most inevitable prospect of entailing the like or greater miseries upon their breed forever.

I profess, in the sincerity of my heart, that I have not the least personal interest in endeavoring to promote this necessary work, having no other motive than the public good of my country, by advancing our trade, providing for infants, relieving the poor, and giving some pleasure to the rich. I have no children by which I can propose to get a single penny; the youngest being nine years old, and my wife past childbearing.

STUDY QUESTIONS

1. What does Swift's SPEAKER propose that the people of Ireland do with their children? Why is he making this PROPOSAL?

2. Consider Swift's persona in this essay. How does the speaker establish his ETHOS? Is it credible? Compassionate? Reasonable? Explain.

3. At what point in this proposal do you begin to suspect that Swift is engaging in SATIRE? How does he employ PATHOS and LOGOS within his satire? Where and for what purpose does he break from his satirical stance?

4. *For Writing.* Write a satirical "modest proposal" of your own, dealing with a social or political issue that you are familiar with, such as music downloading or health care reform. Make sure that your proposal, like Swift's, is impossible to take seriously but highlights a real problem. Create a speaker and address your proposal toward a specific AUDIENCE.

GEORGE F. WILL { *The Biofuel Follies*

GEORGE F. WILL (b. 1941) earned his BA from Trinity College in
Hartford, Connecticut, a second BA and an MA from Magdalen College,
Oxford University, and a second MA and a PhD from Princeton University.
Before becoming a journalist, he taught political philosophy at James
Madison College and the University of Toronto and served on the staff of
Senator Gordon Allott. Will edited the conservative *National Review* from
1972 to 1978, when he began writing a syndicated column for the
Washington Post. In 1976 he joined *Newsweek* magazine, where, just a year
later, his biweekly back-page column "The Last Word" won him a Pulitzer
Prize. Will has been a news analyst for ABC and has appeared on NBC's
Meet the Press. He has published a number of collections of his columns,
including *The Pursuit of Happiness and Other Sobering Thoughts* (1978), as
well as books on American culture, including *One Man's America: The
Pleasures and Provocations of Our Singular America* (2008).

In "The Biofuel Follies," originally published in *Newsweek*, Will argues
for increased petroleum production and against the production of biofuels.
He disputes environmentalists who want to keep the Arctic National
Wildlife Refuge (ANWR) in Alaska protected from oil drilling, and then he
takes on the farmers and farm-state politicians who urge that ethanol—that
is, biofuel—is a viable alternative to petroleum. As you read, think about
both the content of this opinion piece and Will's rhetorical style. Whom
does he seem to be writing for—those who might be persuaded to change
their minds or those who probably agree with him already?

IOWA'S CAUCUSES,[1] A SOURCE OF so much turbulence, might even have helped cause the recent demonstration by 10,000 Indonesians in Jakarta. Savor the multiplying irrationalities of the government-driven mania for ethanol and other biofuels, and energy policy generally.

Indonesians, like most Asians, love soybeans, the world price of which has risen 50 percent in a month and 125 percent in a year, partly because of increasing world population and incomes, but also because many farmers have switched land from soybeans to crops that can be turned into biofuels. In 2005, America used 15 percent of its corn crop to supplant less than 2 percent of its gasoline use. In 2007, the government-contrived U.S. demand for ethanol was more than half the global increase in demand. The political importance of corn-growing, ethanol-making Iowa is one reason that biofuel mandates flow from Washington the way oil would flow from the Arctic National Wildlife Refuge if it had nominating caucuses.

ANWR's 10.4 billion barrels of oil have become hostage to the planet's saviors (e.g., John McCain, Hillary Clinton, Barack Obama), who block drilling in even a tiny patch of ANWR. You could fit Massachusetts, New Jersey, Rhode Island, Connecticut and Delaware into ANWR's frozen desolation; the "footprint" of the drilling operation would be one sixth the size of Washington's Dulles airport.

Clinton has an alternative to drilling: Oil should be released from the Strategic Petroleum Reserve—which exists to protect the nation against major interruptions of supply—as "a signal to the market." A signal of what? Readiness to release more? All 698 million barrels? Then what?

Americans can still drill for . . . water. Water rights (T. Boone Pickens[2] has bought 400,000 acres of them in the Texas Panhandle) are becoming more valuable as ethanol production, which is extremely water-intensive, puts pressure on supplies. 5

To avoid drilling for oil in ANWR's moonscape, the planet savers evidently prefer destroying forests, even though they absorb greenhouse gases. Will ethanol prevent more carbon-dioxide emissions than

[1]Iowa's caucuses are the first state primary in the race for the U.S. presidency.
[2]American businessman (b. 1928), chairman of BP Capital Management, a hedge fund.

would have been absorbed by the trees cut down to clear land for the production of crops for ethanol? Be that as it may, governments mandating the use of biofuels are one reason for the global rise in food prices, which is driving demand for more arable land. That demand is driving the destruction of forests—and animal habitats. In Indonesia alone, 44 million acres have been razed to make way for production of palm oil.

The destruction of forests is one reason European governments are rethinking their biofuel enthusiasm. The European Union has awakened to the fact that growing crops (which requires diesel fuel for tractors, and nitrogen fertilizer made with natural gas) and turning them into biofuel (transporting them to energy-devouring manufacturing plants) takes a toll on the environment. So the EU might require—talk about lowered expectations—that any biofuel represent "a minimal level of greenhouse-gas savings."

The environmental argument for ethanol and other biofuels is, to say no more, rickety. The economic argument is refuted by the need to mandate and subsidize the fuels. The argument that biofuels are important for reducing our energy dependence on unreliable or dangerous Middle Eastern nations (the two largest sources of U.S. oil imports are turbulent Canada and militant Mexico) is mocked by the 54-cents-a-gallon tariff penalizing Brazilian ethanol. The theory behind that tariff is as old as American history. It is that "infant industries"— in this case, the ethanol industry that the government has ordered into existence—require protection. But protection permanently infantilizes industries.

If the argument for ethanol is that domestically produced energy should be increased, there are better ways of doing that. On the outer continental shelf there is a 50-year supply of clean-burning natural gas, 420 trillion cubic feet of it, that the government, at the behest of the planet's saviors, will not allow to be extracted. But, then, consider what was done in 1996 by the dominant half of today's Clinton tandem presidential candidacy.

Bill Clinton, by executive edict, declared 1.7 million acres of Utah 10 to be a national monument. Under those acres are the largest known deposit—more than 60 billion tons—of low-sulfur, clean-burning coal.

The second largest deposit, the value of which rose because of Clinton's action locking up an alternative supply, is in Indonesia and is owned by a member of the Indonesian Riady family, of fragrant memory,[3] which was generous to Clinton's 1992 campaign.

James and Stephen Eaves, writing in *Regulation* quarterly, note that if the entire U.S. corn crop were turned into ethanol—it might have to be to meet the goal of 35 billion gallons of biofuels by 2017—it would displace 3.5 percent of gasoline use, just slightly more than would be displaced if drivers properly inflated their tires. And because the United States produces 40 percent of the world's corn supply and 70 percent of global corn exports, turning corn into fuel will damage the world's poor at a time when rising demand will require a tripling of world food production by 2050.

Energy policy has become a mare's nest[4] of environmental and national-security fallacies. Energetic rethinking is in order.

---

[3]A reference to corruption controversies surrounding the family, including campaign finance violations resulting in the largest fines ever imposed for such charges.

[4]That is, a tangle of confusion and disorder.

STUDY QUESTIONS

1. Why are corn crops are at the center of Will's opinion piece? Why does Will criticize biofuel mandates from the government? How do other countries respond to the push for biofuel?

2. Who is Will's AUDIENCE? How can you tell?

3. What REASONS and what kinds of EVIDENCE does Will employ to support his CLAIM that ANWR should be drilled and that corn-produced biofuels are an inefficient means of meeting our energy needs? Which of these are the most and the least convincing, and why? To what other solutions does Will allude?

4. *For Writing.* RESEARCH the arguments for and against biofuel production, as well as the current state of biofuel technology. In an essay, use your findings to RESPOND to Will's claims and to take a POSITION on the issue.

Food Politics

ANN HODGMAN { *No Wonder They Call* *Me a Bitch*

ANN HODGMAN (b. 1956) writes children's books, cookbooks, and
nonfiction; her work is marked by a humorous tone and conversational
style, as well as vivid descriptions. Hodgman grew up in Rochester,
New York, earned a degree in English from Harvard, and now lives in
Connecticut with her husband and a houseful of pets. Her work has
appeared in the *Atlantic Monthly, Gourmet, Eating Well, Food & Wine,*
The New Yorker, Spy, and numerous other publications.

   In her well-known descriptive essay "No Wonder They Call Me a
Bitch," which appeared in the satiric magazine *Spy* in 1989, Hodgman
taste-tests a variety of dog foods and treats, describing their tastes,
textures, appearance, and oftentimes questionable ingredients. She
compares her own experience of the products to the claims advertisers
have made, demonstrating a clear gap between the two. As you read this
essay, consider the strategies Hodgman uses to make her writing
humorous.

──────────

I'VE ALWAYS WONDERED ABOUT DOG food. Is a Gaines-burger really
like a hamburger? Can you fry it? Does dog food "cheese" taste like
real cheese? Does Gravy Train actually make gravy in the dog's bowl,
or is that brown liquid just dissolved crumbs? And exactly what *are*
by-products?

   Having spent the better part of a week eating dog food, I'm sorry
to say that I now know the answers to these questions. While my

dachshund, Shortie, watched in agonies of yearning, I gagged my way through can after can of stinky, white-flecked mush and bag after bag of stinky, fat-drenched nuggets. And now I understand exactly why Shortie's breath is so bad.

Of course, Gaines-burgers are neither mush nor nuggets. They are, rather, a miracle of beauty and packaging—or at least that's what I thought when I was little. I used to beg my mother to get them for our dogs, but she always said they were too expensive. When I finally bought a box of cheese-flavored Gaines-burgers—after twenty years of longing—I felt deliciously wicked.

"Dogs love real beef," the back of the box proclaimed proudly. "That's why Gaines-burgers is the only beef burger for dogs with real beef and no meat by-products!" The copy was accurate: meat by-products did not appear in the list of ingredients. Poultry by-products did, though—right there next to preserved animal fat.

One Purina spokesman told me that poultry by-products consist of 5 necks, intestines, undeveloped eggs and other "carcass remnants," but not feathers, heads, or feet. When I told him I'd been eating dog food, he said, "Oh, you're kidding! Oh, *no!*" (I came to share his alarm when, weeks later, a second Purina spokesman said that Gaines-burgers *do* contain poultry heads and feet—but not undeveloped eggs.)

Up close my Gaines-burger didn't much resemble chopped beef. Rather, it looked—and felt—like a single long, extruded piece of redness that had been chopped into segments and formed into a patty. You could make one at home if you had a Play-Doh Fun Factory.

I turned on the skillet. While I waited for it to heat up I pulled out a shred of cheese-colored material and palpated it. Again, like Play-Doh; it was quite malleable. I made a little cheese bird out of it; then I counted to three and ate the bird.

There was a horrifying rush of cheddar taste, followed immediately by the dull tang of soybean flour—the main ingredient in Gaines-burgers. Next I tried a piece of red extrusion. The main difference between the meat-flavored and cheese-flavored extrusions is one of texture. The "cheese" chews like fresh Play-Doh, whereas the "meat" chews like Play-Doh that's been sitting out on a rug for a couple of hours.

Frying only turned the Gaines-burger black. There was no melting no sizzling, no warm meat smells. A cherished childhood illusion was gone. I flipped the patty into the sink, where it immediately began leaking rivulets of red dye.

As alarming as the Gaines-burgers were, their soy meal began to 10 seem like an old friend when the time came to try some *canned* dog foods. I decided to try the Cycle foods first. When I opened them, I thought about how rarely I use can openers these days, and I was suddenly visited by a long-forgotten sensation of can-opener distaste. *This* is the kind of unsavory place can openers spend their time when you're not watching! Every time you open a can of, say, Italian plum tomatoes, you infect them with invisible particles of by-product.

I had been expecting to see the usual homogeneous scrapple inside, but each can of Cycle was packed with smooth, round, oily nuggets. As if someone at Gaines had been tipped off that a human would be tasting the stuff, the four Cycles really were different from one another. Cycle-1, for puppies, is wet and soyish. Cycle-2, for adults, glistens nastily with fat, but it's passably edible—a lot like some canned Swedish meatballs I once got in a care package at college. Cycle-3, the "lite" one, for fatties, had no specific flavor; it just tasted like dog food. But at least it didn't make me fat.

Cycle-4, for senior dogs, had the smallest nuggets. Maybe old dogs can't open their mouths as wide. This kind was far sweeter than the other three Cycles—almost like baked beans. It was also the only one to contain "dried beef digest," a mysterious substance that the Purina spokesman defined as "enzymes" and my dictionary defined as "the products of digestion."

Next on the menu was a can of Kal Kan Pedigree with Chunky Chicken. Chunky *chicken*? There were chunks in the can, certainly— big, purplish-brown chunks. I forked one chunk out (by now I was becoming more callous) and found that while it had no discernible chicken flavor, it wasn't bad except for its texture—like meat loaf with ground-up chicken bones.

In the world of canned dog food, a smooth consistency is a sign of low quality—lots of cereal. A lumpy, frightening, bloody, stringy horror is a sign of high quality—lots of meat. Nowhere in the world of wet dog foods was this demonstrated better than in the fanciest I tried—Kal Kan's Pedigree Select Dinners. These came not in a can but in a tiny foil packet with a picture of an imperious Yorkie. When I pulled open the container, juice spurted all over my hand, and the first chunk I speared was trailing a long gray vein. I shrieked and went instead for a plain chunk, which I was able to swallow only after taking a break to read some suddenly fascinating office equipment catalogues. Once again, though, it tasted no more alarming than, say, canned hash.

Still, how pleasant it was to turn to *dry* dog food! Gravy Train was the 15 first I tried, and I'm happy to report that it really does make a "thick, rich, real beef gravy" when you mix it with water. Thick and rich, anyway. Except for a lingering rancid-fat flavor, the gravy wasn't beefy, but since it tasted primarily like tap water, it wasn't nauseating either.

My poor dachshund just gets plain old Purina Dog Chow, but Purina also makes a dry food called Butcher's Blend that comes in Beef, Bacon & Chicken flavor. Here we see dog food's arcane semiotics at its best: a red triangle with a *T* stamped into it is supposed to suggest beef; a tan curl, chicken; and a brown *S*, a piece of bacon. Only dogs understand these messages. But Butcher's Blend does have an endearing slogan: "Great Meaty Tastes—without bothering the Butcher!" *You know, I wanted to buy some meat, but I just couldn't bring myself to bother the butcher . . .*

Purina O.N.E. ("Optimum Nutritional Effectiveness") is targeted at people who are unlikely ever to worry about bothering a tradesperson. "We chose chicken as a primary ingredient in Purina O.N.E. for several reasonings," the long, long essay on the back of the bag announces. Chief among these reasonings, I'd guess, is the fact that chicken appeals to people who are—you know—*like us.* Although our dogs do nothing but spend eighteen-hour days alone in the apartment, we still want them to be *premium* dogs. We want them to cut down on red meat, too. We also want dog food that comes in a bag with an attractive design, a subtle typeface, and no kitschy pictures of slobbering golden retrievers.

Besides that, we want a list of the Nutritional Benefits of our dog food—and we get it on O.N.E. One thing I especially like about this list is its constant references to a dog's "hair coat," as in "Beef tallow is good for the dog's skin and hair coat." (On the other hand, beef tallow merely provides palatability, while the dried beef digest in Cycle provides palatability *enhancement.*)

I hate to say it, but O.N.E. was pretty palatable. Maybe that's because it has about 100 percent more fat than, say, Butcher's Blend. Or maybe I'd been duped by the packaging; that's been known to happen before.

As with people food, dog snacks taste much better than dog meals. They're better-looking too. Take Milk-Bone Flavor Snacks. The loving-hands-at-home prose describing each flavor is colorful; the writers practically choke on their own exuberance. Of bacon they say, "It's so good, your dog will think it's hot off the frying pan." Of liver: "The only taste your dog wants more than liver—is even more liver!" Of poultry: "All those farm fresh flavors deliciously mixed in one biscuit. Your dog will bark with delight!" And of vegetable: "Gardens of taste! Specially blended to give your dog that vegetable flavor he wants—but can rarely get!"

Well, I may be a sucker, but advertising this emphatic just doesn't convince me. I lined up all seven flavors of Milk-Bone Flavor Snacks on the floor. Unless my dog's palate is a lot more sensitive than mine— and considering that she steals dirty diapers out of the trash and eats them, I'm loath to think it is—she doesn't detect any more difference in the seven flavors than I did when I tried them.

I much preferred Bonz, the hard-baked, bone-shaped snack stuffed with simulated marrow. I liked the bone part, that is; it tasted almost exactly like the cornmeal it was made of. The mock marrow inside was a bit more problematic: in addition to looking like the sludge that collects in the treads of my running shoes, it was bursting with tiny hairs.

I'm sure you have a few dog food questions of your own. To save us time, I've answered them in advance.

Q. *Are those little cans of Mighty Dog actually branded with the sizzling word* BEEF, *the way they show in the commercials?*

A. You should know by now that that kind of thing never happens.

Q. *Does chicken-flavored dog food taste like chicken-flavored cat food?*

A. To my surprise, chicken cat food was actually a little better— more chickeny. It tasted like inferior canned pâté.

Q. Was there any dog food that you just couldn't bring yourself to try?

A. Alas, it was a can of Mighty Dog called Prime Entree with Bone Marrow. The meat was dark, dark brown, and it was surrounded by gelatin that was almost black. I knew I would die if I tasted it, so I put it outside for the raccoons.

STUDY QUESTIONS

1. What do you think Hodgman's PURPOSE was in sampling different kinds of dog foods and describing the results of her taste-testing? Why do you think she doesn't explicitly indicate why she did so?

2. What was the effect of Hodgman's title? Did her title give you any idea of what the article would be about, or help shape her ETHOS?

3. In order to DESCRIBE tastes and textures that may be unfamiliar to readers, Hodgman makes COMPARISONS (often through SIMILES) to products that may be more familiar to readers (Play-Doh, baked beans, Swedish meatballs, etc.). Which comparisons do you find most successful? Why?

4. Why do you think Hodgman chose to begin and end her essay with a series of questions? Do those questions help define her TONE? How?

5. *For Writing.* Write a three- to four-page humorous descriptive essay about a product for which advertisers make particular claims that few people have actually researched for themselves (e.g., deodorants, tissues, face creams, etc.).

MARION NESTLE { *The Supermarket:*
Prime Real Estate

MARION NESTLE (b. 1936) teaches courses in food studies, nutrition, and public health at New York University. At the University of California, Berkeley, Nestle earned a PhD in molecular biology in 1968 and an MPH in public health nutrition in 1986. From 1986 to 1988 she worked as a policy adviser for the Department of Health and Human Services and served as an editor of *The Surgeon General's Report on Nutrition and Health.* She is the author of several books on nutrition and food safety, including *Food Politics: How the Food Industry Influences Nutrition and Health* (2002); *Safe Food: The Politics of Food Safety* (2003); *What to Eat* (2006); and *Pet Food Politics: The Chihuahua in the Coal Mine* (2008).

"The Supermarket: Prime Real Estate" is the first chapter of *What to Eat.* Nestle's overview of supermarket design reveals the ways in which marketing and design influence consumer purchases—and what is profitable for the supermarket often comes at the expense of consumer health. Marketers, of course, encourage consumers to buy large amounts of processed foods. Nestle's goal, instead, is to guide readers to make healthier food choices.

A VISIT TO A LARGE supermarket can be a daunting experience: so many aisles, so many brands and varieties, so many prices to keep track of and labels to read, so many choices to make. No wonder. To repeat: An astonishing 320,000 edible products are for sale in the United States, and any large supermarket might display as many as 40,000 of them. You are supposed to feel daunted—bewildered by all the choices and forced to wander through the aisles in search of the items you came to buy. The big companies that own most supermarkets want you to do as much searching as you can tolerate. It is no coincidence that one supermarket is laid out much like another: breathtaking amounts of research have gone into designing these places. There are precise reasons why milk is at the back of the store and the center aisles are so long. You are forced to go past thousands of other products on your way to get what you need.

Supermarkets say they are in the business of offering "choice." Perhaps, but they do everything possible to make the choice theirs, not yours. Supermarkets are not social service agencies providing food for the hungry. Their job is to sell food, and more of it. From their perspective, it is *your* problem if what you buy makes you eat more food than you need, and more of the wrong kinds of foods in particular.

And supermarket retailers know more than you could possibly imagine about how to push your "buy" buttons. Half a century ago, Vance Packard revealed their secrets in his book *The Hidden Persuaders*. His most shocking revelation? Corporations were hiring social scientists to study unconscious human emotions, not for the good of humanity but to help companies manipulate people into buying products. Packard's chapter on supermarket shopping, "Babes in Consumerland," is as good a guide as anything that has been written since to methods for getting you—and your children—to "reach out, hypnotically . . . and grab boxes of cookies, candies, dog food, and everything else that delights or interests [you]."

More recent research on consumer behavior not only confirms his observations but continues to be awe-inspiring in its meticulous attention to detail. Your local library has entire textbooks and academic journals devoted to investigations of consumer behavior and ways to use the results of that research to sell products. Researchers are constantly interviewing shoppers and listening carefully to what they are told. Because of scanners, supermarkets can now track your purchases and compare what you tell researchers to what you actually buy. If you belong to a supermarket discount "shoppers club," the store gains your loyalty but gets to track your personal buying habits in exchange. This research tells food retailers how to lay out the stores, where to put specific products, how to position products on shelves, and how to set prices and advertise products. At the super-market, you exercise freedom of choice and personal responsibility every time you put an item in your shopping cart, but massive efforts have gone into making it more convenient and desirable for you to choose some products rather than others.

As basic marketing textbooks explain, the object of the game is to 5 "maximize sales and profit consistent with customer convenience." Translated, this means that supermarkets want to expose you to the largest possible number of items that you can stand to see, without annoying you so much that you run screaming from the store. This strategy is based on research proving that "the rate of exposure is directly related to the rate of sale of merchandise." In other words, the more you see, the more you buy. Supermarkets dearly wish they could expose you to every single item they carry, every time you shop. Ter-rific as that might be for your walking regimen, you are unlikely to endure having to trek through interminable aisles to find the few items you came in for—and retailers know it. This conflict creates a serious dilemma for the stores. They have to figure out how to get you to walk up and down those aisles for as long as possible, but not so long that you get frustrated. To resolve the dilemma, the stores make some compromises—but as few as possible. Overall, supermarket design fol-lows fundamental rules, all of them based firmly on extensive research.

- Place the highest-selling food departments in the parts of the store that get the greatest flow of traffic—the periphery. Perishables—meat, produce, dairy, and frozen foods—generate the most sales, so put them against the back and side walls.

- Use the aisle nearest the entrance for items that sell especially well on impulse or look or smell enticing—produce, flowers, or freshly baked bread, for example. These must be the first things customers see in front or immediately to the left or right (the direction, according to researchers, doesn't matter).

- Use displays at the ends of aisles for high-profit, heavily adver-tised items likely to be bought on impulse.

- Place high-profit, center-aisle food items sixty inches above the floor where they are easily seen by adults, with or without eyeglasses.

- Devote as much shelf space as possible to brands that generate frequent sales; the more shelf space they occupy, the better they sell.

- Place store brands immediately to the right of those high-traffic items (people read from left to right), so that the name brands attract shoppers to the store brands too.

- Avoid using "islands." These make people bump into each other and want to move on. Keep the traffic moving, but slowly.

- Do not create gaps in the aisles that allow customers to cross over to the next one unless the aisles are so long that shoppers complain. If shoppers can escape mid-aisle, they will miss seeing half the products along that route.

Additional principles, equally well researched, guide every other aspect of supermarket design: product selection, placement on shelves, and display. The guiding principle of supermarket layout is the same: products seen most sell best. Think of the supermarket as a particularly intense real estate market in which every product competes fiercely against every other for precious space. Because you can see products most easily at eye level, at the ends of aisles, and at the checkout counters, these areas are prime real estate. Which products get the prime space? The obvious answer: the ones most profitable for the store.

But store profitability is not simply a matter of the price charged for a product compared to its costs. Stores also collect revenue by "renting" real estate to the companies whose products they sell. Product placement depends on a system of "incentives" that sometimes sound suspiciously like bribes. Food companies pay supermarkets "slotting fees" for the shelf space they occupy. The rates are highest for premium, high-traffic space, such as the shelves near cash registers. Supermarkets demand and get additional sources of revenue from food companies in "trade allowances," guarantees that companies will buy local advertising for the products for which they pay slotting fees. The local advertising, of course, helps to make sure that products in prime real estate sell quickly.

This unsavory system puts retail food stores in firm control of the marketplace. They make the decisions about which products to sell and, therefore, which products you buy. This system goes beyond a simple matter of supply and demand. The stores *create* demand by putting some products where you cannot miss them. These are often "junk" foods full of cheap, shelf-stable ingredients like hydrogenated oils and corn sweeteners, made and promoted by giant food companies that can afford slotting fees, trade allowances, and advertising. This is why entire aisles of prime supermarket real estate are devoted to soft drinks, salty snacks, and sweetened breakfast cereals, and why you can always find candy next to cash registers. Any new product that comes into a store must come with guaranteed advertising, coupons, discounts, slotting fees, and other such incentives.

Slotting fees emerged in the 1980s as a way for stores to cover the added costs of dealing with new products: shelving, tracking inventory, and removing products that do not sell. But the system is so corrupt and so secret that Congress held hearings about it in 1999. The industry people who testified at those hearings were so afraid of retribution that they wore hoods and used gadgets to prevent voice recognition. The General Accounting Office, the congressional watchdog agency (now called the Government Accountability Office), was asked to do its own investigation but got nowhere because the retail food industry refused to cooperate.

The defense of the current system by both the retailers who demand 10 the fees and the companies that agree to pay them comes at a high cost—out of your pocket. You pay for this system in at least three ways: higher prices at the supermarket; taxes that in part compensate for business tax deductions that food companies are allowed to take for slotting fees and advertising; and the costs of treating illnesses that might result from consuming more profitable but less healthful food products.

In 2005, supermarkets sold more than $350 billion worth of food in the United States, but this level of sales does not stop them from complaining about low after-tax profit margins—just 1 to 3 percent of sales. One percent of $350 billion is $3.5 billion, of course, but by some corporate standards that amount is too little to count. In any case, corporations have to grow to stay viable, so corporate pressures on supermarkets to increase sales are unrelenting. The best way to expand sales, say researchers, is to increase the size of the selling area and the number of items offered. Supermarkets do both. In the last decade, mergers and acquisitions have turned the top-ranking supermarkets—Kroger, Albertsons, and Safeway—into companies with annual sales of $56, $40, and $36 billion, respectively. Small chains, like Whole Foods and Wegmans, have sales in the range of just $4 billion a year.

But sales brought in by these small chains are peanuts compared to those of the store that now dominates the entire retail food marketplace: Wal-Mart. Wal-Mart sold $284 billion worth of goods in 2005. Groceries accounted for about one-quarter of that amount, but that meant $64 billion, and rising. Many food companies do a third of their business with this one retailer. Wal-Mart does not have to demand slotting fees. If a food company wants its products to be in Wal-Mart, it has to offer rock-bottom prices. Low prices sound good for people without much money, but nutritionally, there's a catch. Low prices encourage everyone to buy more food in bigger packages. If you buy more, you are quite likely to eat more. And if you eat more, you are more likely to gain weight and become less healthy.

Food retailers argue that if you eat too much it is your problem, not theirs. But they are in the business of encouraging you to buy more food, not less. Take the matter of package size and price. I often talk to business groups about such matters and at a program for food executives at Cornell University, I received a barrage of questions about where personal responsibility fits into this picture. One supermarket manager insisted that his store does not force customers to buy Pepsi in big bottles. He also offers Pepsi in 8-ounce cans. The sizes and prices are best shown in a Table (see next page).

PRICE OF PEPSI-COLA, P&C MARKET, ITHACA, NEW YORK, JULY 2005

CONTAINER SIZE	TOTAL OUNCES	PRICE	PRICE PER QUART
2-liter bottle	67	$1.49	$0.71
24-ounce bottles (6-pack)	144	$3.00*	$0.67
16-ounce bottles (6-pack)	96	$2.99	$1.00
12-ounce cans (12-pack)	144	$4.49	$1.00
8-ounce cans (6-pack)	48	$2.25	$1.50

*This is with a P&C store membership "Wild Card."

In this store, the 2-liter container and the special-for-members 6-pack of 24-ounce bottles were less than half the cost of the equivalent volume in 8-ounce cans. Supermarket managers tell me that this kind of pricing is not the store's problem. If you want smaller sizes, you should be willing to pay more for them. But if you care about how much you get for a price, you are likely to pick the larger sizes. And if you buy the larger sizes, you are likely to drink more Pepsi and take in more calories; the 8-ounce cans of Pepsi contain 100 calories each, but the 2-liter bottle holds 800 calories.

Sodas of any size are cheap because they are mostly water and corn 15 sweeteners—water is practically free, and your taxes pay to subsidize corn production. This makes the cost of the ingredients trivial compared to labor and packaging, so the larger sizes are more profitable to the manufacturer and to the stores. The choice is yours, but anyone would have a hard time choosing a more expensive version of a product when a cheaper one is right there. Indeed, you have to be strong and courageous to hold out for healthier choices in the supermarket system as it currently exists.

You could, of course, bring a shopping list, but good luck sticking to it. Research says that about 70 percent of shoppers bring lists into supermarkets, but only about 10 percent adhere to them. Even with a list, most shoppers pick up two additional items for every item on it. The additions are "in-store decisions," or impulse buys. Stores directly appeal to your senses to distract you from worrying about lists. They hope you will:

- Listen to the background music. The slower the beat, the longer you will tarry.

- Search for the "loss leaders" (the items you always need, like meat, coffee, or bananas, that are offered at or below their actual cost). The longer you search, the more products you will see.

- Go to the bakery, prepared foods, and deli sections; the sights and good smells will keep you lingering and encourage sales.

- Taste the samples that companies are giving away. If you like what you taste, you are likely to buy it.

- Put your kids in the play areas; the longer they play there, the more time you have to walk those tempting aisles.

If you find yourself in a supermarket buying on impulse and not minding it a bit, you are behaving exactly the way store managers want you to. You will be buying the products they have worked long and hard to make most attractive and convenient for you—and most profitable for them.

STUDY QUESTIONS

1. Nestle lists eight fundamental rules of supermarket design. What are they? Had you been aware of these design features before you read this piece?

2. Nestle uses CAUSE AND EFFECT as a method for developing her argument that supermarket retailers use research to influence consumer behavior. What do supermarket retailers do (cause), and how do those practices influence consumer behavior (effect)?

3. Nestle uses a table and two bulleted lists as design features of her essay. How do these design features support her ARGUMENT? Do you find them effective? Why?

4. *For Writing.* Nestle did much of her research for her essay in 2005. With her claims in mind, visit a local supermarket. Have any design features or food marketing strategies changed in the years since her book was published in 2006? Using your FIELD RESEARCH as your primary source, write a four- to six-page report about the design features and marketing strategies you see at your local supermarket. Like Nestle, use at least one table and one bulleted list to report your findings.

ERIC SCHLOSSER { *Why McDonald's*
French Fries
Taste So Good }

ERIC SCHLOSSER (b. 1959) received his BA from Princeton University and his MA from Oxford University. A contributing editor for *The Atlantic Monthly*, Schlosser has also had articles published in *Rolling Stone, Vanity Fair, The Nation,* and *The New Yorker.* His book *Reefer Madness* (2003) probes America's anti-marijuana laws and the "war on drugs." Schlosser's best-known book is *Fast Food Nation* (2001), from which this selection was taken.

In this expository essay, Schlosser moves outward from the specific example of McDonald's French fries to examine the processed-food industry, how our sense of taste works, artificial additives, and the chemistry of "flavor." He describes the various ways manufacturers make food taste the way it does in order to satisfy—and create—consumer demand. Additionally, Schlosser demonstrates how industry profits from the preferences consumers formed in childhood and points out legal but possibly deadly ommissions from food ingredient labels. In other words, the author reveals that there is a lot more to the food industry than just food.

THE FRENCH FRY WAS "ALMOST sacrosanct for me," Ray Kroc, one of the founders of McDonald's, wrote in his autobiography, "its preparation a ritual to be followed religiously." During the chain's early years french fries were made from scratch every day. Russet Burbank potatoes were peeled, cut into shoestrings, and fried in McDonald's kitchens. As the chain expanded nationwide, in the mid-1960s, it sought to cut labor costs, reduce the number of suppliers, and ensure that its fries tasted the same at every restaurant. McDonald's began switching to frozen french fries in 1966—and few customers noticed the difference. Nevertheless, the change had a profound effect on the nation's agriculture and diet. A familiar food had been transformed into a highly processed industrial commodity. McDonald's fries now come from huge manufacturing plants that can peel, slice, cook, and freeze two million pounds of potatoes a day. The rapid expansion of McDonald's and the popularity of its low-cost, mass-produced fries changed the way Americans eat. In 1960 Americans consumed an average of about eighty-one pounds of fresh potatoes and four pounds of frozen french fries. In 2000 they consumed an average of about fifty pounds of fresh potatoes and thirty pounds of frozen fries. Today McDonald's is the largest buyer of potatoes in the United States.

The taste of McDonald's french fries played a crucial role in the chain's success—fries are much more profitable than hamburgers—and was long praised by customers, competitors, and even food critics. James Beard[1] loved McDonald's fries. Their distinctive taste does not stem from the kind of potatoes that McDonald's buys, the technology that processes them, or the restaurant equipment that fries them: other chains use Russet Burbanks, buy their french fries from the same large processing companies, and have similar fryers in their restaurant kitchens. The taste of a french fry is largely determined by the cooking oil. For decades McDonald's cooked its french fries in a mixture of about seven percent cottonseed oil and 93 percent beef tallow. The mixture gave the fries their unique flavor—and more saturated beef fat per ounce than a McDonald's hamburger.

In 1990, amid a barrage of criticism over the amount of cholesterol in its fries, McDonald's switched to pure vegetable oil. This presented the company with a challenge: how to make fries that subtly taste like beef without cooking them in beef tallow. A look at the ingredients in McDonald's french fries suggests how the problem was solved. Toward the end of the list is a seemingly innocuous yet oddly mysterious phrase: "natural flavor." That ingredient helps to explain not only

[1] American food writer and chef (1903–85).

why the fries taste so good but also why most fast food—indeed, most of the food Americans eat today—tastes the way it does.

Open your refrigerator, your freezer, your kitchen cupboards, and look at the labels on your food. You'll find "natural flavor" or "artificial flavor" in just about every list of ingredients. The similarities between these two broad categories are far more significant than the differences. Both are man-made additives that give most processed food most of its taste. People usually buy a food item the first time because of its packaging or appearance. Taste usually determines whether they buy it again. About 90 percent of the money that Americans now spend on food goes to buy processed food. The canning, freezing, and dehydrating techniques used in processing destroy most of food's flavor—and so a vast industry has arisen in the United States to make processed food palatable. Without this flavor industry today's fast food would not exist. The names of the leading American fast-food chains and their best-selling menu items have become embedded in our popular culture and famous worldwide. But few people can name the companies that manufacture fast food's taste.

The flavor industry is highly secretive. Its leading companies will 5 not divulge the precise formulas of flavor compounds or the identities of clients. The secrecy is deemed essential for protecting the reputations of beloved brands. The fast-food chains, understandably, would like the public to believe that the flavors of the food they sell somehow originate in their restaurant kitchens, not in distant factories run by other firms. A McDonald's french fry is one of countless foods whose flavor is just a component in a complex manufacturing process. The look and the taste of what we eat now are frequently deceiving—by design.

THE FLAVOR CORRIDOR

The New Jersey Turnpike runs through the heart of the flavor industry, an industrial corridor dotted with refineries and chemical plants. International Flavors & Fragrances (IFF), the world's largest flavor company, has a manufacturing facility off Exit 8A in Dayton, New Jersey; Givaudan, the world's second-largest flavor company, has a plant in East Hanover. Haarmann & Reimer, the largest German flavor company, has a plant in Teterboro, as does Takasago, the largest Japanese flavor company. Flavor Dynamics had a plant in South Plainfield; Frutarom is in North Bergen; Elan Chemical is in Newark. Dozens of companies manufacture flavors in the corridor between Teaneck and South Brunswick. Altogether the area produces about two thirds of the flavor additives sold in the United States.

The IFF plant in Dayton is a huge pale-blue building with a modern office complex attached to the front. It sits in an industrial park, not far from a BASF plastics factory, a Jolly French Toast factory, and a plant that manufactures Liz Claiborne cosmetics. Dozens of tractor-trailers were parked at the IFF loading dock the afternoon I visited, and a thin cloud of steam floated from a roof vent. Before entering the plant, I signed a nondisclosure form, promising not to reveal the brand names of foods that contain IFF flavors. The place reminded me of Willy Wonka's chocolate factory.[2] Wonderful smells drifted through the hallways, men and women in neat white lab coats cheerfully went about their work, and hundreds of little glass bottles sat on laboratory tables and shelves. The bottles contained powerful but fragile flavor chemicals, shielded from light by brown glass and round white caps shut tight. The long chemical names on the little white labels were as mystifying to me as medieval Latin. These odd-sounding things would be mixed and poured and turned into new substances, like magic potions.

I was not invited into the manufacturing areas of the IFF plant, where, it was thought, I might discover trade secrets. Instead I toured various laboratories and pilot kitchens, where the flavors of well-established brands are tested or adjusted, and where whole new flavors are created. IFF's snack-and-savory lab is responsible for the flavors of potato chips, corn chips, breads, crackers, breakfast cereals, and pet food. The confectionery lab devises flavors for ice cream, cookies, candies, toothpastes, mouthwashes, and antacids. Everywhere I looked, I saw famous, widely advertised products sitting on laboratory desks

---

[2] A reference to the 1964 novel by Roald Dahl, *Charlie and the Chocolate Factory*, which was adapted into the 1971 movie *Willy Wonka and the Chocolate Factory*.

and tables. The beverage lab was full of brightly colored liquids in clear bottles. It comes up with flavors for popular soft drinks, sports drinks, bottled teas, and wine coolers, for all-natural juice drinks, organic soy drinks, beers, and malt liquors. In one pilot kitchen I saw a dapper food technologist, a middle-aged man with an elegant tie beneath his crisp lab coat, carefully preparing a batch of cookies with white frosting and pink-and-white sprinkles. In another pilot kitchen I saw a pizza oven, a grill, a milk-shake machine, and a french fryer identical to those I'd seen at innumerable fast-food restaurants.

In addition to being the world's largest flavor company, IFF manufactures the smells of six of the ten best-selling fine perfumes in the United States, including Estée Lauder's Beautiful, Clinique's Happy, Lancôme's Tresor, and Calvin Klein's Eternity. It also makes the smells of household products such as deodorant, dishwashing detergent, bath soap, shampoo, furniture polish, and floor wax. All these aromas are made through essentially the same process: the manipulation of volatile chemicals. The basic science behind the scent of your shaving cream is the same as that governing the flavor of your TV dinner.

"NATURAL" AND "ARTIFICIAL"

Scientists now believe that human beings acquired the sense of taste 10 as a way to avoid being poisoned. Edible plants generally taste sweet, harmful ones bitter. The taste buds on our tongues can detect the presence of half a dozen or so basic tastes, including sweet, sour, bitter, salty, astringent, and umami, a taste discovered by Japanese researchers—a rich and full sense of deliciousness triggered by amino acids in foods such as meat, shellfish, mushrooms, potatoes, and seaweed. Taste buds offer a limited means of detection, however, compared with the human olfactory system, which can perceive thousands of different chemical aromas. Indeed, "flavor" is primarily the smell of gases being released by the chemicals you've just put in your mouth. the aroma of a food can be responsible for as much as 90 percent of its taste.

The act of drinking, sucking, or chewing a substance releases its volatile gases. They flow out of your mouth and up your nostrils, or up the passageway in the back of your mouth, to a thin layer of nerve cells called the olfactory epithelium, located at the base of your nose, right between your eyes. Your brain combines the complex smell signals from your olfactory epithelium with the simple taste signals from your tongue, assigns a flavor to what's in your mouth, and decides if it's something you want to eat.

A person's food preferences, like his or her personality, are formed during the first few years of life, through a process of socialization. Babies innately prefer sweet tastes and reject bitter ones; toddlers can learn to enjoy hot and spicy food, bland health food, or fast food, depending on what the people around them eat. The human sense of smell is still not fully understood. It is greatly affected by psychological factors and expectations. The mind focuses intently on some of the aromas that surround us and filters out the overwhelming majority. People can grow accustomed to bad smells or good smells; they stop noticing what once seemed overpowering. Aroma and memory are somehow inextricably linked. A smell can suddenly evoke a long-forgotten moment. The flavors of childhood foods seem to leave an indelible mark, and adults often return to them, without always knowing why. These "comfort foods" become a source of pleasure and reassurance—a fact that fast-food chains use to their advantage. Childhood memories of Happy Meals, which come with french fries, can translate into frequent adult visits to McDonald's. On average, Americans now eat about four servings of french fries every week.

The human craving for flavor has been a largely unacknowledged and unexamined force in history. For millennia royal empires have been built, unexplored lands traversed, and great religions and philosophies forever changed by the spice trade. In 1492 Chirstopher Columbus set sail to find seasoning. Today the influence of flavor in the world marketplace is no less decisive. The rise and fall of corporate empires—of soft-drink companies, snack-food companies, and fast-food chains—is often determined by how their products taste.

The flavor industry emerged in the mid-nineteenth century, as processed foods began to be manufactured on a large scale. Recognizing the need for flavor additives, early food processors turned to perfume companies that had long experience working with essential oils and volatile aromas. The great perfume houses of England, France, and the Netherlands produced many of the first flavor compounds. In the early part of the twentieth century Germany took the technological lead in flavor production, owing to its powerful chemical industry. Legend has it that a German scientist discovered methyl anthranilate, one of the first artificial flavors, by accident while mixing chemicals in his laboratory. Suddenly the lab was filled with the sweet smell of grapes. Methyl anthranilate later became the chief flavor compound in grape Kool-Aid. After World War II much of the perfume industry shifted from Europe to the United States, settling in New York City near the garment district and the fashion houses. The flavor industry came with it, later moving to New Jersey for greater plant capacity. Man-made flavor additives were used mostly in baked goods, candies, and sodas until the 1950s, when sales of processed food began to soar. The invention of gas chromatographs and mass spectrometers—machines capable of detecting volatile gases at low levels—vastly increased the number of flavors that could be synthesized. By the mid-1960s flavor companies were churning out compounds to supply the taste of Pop Tarts, Bac-Os, Tab, Tang, Filet-O-Fish sandwiches, and literally thousands of other new foods.

The American flavor industry now has annual revenues of about 15 $1.4 billion. Approximately 10,000 new processed-food products are introduced every year in the United States. Almost all of them require flavor additives. And about nine out of ten of these products fail. The latest flavor innovations and corporate realignments are heralded in publications such as *Chemical Market Reporter, Food Chemical News, Food Engineering,* and *Food Product Design.* The progress of IFF has mirrored that of the flavor industry as a whole. IFF was formed in 1958, through the merger of two small companies. Its annual revenues have grown almost fifteenfold since the early 1970s, and it currently has manufacturing facilities in twenty countries.

Today's sophisticated spectrometers, gas chromatographs, and headspace-vapor analyzers provide a detailed map of a food's flavor components, detecting chemical aromas present in amounts as low as one part per billion. The human nose, however, is even more sensitive. A nose can detect aromas present in quantities of a few parts per trillion—an amount equivalent to about 0.000000000003 percent. Complex aromas, such as those of coffee and roasted meat, are composed of volatile gases from nearly a thousand differnet chemicals. The smell of a strawberry arises from the interaction of about 350 chemicals that are present in minute amounts. The quality that people seek most of all in a food—flavor—is usually present in a quantity too infinitesimal to be measured in traditional culinary terms such as ounces or teaspoons. The chemical that provides the dominant flavor of bell pepper can be tasted in amounts as low as 0.02 parts per billion; one drop is sufficient to add flavor to five average-size swimming pools. The flavor additive usually comes next to last in a processed food's list of ingredients and often costs less than its packaging. Soft drinks contain a larger proportion of flavor additives than most products. The flavor in a twelve-ounce can of Coke costs about half a cent.

The color additives in processed foods are usually present in even smaller amounts than the flavor compounds. Many of New Jersey's flavor companies also manufacture these color additives, which are used to make processed foods look fresh and appealing. Food coloring serves many of the same decorative purposes as lipstick, eye shadow, mascara—and is often made from the same pigments. Titanium dioxide, for example, has proved to be an especially versatile mineral. It gives many processed candies, frostings and icings their bright white color; it is a common ingredient in women's cosmetics; and it is the pigment used in many white oil paints and house paints. At Burger King, Wendy's, and McDonald's coloring agents have been added to many of the soft drinks, salad dressings, cookies, condiments, chicken dishes, and sandwich buns.

Studies have found that the color of a food can greatly affect how its taste is perceived. Brightly colored foods frequently seem to taste better than bland-looking foods, even when the flavor compounds are identical. Foods that somehow look off-color often seem to have off tastes. For thousands of years human beings have relied on visual cues to help determine what is edible. The color of fruit suggests whther it is ripe, the color of meat whether it is rancid. Flavor researchers sometimes use colored lights to modify the influence of visual cues during taste tests. During one experiment in the early 1970s people were served an oddly tinted meal of steak and french fries that appeared normal beneath colored lights. Everyone thought the meal tasted fine until the lighting was changed. Once it became apparent that the steak was actually blue and the fries were green, some people became ill.

The federal Food and Drug Administration does not require companies to disclose the ingredients of their color or flavor additives so long as all the chemicals in them are considered by the agency to be GRAS ("generally recognized as safe"). This enables companies to maintain the secrecy of their formulas. It also hides the fact that flavor compounds often contain more ingredients than the foods to which they give taste. The phrase "artificial strawberry flavor" gives little hint of the chemical wizardry and manufacturing skill that can make a highly processed food taste like strawberries. A typical artificial strawberry flavor, like the kind found in a Burger King strawberry milk shake, contains the following ingredients: amyl acetate, amyl butyrate, amyl valerate, anethol, anisyl formate, benzyl acetate, benzyl isobutyrate, butyric acid, cinnamyl isobutyrate, cinnamyl valerate, cognac essential oil, diacetyl, dipropyl ketone, ethyl acetate, ethyl amyl ketone, ethyl butyrate, ethyl cinnamate, ethyl heptanoate, ethyl heptylate, ethyl lactate, ethyl methylphenylglycideate, ethyl nitrate, ethyl propionate, ethyl valerate, heliotropin, hydroxyphenyl-2-butanone (10 percent solution in alcohol), a-ionone, isobutyl anthranilate, isobutyl butyrate, lemon essential oil, maltol, 4-methylacetophenone, methyl anthranilate, methyl benzoate, methyl cinnamate, methyl heptine carbonate, methyl naphthyl ketone, methyl salicylate, mint essential oil, neroli essential oil, nerolin, neryl isobutyrate, orris butter, phenethyl alcohol, rose, rum ether, gamma-undecalactone, vanillin, and solvent.

Although flavors usually arise from a mixture of many different 20 volatile chemicals, often a single compound supplies the dominant aroma. Smelled alone, that chemical provides an unmistakable sense of the food. Ethyl-2-methyl butyrate, for example, smells just like an apple. Many of today's highly processed foods offer a blank palette:

whatever chemicals are added to them will give them specific tastes. Adding methyl-2-pyridyl ketone makes something taste like popcorn. Adding ethyl-3-hydroxy butanoate makes it taste like marshmallow. The possibilities are now almost limitless. Without affecting appearance or nutritional value, processed foods could be made with aroma chemicals such as hexanal (the smell of freshly cut grass), or 3-methyl butanoic acid (the smell of body odor).

The 1960s were the heyday of artificial flavors in the United States. The synthetic versions of flavor compounds were not subtle, but they did not have to be, given the nature of most processed food. For the past twenty years food processors have tried hard to use only "natural flavors" in their products. According to the FDA, these must be derived entirely from natural sources—from herbs, spices, fruits, vegetables, beef, chicken, yeast, bark, roots, and so forth. Consumers prefer to see natural flavors on a label, out of a belief that they are more healthful. Distinctions between artificial and natural flavors can be arbitrary and somewhat absurd, based more on how the flavor has been made than on what it actually contains.

"A natural flavor," says Terry Acree, a professor of food science at Cornell University, "is a flavor that's been derived with an out-of-date technology." Natural flavors and artificial flavors sometimes contain exactly the same chemicals, produced through different methods. Amyl acetate, for example, provides the dominant note of banana flavor. When it is distilled from bananas with a solvent, amyl acetate is a natural flavor. When it is produced by mixing vinegar with amyl alcohol and adding sulfuric acid as a catalyst, amyl acetate is an artificial flavor. Either way it smells and tastes the same. "Natural flavor" is now listed among the ingredients of everything from Health Valley Blueberry Granola Bars to Taco Bell Hot Taco Sauce.

A natural flavor is not necessarily more healthful or purer than an artificial one. When almond flavor—benzaldehyde—is derived from natural sources, such as peach and apricot pits, it contains traces of hydrogen cyanide, a deadly poison. Benzaldehyde derived by mixing oil of clove and amyl acetate does not contain any cyanide. Nevertheless, it is legally considered an artificial flavor and sells at a much lower price. Natural and artificial flavors are now manufactured at the same chemical plants, places that few people would associate with Mother Nature.

A TRAINED NOSE AND A POETIC SENSIBILITY

The small and elite group of scientists who create most of the flavor in most of the food now consumed in the United States are called "flavorists." They draw on a number of disciplines in their work: biology, psychology, physiology, and organic chemistry. A flavorist is a chemist with a trained nose and a poetic sensibility. Flavors are created by blending scores of different chemicals in tiny amounts—a process governed by scientific principles but demanding a fair amount of art. In an age when delicate aromas and microwave ovens do not easily co-exist, the job of the flavorist is to conjure illusions about processed food and, in the words of one flavor company's literature, to ensure "consumer likeability." The flavorists with whom I spoke were discreet, in keeping with the dictates of their trade. They were also charming, cosmopolitan, and ironic. They not only enjoyed fine wine but could identify the chemicals that give each grape its unique aroma. One flavorist compared his work to composing music. A well-made flavor compound will have a "top note" that is often followed by a "dry-down" and a "leveling-off," with different chemicals responsible for each stage. The taste of a food can be radically altered by minute changes in the flavoring combination. "A little odor goes a long way," one flavorist told me.

In order to give a processed food a taste that consumers will find 25 appealing, a flavorist must always consider the food's "mouthfeel"—the unique combination of textures and chemical interactions that affect how the flavor is perceived. Mouthfeel can be adjusted through the use of various fats, gums, starches, emulsifiers, and stabilizers. The aroma chemicals in a food can be precisely analyzed, but the elements that make up mouthfeel are much harder to measure. How does one quantify a pretzel's hardness, a french fry's crispness? Food technologists are now conducting basic research in rheology, the branch of physics that examines the flow and deformation of materials. A number of companies sell sophisticated devices that attempt to measure mouthfeel. The

TA.XT2i Texture Analyzer, produced by the Texture Technologies Corporation, of Scardsale, New York, performs calculations based on data derived from as many as 250 separate probes. It is essentially a mechanical mouth. It gauges the most-important rheological properties of a food—bounce, creep, breaking point, density, crunchiness, chewiness, gumminess, lumpiness, rubberiness, springiness, slipperiness, smoothness, softness, wetness, juiciness, spreadability, springback, and tackiness.

Some of the most important advances in flavor manufacturing arc now occurring in the field of biotechnology. Complex flavors are being made using enzyme reactions, fermentation, and fungal and tissue cultures. All the flavors created by these methods—including the ones being synthesized by fungi—are considered natural flavors by the FDA. The new enzyme-based processes are responsible for extremely true-to-life dairy flavors. One company now offers not just butter flavor but also fresh creamy butter, cheesy butter, milky butter, savory melted butter, and super-concentrated butter flavor, in liquid or powder form. The development of new fermentation techniques, along with new techniques for heating mixtures of sugar and amino acids, have led to the creation of much more realistic meat flavors.

The McDonald's Corporation most likely drew on these advances when it eliminated beef tallow from its french fries. The company will not reveal the exact origin of the natural flavor added to its fries. In response to inquiries from *Vegetarian Journal,* however, McDonald's did acknowledge that its fries derive some of their characteristic flavor from "an animal source." Beef is the probable source, although other meats cannot be ruled out. In France, for example, fries are sometimes cooked in duck fat or horse tallow.

Other popular fast foods derive their flavor from unexpected ingredients. McDonald's Chicken McNuggets contain beef extracts, as does Wendy's Grilled Chicken Sandwich. Burger King's BK Broiler Chicken Breast Patty contains "natural smoke flavor." A firm called Red Arrow Products specializes in smoke flavor, which is added to barbecue sauces, snack foods, and processed meats. Red Arrow manufactures natural smoke flavor by charring sawdust and capturing the aroma chemicals released into the air. The smoke is captured in water and then bottled, so that other companies can sell food that seems to have been cooked over a fire.

The Vegetarian Legal Action Network recently petitioned the FDA to issue new labeling requirements for foods that contain natural flavors. The group wants food processors to list the basic origins of their flavors on their labels. At the moment vegetarians often have no way of knowing whether a flavor additive contains beef, pork, poultry, or shellfish. One of the most widely used color additives—whose presence is often hidden by the phrase "color added"—violates a number of religious dietary restrictions, may cause allergic reactions in susceptible people, and comes from an unusual source. Cochineal extract (also known as carmine or carminic acid) is made from the desiccated bodies of female *Dactylopius coccus Costa,* a small insect harvested mainly in Peru and the Canary Islands. The bug feeds on red cactus berries, and color from the berries accumulates in the females and their unhatched larvae. The insects are collected, dried, and ground into a pigment. It takes about 70,000 of them to produce a pound of carmine, which is used to make processed foods look pink, red, or purple. Dannon strawberry yogurt gets its color from carmine, and so do many frozen fruit bars, candies, and fruit fillings, and Ocean Spray pink-grapefruit juice drink.

In a meeting room at IFF, Brian Grainger let me sample some of the company's flavors. It was an unusual taste test—there was no food to taste. Grainger is a senior flavorist at IFF, a soft-spoken chemist with graying hair, an English accent, and a fondness for understatement. He could easily be mistaken for a British diplomat or the owner of a West End brasserie with two Michelin stars. Like many in the flavor industry, he has an Old World, old-fashioned sensibility. When I suggested that IFF's policy of secrecy and discretion was out of step with our mass-marketing, brand-conscious, self-promoting age, and that the company should put its own logo on the countless products that bear its flavors, instead of allowing other companies to enjoy the consumer loyalty and affection inspired by those flavors, Grainger politely disagreed, assuring me that such a thing would never be done. In the absence of public credit or acclaim, the small and secretive fraternity of flavor chemists

30

praise one another's work. By analyzing the flavor formula of a product, Grainger can often tell which of his counterparts at a rival firm devised it. Whenever he walks down a supermarket aisle, he takes a quiet pleasure in seeing the well-known foods that contain his flavors.

Grainger had brought a dozen small glass bottles from the lab. After he opened each bottle, I dipped a fragrance-testing filter into it—a long white strip of paper designed to absorb aroma chemicals without producing off notes. Before placing each strip of paper in front of my nose, I closed my eyes. Then I inhaled deeply, and one food after another was conjured from the glass bottles. I smelled fresh cherries, black olives, sauteed onions, and shrimp. Grainger's most remarkable creation took me by surprise. After closing my eyes, I suddenly smelled a grilled hamburger. The aroma was uncanny, almost miraculous—as if somone in the room were flipping burgers on a hot grill. But when I opened my eyes, I saw just a narrow strip of white paper and a flavorist with a grin.

STUDY QUESTIONS

1. What are the perceived and actual differences between "natural flavor" and "artificial flavor"? Describe the relationship between European perfume houses and the flavor industry.

2. Find the PROCESS ANALYSIS paragraphs in the article dealing with smell and taste. Using those paragraphs as your source, explain in your own words how our senses of smell and taste work.

3. How does the inclusion of personal experiences contribute to or detract from Schlosser's ETHOS? Select two experiences that he shares, explain how they affect his ethos, and evaluate their effectiveness in this essay.

4. *For Writing.* Examine the items in your pantry. (If you live in a dorm and have no kitchen or pantry, visit a local grocery store and select ten or fifteen items to examine.) Organize them into the various categories of foods: canned fruits and vegetables, packaged processed foods, and so forth. Carefully read the lists of ingredients on each label. If you do not recognize some of the ingredients, look them up in a dictionary or on the Internet. Write an EXPOSITORY essay about these items and their ingredients. Evaluate the safety and nutritional value of the ingredients, and determine whether each is necessary and whether any might be harmful.

MORGAN SPURLOCK { *A Lunchroom Named Desire*

MORGAN SPURLOCK (b. 1970) was born and reared in West Virginia. In 1993 he earned a BFA in film at New York University's Tisch School of the Arts. A decade later Spurlock made the Academy Award–nominated documentary film *Super Size Me*, in which he ate nothing but McDonald's meals for thirty days, choosing Super Size portions whenever they were offered to him—despite the alarming deterioration of his health. The success of the film led him to write the cultural study *Don't Eat This Book: Fast Food and the Supersizing of America* (2005).

In the following selection from that book, Spurlock analyzes the factors at work behind the lunch menus of most public-school cafeterias. Spurlock argues that they are not designed with nutrition in mind; rather, they are frequently outsourced to commercial food corporations that promote profits instead of children's health. Further, Spurlock dissects the process by which the U.S. Department of Agriculture devised its highly touted "food pyramid" of dietary recommendations with more input from food-industry lobbyists than from doctors or nutritionists. If you eat in a cafeteria on a daily basis, what kinds of foods do you choose? And more importantly, what kinds are available there in the first place?

IT'S LUNCHTIME IN THE CAFETERIA at Madison Junior High in Naperville, Illinois. Cute adolescents milling around, lining up at the counter, carrying trays to the long tables, where I'm sure there are complicated social rules for who gets to sit with which crowd. Giggling, laughing, talking over one another. Generating that bubbly hubbub of energy that kids throw off.

Several kids are crowded around the near end of the counter, where pizzas are stacked one above the other, slowly spinning to display all their cheesy, doughy goodness. A Tower of Pizza. Kids reach in, grab a slice or two, and push their trays down the line.

Let's see what else they're being tempted with. *Mmmm,* a big aluminum tub of mac and cheese, glowing an artificial neon orange under the fluorescents. A tub of spaghetti and meatballs you just know was reheated out of an industrial-size can. A tub of succotash that's more gray than green and yellow.

Down at the end of the line is where all the fun stuff is. Tubs of french fries and ketchup packets. Piles of plastic-wrapped cinnamon buns and snack cakes. Rows of candy bars. To drink, your choice of milk, water, "fruit" beverages, canned lemonade, or bottles of Gatorade.

Most kids cluster at the two ends of the line. A few kids lean over the 5 succotash, sniff at it and move on. Yeah, the staff is gonna haul a lot o' succotash to the dumpster this afternoon. Unless they just reheat it and try again tomorrow?

Now, it's no surprise that adolescents choose pizza, fries, and candy. If you were a kid, which would you choose? *That's why kids need adults to supervise how they eat.*

At home, it's the parents' job. It's your mom or dad who says, "No, you can't just have fries for dinner. Eat some string beans, then you can have some fries." Or, under extreme conditions, "Young lady, you will sit there until you eat your vegetables." How many nights when you were a kid did you sit at the table for hours, staring at a pile of Brussels sprouts as they got colder and colder? You may not have eaten them that night, but a message was imparted, and later, as you got older, you discovered that vegetables actually taste good.

The average kid spends one-third of the day at home, one-third asleep, and one-third in school. During those school hours, teachers and administrators are the surrogate parents. But in too many of our schools, the surrogate parents abandon the kids in the cafeteria. No adult is there monitoring what they eat—certainly not the people behind the counter. The kids are left to make "wise" food choices on their own.

Is it any wonder that they don't? We don't expect adolescents to make other kinds of crucial health choices on their own. We don't hand a thirteen-year-old the car keys and let the kid go joyriding. We don't hand a thirteen-year-old a rifle to play with. We don't say to our kids, "It's okay if you want to raid the liquor cabinet. Just be smart about how much of my vodka you drink."

But that's pretty much what we say to kids in schools. That's certainly 10 what the food lobbyists say. Whenever they hear criticism about the kinds of foods kids choose to eat in school, one of their stock answers is, "Proper nutrition should be taught in the home, then the children would make the right choices here," or they'll proclaim, "Teach the kids proper nutrition in class, and when they come to the cafeteria they'll choose a balanced meal." The buck is passed, and passed again. But the fact remains, given the choice between peas and pizza, we know what nine out of ten kids will eat. Hell, that's the way many adults will eat. I've stood in line behind you at McDonald's—I know!

The cafeteria staff and school nutritionists try to put the best face on it. They'll tell you that, yes, kids buy a lot of fries, but they eat them as a side dish with a sandwich. But what I observed were kids—not just a few kids but *lots* of kids—whose entire lunch consisted of fries, cookies, and a lemonade, or fries and milk or even a tray loaded up with bags of chips and candy. When I followed them to their tables to see if they'd brown-bagged a sandwich to have with those goodies, they rarely had. Fries and ketchup was their lunch. (Well, ketchup is a vegetable. Reagan told us so.[1]) Some schools won't serve sodas, but they'll sell so-called fruit drinks that are just water, a little artificial fruit flavoring and coloring and 36 grams of sugar per bottle. In other schools, Coke and Pepsi and the like are prevalent. One girl I saw bought two

---

[1]In September 1981, early in the administration of President Ronald Reagan, the U.S. Department of Agriculture proposed reclassifying ketchup as a "vegetable," arguing that this would save the government nearly $1 billion a year in subsidies to school hot-lunch programs for lower-income students. The proposal met with outrage and derision, and was never implemented. [Ed.]

packs of Ruffles, a Twix bar, a soft pretzel, and a Gatorade for lunch. When I followed her back to the table, I saw that she also had brought a Coke from home to drink with all that!

The sad fact is that in many, many of our schools, we're teaching kids terrible habits of diet and health. Often they get no gym class. They get no nutrition education. And they get few good choices in the lunchroom. Whether it's through the federal government's school lunch program or because the school district has farmed out the feeding of kids to a lowest-bidding commercial outfit, cafeteria food is distinctly sub-par.

Worse, while schools should be the one place kids aren't inundated with junk food messages, fast food, and lousy processed food, it's just the opposite. In fact, a lot of school lunchrooms look like mall food courts. Coke, Pepsi, Taco Bell, Burger King, McDonald's, and the rest have taken over thousands of American schools.

And for that we have no one to blame but ourselves. As voters, as taxpayers, and as parents, we've sold out our schools to the corporate takeover artists because we don't want to pay more local taxes. As federal and state officials continue to slash education budgets, these corporations step into the "funding gap." We're sacrificing our children's health so that they can turn a profit in our schools.

First, let's look at those cafeteria lines.   15

Since the mid-1990s, an increasing number of school districts have been licensing out the management of their cafeterias to commercial food-service outfits like Sodexho, Aramark, and Daka. Sodexho manages the school district that is the home to the Madison Junior High cafeteria and a few hundred others across the United States. These are the same companies that provide food service to prisons, hospitals, and many college campuses. And now they run the lunchrooms in thousands of school districts.

Why are public schools farming out their lunchrooms to these companies? For the same reason many of them don't have gym equipment, or instruments for a school band, or biology labs, or any books in their libraries that aren't twenty years out of date: They're broke. Broke because we don't fund them.

Farming out lunchroom management is one way school districts cut costs. They may even make a little money out of the deal. These companies are supposed to follow those federal nutrition guidelines, ensuring that our kids are eating right, but it's all very loosey-goosey, and the kids' welfare is more observed in theory than in fact.

But even schools that aren't outsourcing their lunchrooms are failing our kids nutritionally—and they're doing it with the full support of our friends in the federal government. Through the National School Lunch Program (NSLP),[2] the United States Department of Agriculture provides lunches for some 26 million children each schoolday. About 99 percent of all public elementary, junior high, and senior high schools, along with a number of private schools and residential child-care institutions, participate in the program. Schools get a cash reimbursement and donated goods for serving the meals.

Any student can avail herself of these meals, but kids from households below certain income levels get them free or for a greatly reduced price (40 cents max); students who aren't from poor homes pay more for them. Of course, kids don't have to participate, and can bring their own lunches from home. 20

All NSLP lunches are supposed to meet federal nutrition requirements, based on the USDA's own Dietary Guidelines for Americans: no more than 35 percent of calories from fat, with less than 10 percent from saturated fat. Plus the meal should provide one-third of the Recommended Dietary Allowances for calories, protein, vitamins A and C, iron, and calcium.

Sounds great, right? Good ol' USDA, feeding all those poor kids nutritious, wholesome meals every day!

Well . . . not exactly.

An encyclopedia (Wikipedia) definition of the USDA[3] reads like this: "The United States Department of Agriculture, also called the Agriculture Department, or USDA, is a Cabinet department of the United States Federal Government. Its purpose is to develop and execute policy on farming, agriculture, and food. It aims to meet the needs of farmers

---

[2]Marion Nestle, *Food Politics* (Berkeley: University of California Press).
[3]http://www.wikipedia.org.

and ranchers, promote agricultural trade and production, work to assure food safety, protect natural resources, foster rural communities, and end hunger in America and abroad."

Notice the priorities. The interests of agriculture and ranching 25 come first. In the twenty-first century, that means corporate agribusiness, the corporate beef industry, the corporate poultry and dairy industries—in short, Big Food. Notice how the interests of the consumer—things like food safety and hunger—come last.

That's a pretty apt description of the USDA's agenda. Some critics call it "USDA Inc.,"[4] and say it's basically agribusiness's department in Washington.

It hasn't always been that way. In Abe Lincoln's day, it was known as "the People's Department," because it represented the needs and interests of American farmers and farm workers, which meant most of the people in America. In the early twentieth century, largely as a result of the uproar about unsanitary meatpacking plants described by Upton Sinclair in his muckraking book *The Jungle*,[5] the USDA took on a more regulatory role—and took it seriously.

But as the century progressed and nearly all the family farms and ranches were swallowed up by giant corporations, the USDA became less and less about serving the needs of the People and more and more about protecting the profits of Big Business. Nowadays, the only time the USDA seems to take its regulatory role seriously is when it's forced to by a huge public scandal like the mad-cow scare.[6]

In fact, a lot of the time the USDA seems to function like a Big Food lobby that conveniently just happens to be a wing of the federal government. That's partly because so many of its executive offices, from the Secretary of Agriculture on down, are occupied by people who came from the executive offices of the Big Food corporations and will go

[4]Philip Mattera, "USDA Inc.: How Agribusiness Has Hijacked Regulatory Policy at the U.S. Department of Agriculture," report released at the Food and Agricultural Conference of the Organization of Competitive Markets, Omaha, Nebraska, July 23, 2004.

[5]Sinclair's (1878–1968) novel *The Jungle* (1906) exposed horrifically unsanitary practices in the U.S. meatpacking industry and sparked a wave of regulatory intervention by lawmakers. [Ed.]

[6]Bovine Spongiform Encephalopathy (BSE), commonly known as "mad-cow disease," is a fatal illness originating in cattle that affects the nervous system; in the late 1980s it was discovered

back there when their tour of duty in D.C. is completed. In 2004, something like forty-five of the top offices of the USDA[7] were filled by people recruited from Big Food and its lobbies. "Incestuous" hardly seems like a strong enough word to describe the revolving-door relationship between the USDA and Big Food.

In 2004, according to their bios on the USDA's own website:

- Former Secretary Ann M. Veneman served on the board of the biotech company Colgene.
- Her chief of staff, Dale Moore, had been an executive of the National Cattlemen's Beef Association, the enormously powerful corporate meatpackers' lobby.
- So had her director of communications, Alisa Harrison.
- Her deputy chief of staff (who left in 2004) was a vice president of the International Dairy Foods Association, the also extremely powerful milk-and-cheese industry's lobby.
- Deputy Secretary of Agriculture James Moseley was a partner in Infinity Pork LLC, a corporate pig farm in Indiana.
- Under Secretary J. B. Penn was an agribusiness consultant.
- Under Secretary Joseph Jen came from Campbell Soup.

"Conflict of interests" is hardly apt. These people have no conflict of interests. They know exactly whose interests they serve. 30

These are the people you're trusting to inspect the National Cattlemen's Beef Association members' meatpacking plants. To keep an eye on what the International Dairy Foods Association's members are feeding their milk cows. To make sure the pork chops you get from Infinity Pork don't give you trichinosis. Last time I checked, banks weren't guarded by bank robbers. How can this be happening in the highest branches of our government?

that BSE was spreading and had entered the human food supply, particularly in Britain, because brain and spinal cord material of infected cattle had been included in cattle feed. [Ed.]
[7]Mattera, "USDA Inc."

But wait—they're also the ones responsible for disseminating the one bit of nutritional education every kid, and every adult, is supposed to know by heart: the Food Pyramid. Which boils down the USDA's Dietary Guidelines into an easy-to-follow, at-a-glance graphic. Eat more of the foods at the bottom, less of the ones at the top. Simple. Couldn't be clearer.

Yet nothing illustrates the USDA's conflicts of interest like the wheeling and dealing that have gone on over the last couple of years as the department has tried to figure out how to revise and update both the Guidelines and the Pyramid.[8] The Guidelines are updated every five years by a panel of experts jointly appointed by the USDA and the Department of Health and Human Services. The Pyramid, however, had not been changed since it was introduced in 1992.

The friggin' Great Pyramid in Egypt wasn't as hard to build as this revised Food Pyramid. All the Big Food lobbies—meat, sugar, dairy, even salt (who even knew salt had its own lobbyists?)—have been jockeying to get the best positions on the new Pyramid and to soften anything said about them in the new Guidelines. Even the Fatkins Diet[9] lobby got into the act, demanding that the Guidelines reflect the late, great, and overweight Dr. Atkins' anti-carbs campaign. It's also worth mentioning that the panel appointed to update the Guidelines was packed with more Big Food industry types than a fruitcake has cherries.

Everybody got to throw their two cents in. The Peanut Institute, the   35 California Walnut Commission, and the National Barley Food Council all fought for their fair share. The lobby for the vitamin-supplements industry tried to convince the panel that the Pyramid should have a little flag waving from the top of it—the flag would represent vitamin supplements.

Private citizens were allowed to write to the panel to express their views, too.[10] Hey, it's the democratic way, even if it does open up the

[8]Amy Lanou and Patrick Sullivan, "Recipe for Disaster: Scientists with Industry Ties Dominate Dietary Guidelines Advisory Committee," September 23, 2003, http://www.tompaine.com.

[9]American physician and cardiologist Robert Atkins (1930–2003) promoted a controversial weight-control regimen, popularly known as the "Atkins Diet," based mainly on limiting the consumption of carbohydrates.

[10]USDA website, http://www.usda.gov/cnpp/pyramid-update/comments/index.html.

process to the lunatic fringe. Between the lobbies and the loonies, there were numerous arguments that the Pyramid shouldn't be a pyramid at all, but a clock, a wheel, a plate, a pie, balloons, a mountain range, an hour glass, a cross-section of a diamond, a menu, an upside-down pyramid superhero, or a "nourishment tree."

One guy, who claimed to be a "foodician," wrote in to argue strenuously that the Pyramid should be a Food Merkabah. (For those of you who haven't been shopping for incense and New Age reading materials lately, a merkabah is a kind of multidimensional mandala.) He also complained that "the cleansing properties of urine are not even addressed in the food pyramid. This must be corrected. We cannot allow small minds and prejudice to bury this useful health information from our brothers and sisters in light." He went on: "Write back IMMEDIATELY and tell me where to report with my diagrams. I am including corn muffins prominently in my calculations. That alone should tell you that I know what I am doing!"

Thank you, Gandalf.[11] We'll get back to you.

The Food Pyramid got the USDA into trouble[12] the very first time it was unveiled, in 1991. The department's friends in the beef industry were outraged at what a small space they got on it, and it took a year of haggling to come up with a version that pleased them. So, right from the start, the USDA was compromising your health to appease one of its true constituents.

When the USDA released its preliminary and unofficial 2005 Dietary Guidelines report in the summer of 2004, it appeared that sugar would come out as the big winner. Previous editions of the Guidelines used to say choose a diet "moderate in sugar" or "avoid too much sugar." Big Sugar has lobbied[13] long and hard to get that wording softened over the years, and the *New York Times* reported in August 2004 that the new

[11]Fictional wizard character in J. R. R. Tolkien's fantasy novels *The Hobbit* (1937) and *The Lord of the Rings* trilogy (1954–5).

[12]Neal Barnard, M.D., "U.S. Dietary Guidelines: Victory in Court," *PCRM Magazine*, Winter 2001.

[13]"OUCH!: Congressional Candyland," *Alternet*, June 20, 2000; Cindi Ross Scoppe, "How Sweet It Is to Manipulate Government Diet Guidelines," *The Slate*, September 14, 2004, http://www.slate.com.

guidelines wouldn't even list sugar among the foods that are bad for you.[14] But thankfully, that part of the preliminary report didn't quite make the final cut. The official Guidelines released in January 2005 make clear statements about limiting added sugars, much to the chagrin of those at Big Sugar who defended their lobbying efforts, saying they stood firm in their assertion "that there is not a direct link between added sugars intake and any lifestyle disease, including obesity." That was Andy Briscoe, president and CEO of the Sugar Association, who went on: "For the guidelines to infer any type of limit on added sugars is not science-based." Better luck next time, guys.

I presume the government's recent focus on combating obesity had a lot to do with this small but important victory for our health. The Guidelines also include more and more advice on preventing obesity, including a recommendation to exercise for sixty to ninety minutes daily, up from thirty minutes in previous guidelines.

The sugar lobby also tried to throw its weight around with the UN's World Health Organization.[15] As draft versions of the WHO's new dietary guidelines, which were released in November 2004, became public in 2003, it became clear that the final report would recommend stiff restrictions in sugar consumption. The Sugar Association went ballistic, firing off letters to the WHO's director general grumbling that the "report reflects poorly on WHO and, if allowed to stand, will mislead and confuse the public," calling it a "shabby affair" and saying, "It is difficult to believe the standards of the World Health Organization have slipped to such a low point. . . ."

The Sugar Association CEO wrote to the WHO, promising, "We will exercise every avenue available to expose the dubious nature of the 'Diet, Nutrition, and the Prevention of Chronic Diseases' Report, including asking Congressional appropriators to challenge future funding of the U.S.'s $406 million contributions (including both regular and

---

[14]"Added Sugars, Less Urgency? Fine Print and the Guidelines," Marion Burros, *New York Times*, August 25, 2004.

[15]"Sugar Lobbyists Sour on Study," Associated Press, April 23, 2003; "Big Sugar's 'Thuggish' Tactics Come Under Fire, Center for Science in the Public Interest press release, April 21, 2003; Sarah Baseley, "Sugar Industry Threatens to Scupper WHO," *The Guardian*, April 21, 2003.

voluntary funding) to the WHO." And the association got its people in the Senate—Louisiana Democrat John Breaux and Idaho Republican Larry Craig, cochairs of the Senate Sweetener Caucus (who knew?)—to complain to cabinet members as well. The WHO didn't cave.

It's also worth noting that advice on carbohydrates warranted its own section in the new Guidelines, whereas past reports barely mentioned carbs. Thanks to relentless lobbying on the part of the Atkins folks, the USDA now tells us to "choose carbohydrates wisely."

The dairy lobby is also celebrating.[16] Reporting in August 2004 on the 45 USDA's preliminary Guidelines, *The Wall Street Journal* said, "In a shift that has major implications for the U.S. dairy industry, the Dietary Guidelines Advisory Committee on Friday endorsed what amounts to a 50% boost in milk consumption, up from the two servings long suggested for many adults. . . . The new advice is a major victory for the $50 billion U.S. dairy industry, which has long lobbied for increased consumption guidelines. Currently, Americans eat or drink about 1.5 servings of dairy products per day, according to the Agriculture Department. Despite the dairy industry's iconic 'Got Milk?' ad campaign, per-capita fluid milk sales have fallen nearly 3% over the past five years. The suggested boost in dairy intake could spell big profits for the industry, as federal nutrition programs such as school lunch menus are adjusted to conform." When the final version of the 2005 Dietary Guidelines were unveiled six months later, the 50 percent recommended boost in milk intake held steady. (Actually, the article was misleading: That ubiquitous "Got Milk?" ad campaign was produced by none other than the USDA,[17] yet another example of the department doing Big Food's work for it.)

Actually, the "Got Milk?" ad campaign was a product of what are called checkoff programs, which are designed by the USDA and made

[16]Nicholas Zamiska, "How Milk Got a Major Boost," *Wall Street Journal*, August 30, 2004.

[17]http://www.beefboard.org, Frequently Asked Questions About National Checkoff Programs. See also USDA's Agricultural Marketing Service, http://www.ams.usda.gov; Pork Promotion, Research and Consumer Information Order, http://www.ams. usda.gov; "New Milk at McDonald's Fact Sheet," Dairy Management, Inc. press release, May 25, 2004, http://www.dairycheckoff.com/news/release-mcdonaldsfacts.asp.

mandatory by acts of Congress to help promote various agricultural commodities. The USDA oversees and must approve all checkoff activities. In this case, milk producers forked over a percentage of their revenues to the Dairy Board, which in turn paid for the "Got Milk?" and other promotions. Have you seen the new McDonald's Milk Jugs? If you think that was a McDonald's idea, think again.

And don't forget pork—the National Pork Board paid McDonald's thousands of dollars to help create and promote the McRib Sandwich.[18] It's not just dairy and pork, either. The USDA uses checkoff programs to gouge farmers from almost any area—beef, eggs, cotton, mushrooms, honey, watermelon, popcorn, soybeans, potatoes, lamb, etc. Farmers from across the spectrum hate these programs, and in 2001 they cheered when the U.S. Supreme Court declared the mushroom checkoff program unconstitutional because "it compels producers to finance and/or to be associated with political or ideological speech to which they are opposed."[19] At the time of this writing, beef producers are awaiting what they hope to be a similar Supreme Court decision,[20] and the pork checkoff has been flopping around the courts for years.[21]

Never mind the fact that, as the article notes, "Walter Willett, a physician and chairman of the department of nutrition at Harvard University's School of Public Health, calls the committee report 'egregious,' saying it excludes at least six major studies linking dairy consumption to prostate cancer. 'There is no nutritional requirement for dairy at all,' he insists. 'Huge parts of the world do not even consume dairy.' "

[18]Physicians Committee for Responsible Medicine provided the author with internal Pork Board documents requested through the Freedom of Information Act; *Pork Leader* newsletter 23, no. 5 (March 7, 2003).

[19]"Mushroom Checkoff Declared Unconstitutional by Nation's Highest Court," *In Motion Magazine,* July 5, 2001.

[20]Troy Marshall, "Beef Checkoff Case Now Before the Supreme Court," *Beef,* December 13, 2004.

[21]Farmers Legal Action Group (FLAG), http://www.flaginc.org/news/checkoff/checkoff.htm.

One reason the Get More Milk lobby may have won out over concerned nutritionists like Dr. Willett, according to *The Wall Street Journal*: "At least three of the 13 committee members, Connie Weaver, head of the department of foods and nutrition at Purdue University; Theresa A. Nicklas, a professor of pediatrics at Baylor College of Medicine; and Penny Kris-Etherton, professor at Pennsylvania State University, have received National Dairy Council funding within the past five years." Milk, it does the lobby good.[22] Pass it on.

All I know is, that's gonna be one lopsided friggin' Pyramid.

And these are the same people who are feeding 26 million kids a day in 99 percent of America's public schools.

How did the USDA get in the business of running school cafeterias, you ask?[23] It started during the Depression. The total collapse of consumer markets left the farm industry with tons of surplus product. Meanwhile, millions of American kids were going hungry. The USDA killed two birds with one biscuit: It bought up all those farm surpluses to save the agriculture industry and dumped all that food into the schools and prisons.

The NSLP operates basically the same way to this day, still using schools and prisons as dumping grounds for surplus agri-product, propping up sagging sectors of the food industry like beef and dairy as needed. As of July 2004, 200 of the 26,000 school districts in the country were even serving kids that irradiated beef I talked about earlier. "The meat industry has used the NSLP as a gravy train, and our kids are paying the price," says Jennifer Keller of the Physicians Committee for Responsible Medicine.[24]

It's not hard to tell which of the USDA's constituents, Big Food or impoverished schoolchildren, gets first priority. The USDA's main job is promoting and supporting agribusiness; feeding kids is just a convenient sideline. When dairy prices fall, for instance, the USDA buys

50

---

[22] A play on the slogan "Milk, It Does a Body Good," part of an advertising campaign sponsored by the dairy industry and the USDA. [Ed.]

[23] Nestle, *Food Politics*.

[24] "Congress: Stop Fattening Kids with Giant Meat and Cheese Subsidies, Say Doctors," Physicians Committee for Responsible Medicine press release, October 6, 2003.

up lots of milk and cheese, then ships it off to school cafeterias, prisons, and hospitals. Never mind that although a lot of kids are lactose-intolerant, the USDA won't reimburse schools for serving alternatives to cow's milk, because the powerful dairy lobby won't allow it. Got milk? Boy, do our schools got milk! Similarly, the USDA buys hundreds of millions of pounds of surplus beef, chicken, cheese, and pork every year, and then dumps them on your kids. Like it or not.

STUDY QUESTIONS

1. How do the dairy, meat, and other food industries work with the U.S. Department of Agriculture to promote their products? How is the composition of the "food pyramid" influenced and managed by lobbyists and food producers?

2. Spurlock ANALYZES the CAUSES AND EFFECTS of poor nutritional offerings in school cafeterias. What are the causes he finds? What are the effects? What other causes and effects can you think of?

3. How would you characterize Spurlock's TONE in this piece? Is it appropriate and effective? Explain.

4. *For Writing.* For a week, observe what your cafeteria serves and what your classmates eat there. In an essay, analyze your observations. Are healthy options available? Do students have a variety of food brands from which to choose? To what extent are students making wise dietary decisions? Should junk food be removed from cafeteria menus? Who should decide what foods are to be available?

Food Preparation and
Presentation

LAURIE COLWIN { *How to Fry Chicken*

LAURIE COLWIN (1944–1992) was born in New York City. A prolific writer of both fiction and nonfiction, Colwin is well known for her essays about food, published in both magazines and two collections: *Home Cooking: A Writer in the Kitchen* (1988) and *More Home Cooking* (1993). She also wrote three collections of short stories—*Passion and Affect* (1974), *The Lone Pilgrim* (1981), and *Another Marvelous Thing* (1988)— and five novels: *Shine On, Bright and Dangerous Object* (1975), *Happy All the Time* (1978), *Family Happiness* (1982), *Goodbye without Leaving* (1990), and *A Big Storm Knocked It Over* (1993). Her love of food spilled into all parts of her short life; as a student at Columbia University, she cooked food for protesting classmates during the 1968 demonstrations against the school.

"How to Fry Chicken" was published in *Home Cooking*, portions of which initially appeared in magazines such as *Gourmet, Inside,* and *7 Days.* In the essay she clearly describes a process and does so with her characteristically direct writing made up largely of short sentences, short paragraphs, and lists—a style she might have learned from recipes.

_____

AS EVERYONE KNOWS, THERE IS only one way to fry chicken correctly. Unfortunately, most people think their method is best, but most people are wrong. Mine is the only right way, and on this subject I feel almost evangelical.

It is not that I am a bug on method—I am fastidious about results. Fried chicken must have a crisp, deep (but not too deep) crust. It must be completely cooked, yet juicy and tender. These requirements sound minimal, but achieving them requires technique. I have been frying chicken according to the correct method for about ten years, and I realize that this skill improves over time. The last batch fried was far, far better than the first. The lady who taught my sister and me, a black woman who cooked for us in Philadelphia, was of course the apotheosis: no one will ever be fit to touch the top of her chicken fryer.

I have had all kinds of nasty fried chicken served to me, usually with great flourish: crisp little baby shoes or hockey pucks turned out by electric frying machines with names such as Little Fry Guy. Beautifully golden morsels completely raw on the inside. Chicken that has been fried and put into the fridge, giving the crust the texture of a wet paper towel.

I have also had described to me Viennese fried chicken, which involves egg and bread crumbs and is put in the oven after frying and drizzled with butter. It sounds very nice, but it is *not* fried chicken.

To fry chicken that makes people want to stand up and sing 5 "The Star-Spangled Banner," the following facts of life must be taken seriously.

- Fried chicken should be served warm. It should never be eaten straight from the fryer—it needs time to cool down and set. Likewise, fried chicken must never see the inside of a refrigerator because this turns the crisp into something awful and cottony.

- Contrary to popular belief, fried chicken should not be deep-fried.

- Anyone who says you merely shake up the chicken in a bag with flour is fooling himself. (More on this later.)

- Fried chicken must be made in a chicken fryer—a steep-sided frying pan with a domed top.

- It must never be breaded or coated with anything except flour (which can be spiced with salt, pepper and paprika). No egg, no crumbs, no crushed Rice Krispies.

Now that the basics have been stated, the preparation is the next step. The chicken pieces should be roughly the same size—this means that the breast is cut into quarters. The breast is the hardest to cook just right as it tends to get dry. People who don't quarter the breast usually end up with either a large, underdone half, or they overcompensate and fry it until it resembles beef jerky.

The chicken should be put in a dish and covered with a little water or milk. This will help to keep the flour on. Let the chicken stand at room temperature. It is not a good thing to put cold raw chicken into hot oil.

Meanwhile, the flour should be put into a deep, wide bowl, with salt, pepper and paprika added to taste. I myself adore paprika and feel it gives the chicken a smoky taste and a beautiful color.

To coat the chicken, lay a few pieces at a time in the bowl and pack the flour on as if you were a child making sand pies. Any excess flour should be packed between the layers. It is important to make sure that every inch of chicken has a nice thick cover. Now heat the oil and let the chicken sit.

And now to the frying. There are people who say, and probably 10 correctly, that chicken should be fried in lard and Crisco, but I am not one of these people. Fried food is bad enough for you. I feel it should not be made worse. The lady who taught me swore by Wesson oil, and I swear by it, too, with the addition of about one-fourth part of light sesame oil. This gives a wonderful taste and is worth the added expense. It also helps to realize that both oils are polyunsaturated in case one cannot fry without guilt.

The oil should come up to just under the halfway mark of your chicken fryer. Heat it slowly until a piece of bread on a skewer fries as soon as you dip it. If it does, you are ready to start.

Carefully slip into the oil as many pieces as will fit. The rule is to crowd a little. Turn down the heat at once and *cover*. The idea of covering frying chicken makes many people squeal, but it is the only correct method. It gets the chicken cooked through. Remember that the chicken must be just done—juicy and crisp. About six minutes or so per side—and you must turn it once—is probably about right, although dark meat takes a little longer. A sharp fork makes a good tester.

When the chicken just slips off the fork, it is done inside. Take the cover off, turn up the heat, and fry it to the color of Colonial pine stain—a dark honey color. Set it on a platter and put it in the oven. If your oven is gas, there is no need for any more warmth than that provided by the pilot light. If electric, turn it up a little in advance and then turn it off. You have now made perfect fried chicken.

And you have suffered. There are many disagreeable things about frying chicken. No matter how careful you are, flour gets all over everything and the oil splatters far beyond the stove. It is impossible to fry chicken without burning yourself at least once. For about twenty-four hours your house smells of fried chicken. This is nice only during dinner and then begins to pall. Waking up to the smell of cooking fat is not wonderful.

Furthermore, frying chicken is just about the most boring thing 15 you can do. You can't read while you do it. Music is drowned out by constant sizzling. Finally, as you fry you are consumed with the realization that fried food is terrible for you, even if you serve it only four times a year.

But the rewards are many, and when you appear with your platter your family and friends greet you with cries of happiness. Soon your table is full of ecstatic eaters, including, if you are lucky, some delirious Europeans—the British are especially impressed by fried chicken. As the cook you get to take the pieces you like best. As for me, I snag the backs, those most neglected and delectable bits, and I do it without a trace of remorse. After all, I did the cooking.

Not only have you mastered a true American folk tradition, but you know that next time will be even better.

STUDY QUESTIONS

1. According to Colwin, what are the drawbacks of frying chicken her way? What are the rewards?

2. How would you characterize the TONE of Colwin's writing? Provide examples to support your answer. Why do you think she would use this tone in writing about cooking?

3. In this PROCESS ANALYSIS, Colwin describes how to fry chicken. In addition to providing a step-by-step process, she also uses DESCRIPTIONS of "nasty fried chicken" (paragraph 3), provides a list of rules, and tells readers both the disagreeable aspects of and rewards of frying chicken. Does this PROCESS and these DESCRIPTIONS make you want to try Colwin's method for frying chicken? Why or why not?

4. *For Writing.* Colwin provides rules for cooking fried chicken "that makes people want to stand up and sing 'The Star-Spangled Banner'" (paragraph 5). Make a list of rules for cooking something you know how to cook but other people tend to prepare badly—at least in your opinion.

ISAK DINESEN { *Babette's Feast*

ISAK DINESEN (1885–1962) is the pseudonym of Karen Dinesen
Blixen, who wrote both memoir and fiction. Born in Denmark, Dinesen
lived most of her life there, although the two decades she spent farming
coffee in Africa became the basis for her best-known work, *Out of Africa*
(1937), which in turn was the basis of the 1985 film of the same title
starring Meryl Streep. Married to and divorced from her second cousin,
a Swedish baron, Dinesen maintained an enigmatic persona, and
biographers differ on many of the details of her life and relationships.
Still, she is hailed for her well-crafted prose.

"Babette's Feast," which was adapted for a 1987 film by the same title, is
set in Jutland in late nineteenth-century Denmark. It follows the lives of
two pious and austere sisters (Martine and Philippa), their suitors (Lorens
Loewenhielm and Achille Papin), and Babette—a former Parisian chef
turned refugee, who becomes the sisters' cook. When Babette wins ten
thousand francs in a lottery, she spends it all on a lavish dinner for twelve
people, many of whom are devoutly religious and, like the sisters,
suspicious of sensual pleasure. Babette, for whom cooking is art, succeeds
in breaking down the barriers among her guests and showing them the
joys of communing over an exquisite meal. Dinesen uses opposites
throughout her story yet creates unity in the end. As you read this story,
note the divisions between Protestants and Catholics, heavenly things,
and earthly things, silence and speech, and restraint and passion.
Notice, too, how Dinesen reconciles these opposites in the end.

I. TWO LADIES OF BERLEVAAG

IN NORWAY THERE IS A fjord—a long narrow arm of the sea between tall mountains—named Berlevaag Fjord. At the foot of the mountains the small town of Berlevaag looks like a child's toy-town of little wooden pieces painted gray, yellow, pink and many other colors.

Sixty-five years ago two elderly ladies lived in one of the yellow houses. Other ladies at that time wore a bustle, and the two sisters might have worn it as gracefully as any of them, for they were tall and willowy. But they had never possessed any article of fashion; they had dressed demurely in gray or black all their lives. They were christened Martine and Philippa, after Martin Luther and his friend Philip Melanchton.[1] Their father had been a Dean and a prophet, the founder of a pious ecclesiastic party or sect, which was known and looked up to in all the country of Norway. Its members renounced the pleasures of this world, for the earth and all that it held to them was but a kind of illusion, and the true reality was the New Jerusalem toward which they were longing. They swore not at all, but their communication was yea yea and nay nay, and they called one another Brother and Sister.

The Dean had married late in life and by now had long been dead. His disciples were becoming fewer in number every year, whiter or balder and harder of hearing; they were even becoming somewhat querulous and quarrelsome, so that sad little schisms would arise in the congregation. But they still gathered together to read and interpret the Word. They had all known the Dean's daughters as little girls; to them they were even now very small sisters, precious for their dear father's sake. In the yellow house they felt that their Master's spirit was with them; here they were at home and at peace.

These two ladies had a French maid-of-all-work, Babette.

It was a strange thing for a couple of Puritan women in a small 5 Norwegian town; it might even seem to call for an explanation. The

[1]Philipp Melanchthon (1497–1560), German theologian and collaborator with the most important figure of the Protestant Reformation, German monk Martin Luther (1483–1546).

people of Berlevaag found the explanation in the sisters' piety and kindness of heart. For the old Dean's daughters spent their time and their small income in works of charity; no sorrowful or distressed creature knocked on their door in vain. And Babette had come to that door twelve years ago as a friendless fugitive, almost mad with grief and fear.

But the true reason for Babette's presence in the two sisters' house was to be found further back in time and deeper down in the domain of human hearts.

II. MARTINE'S LOVER

As young girls, Martine and Philippa had been extraordinarily pretty, with the almost supernatural fairness of flowering fruit trees or perpetual snow. They were never to be seen at balls or parties, but people turned when they passed in the streets, and the young men of Berlevaag went to church to watch them walk up the aisle. The younger sister also had a lovely voice, which on Sundays filled the church with sweetness. To the Dean's congregation earthly love, and marriage with it, were trivial matters, in themselves nothing but illusions; still it is possible that more than one of the elderly Brothers had been prizing the maidens far above rubies[2] and had suggested as much to their father. But the Dean had declared that to him in his calling his daughters were his right and left hand. Who could want to bereave him of them? And the fair girls had been brought up to an ideal of heavenly love; they were all filled with it and did not let themselves be touched by the flames of this world.

All the same they had upset the peace of heart of two gentlemen from the great world outside Berlevaag.

There was a young officer named Lorens Loewenhielm, who had led a gay life in his garrison town and had run into debt. In the year of 1854, when Martine was eighteen and Philippa seventeen, his angry father sent him on a month's visit to his aunt in her old country house

---

[2]Allusion to Proverbs 31:10—"Who can find a virtuous woman? for her price is far above rubies."

of Fossum near Berlevaag, where he would have time to meditate and to better his ways. One day he rode into town and met Martine in the marketplace. He looked down at the pretty girl, and she looked up at the fine horseman. When she had passed him and disappeared he was not certain whether he was to believe his own eyes.

In the Loewenhielm family there existed a legend to the effect that 10 long ago a gentleman of the name had married a Huldre, a female mountain spirit of Norway, who is so fair that the air round her shines and quivers. Since then, from time to time, members of the family had been second-sighted. Young Lorens till now had not been aware of any particular spiritual gift in his own nature. But at this one moment there rose before his eyes a sudden, mighty vision of a higher and purer life, with no creditors, dunning letters[3] or parental lectures, with no secret, unpleasant pangs of conscience and with a gentle, golden-haired angel to guide and reward him.

Through his pious aunt he got admission to the Dean's house, and saw that Martine was even lovelier without a bonnet. He followed her slim figure with adoring eyes, but he loathed and despised the figure which he himself cut in her nearness. He was amazed and shocked by the fact that he could find nothing at all to say, and no inspiration in the glass of water before him. "Mercy and Truth, dear brethren, have met together," said the Dean. "Righteousness and Bliss have kissed one another." And the young man's thoughts were with the moment when Lorens and Martine should be kissing each other. He repeated his visit time after time, and each time seemed to himself to grow smaller and more insignificant and contemptible.

When in the evening he came back to his aunt's house he kicked his shining riding-boots to the corners of his room; he even laid his head on the table and wept.

On the last day of his stay he made a last attempt to communicate his feelings to Martine. Till now it had been easy for him to tell a pretty girl that he loved her, but the tender words stuck in his throat as he looked into this maiden's face. When he had said good-bye to the party, Martine saw him to the door with a candlestick in her hand. The light

---

[3]Letters to customers informing them that their accounts are past due.

shone on her mouth and threw upwards the shadows of her long eye-lashes. He was about to leave in dumb despair when on the threshold he suddenly seized her hand and pressed it to his lips.

"I am going away forever!" he cried. "I shall never, never see you again! For I have learned here that Fate is hard, and that in this world there are things which are impossible!"

When he was once more back in his garrison town he thought his adventure over, and found that he did not like to think of it at all. While the other young officers talked of their love affairs, he was silent on his. For seen from the officers' mess, and so to say with its eyes, it was a pitiful business. How had it come to pass that a lieutenant of the hussars had let himself be defeated and frustrated by a set of long-faced sectarians, in the bare-floored rooms of an old Dean's house?

Then he became afraid; panic fell upon him. Was it the family madness which made him still carry with him the dream-like picture of a maiden so fair that she made the air round her shine with purity and holiness? He did not want to be a dreamer; he wanted to be like his brother-officers.

So he pulled himself together, and in the greatest effort of his young life made up his mind to forget what had happened to him in Berlevaag. From now on, he resolved, he would look forward, not back. He would concentrate on his career, and the day was to come when he would cut a brilliant figure in a brilliant world.

His mother was pleased with the result of his visit to Fossum, and in her letters expressed her gratitude to his aunt. She did not know by what queer, winding roads her son had reached his happy moral standpoint.

The ambitious young officer soon caught the attention of his superiors and made unusually quick advancement. He was sent to France and to Russia, and on his return he married a lady-in-waiting to Queen Sophia. In these high circles he moved with grace and ease, pleased with his surroundings and with himself. He even in the course of time benefited from words and turns which had stuck in his mind from the Dean's house, for piety was now in fashion at Court.

In the yellow house of Berlevaag, Philippa sometimes turned the 20 talk to the handsome, silent young man who had so suddenly made his appearance, and so suddenly disappeared again. Her elder sister would then answer her gently, with a still, clear face, and find other things to discuss.

III. PHILIPPA'S LOVER

A year later a more distinguished person even than Lieutenant Loewenhielm came to Berlevaag.

The great singer Achille Papin of Paris had sung for a week at the Royal Opera of Stockholm, and had carried away his audience there as everywhere. One evening a lady of the Court, who had been dreaming of a romance with the artist, had described to him the wild, grandiose scenery of Norway. His own romantic nature was stirred by the narration, and he had laid his way back to France round the Norwegian coast. But he felt small in the sublime surroundings; with nobody to talk to he fell into that melancholy in which he saw himself as an old man, at the end of his career, till on a Sunday, when he could think of nothing else to do, he went to church and heard Philippa sing.

Then in one single moment he knew and understood all. For here were the snowy summits, the wild flowers and the white Nordic nights, translated into his own language of music, and brought him in a young woman's voice. Like Lorens Loewenhielm he had a vision.

"Almighty God," he thought, "Thy power is without end, and Thy mercy reacheth unto the clouds! And here is a prima donna of the opera who will lay Paris at her feet."

Achille Papin at this time was a handsome man of forty, with curly 25 black hair and a red mouth. The idolization of nations had not spoilt him; he was a kind-hearted person and honest toward himself.

He went straight to the yellow house, gave his name—which told the Dean nothing—and explained that he was staying in Berlevaag for his health, and the while would be happy to take on the young lady as a pupil.

He did not mention the Opera of Paris, but described at length how beautifully Miss Philippa would come to sing in church, to the glory of God.

For a moment he forgot himself, for when the Dean asked whether he was a Roman Catholic he answered according to truth, and the old clergyman, who had never seen a live Roman Catholic, grew a little pale. All the same the Dean was pleased to speak French, which reminded him of his young days when he had studied the works of the great French Lutheran writer, Lefèvre d'Etaples. And as nobody could long withstand Achille Papin when he had really set his heart on a matter, in the end the father gave his consent, and remarked to his daughter: "God's paths run across the sea and the snowy mountains, where man's eye sees no track."

So the great French singer and the young Norwegian novice set to work together. Achille's expectation grew into certainty and his certainty into ecstasy. He thought: "I have been wrong in believing that I was growing old. My greatest triumphs are before me! The world will once more believe in miracles when she and I sing together!"

After a while he could not keep his dreams to himself, but told 30 Philippa about them.

She would, he said, rise like a star above any diva of the past or present. The Emperor and Empress, the Princes, great ladies and *bels esprits*[4] of Paris would listen to her, and shed tears. The common people too would worship her, and she would bring consolation and strength to the wronged and oppressed. When she left the Grand Opera upon her master's arm, the crowd would unharness her horses, and themselves draw her to the Café Anglais, where a magnificent supper awaited her.

Philippa did not repeat these prospects to her father or her sister, and this was the first time in her life that she had had a secret from them.

The teacher now gave his pupil the part of Zerlina in Mozart's opera *Don Giovanni* to study. He himself, as often before, sang Don Giovanni's part.

[4]Literally, fine minds (French), intelligentsia.

He had never in his life sung as now. In the duet of the second act—which is called the seduction duet—he was swept off his feet by the heavenly music and the heavenly voices. As the last melting note died away he seized Philippa's hands, drew her toward him and kissed her solemnly, as a bridegroom might kiss his bride before the altar. Then he let her go. For the moment was too sublime for any further word or movement; Mozart himself was looking down on the two.

Philippa went home, told her father that she did not want any more 35 singing lessons and asked him to write and tell Monsieur Papin so.

The Dean said: "And God's paths run across the rivers, my child."

When Achille got the Dean's letter he sat immovable for an hour. He thought: "I have been wrong. My day is over. Never again shall I be the divine Papin. And this poor weedy garden of the world has lost its nightingale!"

A little later he thought: "I wonder what is the matter with that hussy? Did I kiss her, by any chance?"

In the end he thought: "I have lost my life for a kiss, and I have no remembrance at all of the kiss! Don Giovanni kissed Zerlina, and Achille Papin pays for it! Such is the fate of the artist!"

In the Dean's house Martine felt that the matter was deeper than it 40 looked, and searched her sister's face. For a moment, slightly trembling, she too imagined that the Roman Catholic gentleman might have tried to kiss Philippa. She did not imagine that her sister might have been surprised and frightened by something in her own nature.

Achille Papin took the first boat from Berlevaag.

Of this visitor from the great world the sisters spoke but little; they lacked the words with which to discuss him.

IV. A LETTER FROM PARIS

Fifteen years later, on a rainy June night of 1871, the bell-rope of the yellow house was pulled violently three times. The mistresses of the house opened the door to a massive, dark, deadly pale woman with a bundle on her arm, who stared at them, took a step forward and fell down on the doorstep in a dead swoon. When the frightened ladies had restored her to life she sat up, gave them one more glance from her sunken eyes and, all the time without a word, fumbled in her wet clothes and brought out a letter which she handed to them.

The letter was addressed to them all right, but it was written in French. The sisters put their heads together and read it. It ran as follows:

Ladies!

Do you remember me? Ah, when I think of you I have the heart filled with wild lilies-of-the-valley! Will the memory of a Frenchman's devotion bend your hearts to save the life of a Frenchwoman?

The bearer of this letter, Madame Babette Hersant, like my beautiful Empress herself, has had to flee from Paris. Civil war has raged in our streets.[5] French hands have shed French blood. The noble Communards, standing up for the Rights of Man, have been crushed and annihilated. Madame Hersant's husband and son, both eminent ladies' hairdressers, have been shot. She herself was arrested as a Pétroleuse—(which word is used here for women who set fire to houses with petroleum)—and has narrowly escaped the bloodstained hands of General Galliffet. She has lost all she possessed and dares not remain in France.

A nephew of hers is cook to the boat *Anna Colbioernsson*, bound for Christiania[6]—(as I believe, the capital of Norway)—and he has obtained shipping opportunity for his aunt. This is now her last sad resort!

Knowing that I was once a visitor to your magnificent country she comes to me, asks me if there be any good people in Norway and begs me, if it be so, to supply her with a letter to them. The two words of "good people" immediately bring before my eyes your picture, sacred to my heart. I send her to you. How she is to get from Christiania to Berlevaag I know not, having forgotten the map of Norway. But she is a Frenchwoman, and you will find that in her misery she has still got resourcefulness, majesty and true stoicism.

I envy her in her despair: she is to see your faces.

[5]France's defeat by Germany in the Franco-Prussian War (1870–71) led to the downfall of Emperor Louis Napoleon III and an ensuing period of political chaos, with fighting in the streets of Paris between republicans and anarchists.

[6]Former name of Oslo.

As you receive her mercifully, send a merciful thought back to France.

For fifteen years, Miss Philippa, I have grieved that your voice should never fill the Grand Opera of Paris. When tonight I think of you, no doubt surrounded by a gay and loving family, and of myself: gray, lonely, forgotten by those who once applauded and adored me, I feel that you may have chosen the better part in life. What is fame? What is glory? The grave awaits us all!

And yet, my lost Zerlina, and yet, soprano of the snow! As I write this I feel that the grave is not the end. In Paradise I shall hear your voice again. There you will sing, without fears or scruples, as God meant you to sing. There you will be the great artist that God meant you to be. Ah! how you will enchant the angels.

Babette can cook.

Deign to receive, my ladies, the humble homage of the friend who was once

Achille Papin

At the bottom of the page, as a P.S., were neatly printed the first two 45 bars of the duet between Don Giovanni and Zerlina, like this:

The two sisters till now had kept only a small servant of fifteen to help them in the house and they felt that they could not possibly afford to take on an elderly, experienced housekeeper. But Babette told them that she would serve Monsieur Papin's good people for nothing, and that she would take service with nobody else. If they sent her away she must die. Babette remained in the house of the Dean's daughters for twelve years, until the time of this tale.

V. STILL LIFE

Babette had arrived haggard and wild-eyed like a hunted animal, but in her new, friendly surroundings she soon acquired all the appearance of a respectable and trusted servant. She had appeared to be a beggar; she turned out to be a conqueror. Her quiet countenance and her steady, deep glance had magnetic qualities; under her eyes things moved, noiselessly, into their proper places.

Her mistresses at first had trembled a little, just as the Dean had once done, at the idea of receiving a Papist under their roof. But they did not like to worry a hard-tried fellow-creature with catechization; neither were they quite sure of their French. They silently agreed that the example of a good Lutheran life would be the best means of converting their servant. In this way Babette's presence in the house became, so to say, a moral spur to its inhabitants.

They had distrusted Monsieur Papin's assertion that Babette could cook. In France, they knew, people ate frogs. They showed Babette how to prepare a split cod and an ale-and-bread-soup; during the demonstration the Frenchwoman's face became absolutely expressionless. But within a week Babette cooked a split cod and an ale-and-bread-soup as well as anybody born and bred in Berlevaag.

The idea of French luxury and extravagance next had alarmed 50 and dismayed the Dean's daughters. The first day after Babette had entered their service they took her before them and explained to her that they were poor and that to them luxurious fare was sinful. Their own food must be as plain as possible; it was the soup-pails and baskets for their poor that signified. Babette nodded her head; as a girl, she informed her ladies, she had been cook to an old priest who was a saint. Upon this the sisters resolved to surpass the French priest in asceticism. And they soon found that from the day when Babette took over the housekeeping its cost was miraculously reduced, and the soup-pails and baskets acquired a new, mysterious power to stimulate and strengthen their poor and sick.

The world outside the yellow house also came to acknowledge Babette's excellence. The refugee never learned to speak the language of her new country, but in her broken Norwegian she beat down the prices of Berlevaag's flintiest tradesmen. She was held in awe on the quay and in the marketplace.

The old Brothers and Sisters, who had first looked askance at the foreign woman in their midst, felt a happy change in their little sisters' life, rejoiced at it and benefited by it. They found that troubles and cares had been conjured away from their existence, and that now they had money to give away, time for the confidences and complaints of their old friends and peace for meditating on heavenly matters. In the course of time not a few of the brotherhood included Babette's name in their prayers, and thanked God for the speechless stranger, the dark Martha in the house of their two fair Marys.[7] The stone which the builders had almost refused had become the headstone of the corner.[8]

The ladies of the yellow house were the only ones to know that their cornerstone had a mysterious and alarming feature to it, as if it was somehow related to the Black Stone of Mecca, the Kaaba itself.

Hardly ever did Babette refer to her past life. When in early days the sisters had gently condoled her upon her losses, they had been met with that majesty and stoicism of which Monsieur Papin had written. "What will you ladies?" she had answered, shrugging her shoulders. "It is Fate."

But one day she suddenly informed them that she had for many years held a ticket in a French lottery, and that a faithful friend in Paris was still renewing it for her every year. Some time she might win the *grand prix* of ten thousand francs. At that they felt that their cook's old carpetbag was made from a magic carpet; at a given moment she might mount it and be carried off, back to Paris.

And it happened when Martine or Philippa spoke to Babette that they would get no answer, and would wonder if she had even heard what they said. They would find her in the kitchen, her elbows on the table and her temples on her hands, lost in the study of a heavy black book which they secretly suspected to be a popish prayer-book. Or she would sit immovable on the three-legged kitchen chair, her strong hands in her lap and her dark eyes wide open, as enigmatical and fatal as a Pythia[9] upon her tripod. At such moments they realized

---

[7]In the Bible, Mary and Martha are the sisters of Lazarus (John 11).

[8]See Mark 12:10.

[9]Greek priestess of the Temple of Apollo at Delphi; often called the Oracle of Delphi, she sits on a cauldron atop a tripod.

that Babette was deep, and that in the soundings of her being there were passions, there were memories and longings of which they knew nothing at all.

A little cold shiver ran through them, and in their hearts they thought: "Perhaps after all she had indeed been a Pétroleuse."

VI. BABETTE'S GOOD LUCK

The fifteenth of December was the Dean's hundredth anniversary.

His daughters had long been looking forward to this day and had wished to celebrate it, as if their dear father were still among his disciples. Therefore it had been to them a sad and incomprehensible thing that in this last year discord and dissension had been raising their heads in his flock. They had endeavored to make peace, but they were aware that they had failed. It was as if the fine and lovable vigor of their father's personality had been evaporating, the way Hoffmann's anodyne[1] will evaporate when left on the shelf in a bottle without a cork. And his departure had left the door ajar to things hitherto unknown to the two sisters, much younger than his spiritual children. From a past half a century back, when the unshepherded sheep had been running astray in the mountains, uninvited dismal guests pressed through the opening on the heels of the worshippers and seemed to darken the little rooms and to let in the cold. The sins of old Brothers and Sisters came, with late piercing repentance like a toothache, and the sins of others against them came back with bitter resentment, like a poisoning of the blood.

There were in the congregation two old women who before their conversion had spread slander upon each other, and thereby to each other ruined a marriage and an inheritance. Today they could not remember happenings of yesterday or a week ago, but they remembered this forty-year-old wrong and kept going through the ancient accounts; they scowled at each other. There was an old Brother who suddenly called to mind how another Brother, forty-five years ago, had cheated him in a deal; he could have wished to dismiss the matter

[1]Spirit of ether, used as an anesthetic.

from his mind, but it stuck there like a deep-seated, festering splinter. There was a gray, honest skipper and a furrowed, pious widow, who in their young days, while she was the wife of another man, had been sweethearts. Of late each had begun to grieve, while shifting the burden of guilt from his own shoulders to those of the other and back again, and to worry about the possible terrible consequences, through all eternity, to himself, brought upon him by one who had pretended to hold him dear. They grew pale at the meetings in the yellow house and avoided each other's eyes.

As the birthday drew nearer, Martine and Philippa felt the responsibility growing heavier. Would their ever-faithful father look down to his daughters and call them by name as unjust stewards? Between them they talked matters over and repeated their father's saying: that God's paths were running even across the salt sea, and the snow-clad mountains, where man's eye sees no track.

One day of this summer the post brought a letter from France to Madame Babette Hersant. This in itself was a surprising thing, for during these twelve years Babette had received no letter. What, her mistresses wondered, could it contain? They took it into the kitchen to watch her open and read it. Babette opened it, read it, lifted her eyes from it to her ladies' faces and told them that her number in the French lottery had come out. She had won ten thousand francs.

The news made such an impression on the two sisters that for a full minute they could not speak a word. They themselves were used to receiving their modest pension in small installments; it was difficult to them even to imagine the sum of ten thousand francs in a pile. Then they pressed Babette's hand, their own hands trembling a little. They had never before pressed the hand of a person who the moment before had come into possession of ten thousand francs.

After a while they realized that the happenings concerned themselves as well as Babette. The country of France, they felt, was slowly rising before their servant's horizon, and correspondingly their own existence was sinking beneath their feet. The ten thousand francs which made her rich—how poor did they not make the house she had served! One by one old forgotten cares and worries began to peep out at them from the four corners of the kitchen. The congratulations died on their lips, and the two pious women were ashamed of their own silence.

During the following days they announced the news to their friends 65 with joyous faces, but it did them good to see these friends' faces grow sad as they listened to them. Nobody, it was felt in the Brotherhood, could really blame Babette: birds will return to their nests and human beings to the country of their birth. But did that good and faithful servant realize that in going away from Berlevaag she would be leaving many old and poor people in distress? Their little sisters would have no more time for the sick and sorrowful. Indeed, indeed, lotteries were ungodly affairs.

In due time the money arrived through offices in Christiania and Berlevaag. The two ladies helped Babette to count it, and gave her a box to keep it in. They handled, and became familiar with, the ominous bits of paper.

They dared not question Babette upon the date of her departure. Dared they hope that she would remain with them over the fifteenth of December?

The mistresses had never been quite certain how much of their private conversation the cook followed or understood. So they were surprised when on a September evening Babette came into the drawing room, more humble or subdued than they had ever seen her, to ask a favor. She begged them, she said, to let her cook a celebration dinner on the Dean's birthday.

The ladies had not intended to have any dinner at all. A very plain supper with a cup of coffee was the most sumptuous meal to which they had ever asked any guest to sit down. But Babette's dark eyes were as eager and pleading as a dog's; they agreed to let her have her way. At this the cook's face lighted up.

But she had more to say. She wanted, she said, to cook a French 70 dinner, a real French dinner, for this one time. Martine and Philippa looked at each other. They did not like the idea; they felt that they did not know what it might imply. But the very strangeness of the request disarmed them. They had no arguments wherewith to meet the proposition of cooking a real French dinner.

Babette drew a long sigh of happiness, but still she did not move. She had one more prayer to make. She begged that her mistresses would allow her to pay for the French dinner with her own money.

"No, Babette!" the ladies exclaimed. How could she imagine such a thing? Did she believe that they would allow her to spend her precious money on food and drink—or on them? No, Babette, indeed.

Babette took a step forward. There was something formidable in the move, like a wave rising. Had she stepped forth like this, in 1871, to plant a red flag on a barricade? She spoke, in her queer Norwegian, with classical French eloquence. Her voice was like a song.

Ladies! Had she ever, during twelve years, asked you a favor? No! And why not? Ladies, you who say your prayers every day, can you imagine what it means to a human heart to have no prayer to make? What would Babette have had to pray for? Nothing! Tonight she had a prayer to make, from the bottom of her heart. Do you not then feel tonight, my ladies, that it becomes you to grant it her, with such joy as that with which the good God has granted you your own?

The ladies for a while said nothing. Babette was right; it was her first request these twelve years; very likely it would be her last. They thought the matter over. After all, they told themselves, their cook was now better off than they, and a dinner could make no difference to a person who owned ten thousand francs.

Their consent in the end completely changed Babette. They saw that as a young woman she had been beautiful. And they wondered whether in this hour they themselves had not, for the very first time, become to her the "good people" of Achille Papin's letter.

VII. THE TURTLE

In November Babette went for a journey.

She had preparations to make, she told her mistresses, and would need a leave of a week or ten days. Her nephew, who had once got her to Christiania, was still sailing to that town; she must see him and talk things over with him. Babette was a bad sailor; she had spoken of her one sea-voyage, from France to Norway, as of the most horrible experience of her life. Now she was strangely collected; the ladies felt that her heart was already in France.

After ten days she came back to Berlevaag.

Had she got things arranged as she wished? the ladies asked. Yes, 80 she answered, she had seen her nephew and given him a list of the goods which he was to bring her from France. To Martine and Philippa this was a dark saying, but they did not care to talk of her departure, so they asked her no more questions.

Babette was somewhat nervous during the next weeks. But one December day she triumphantly announced to her mistresses that the goods had come to Christiania, had been transshipped there, and on this very day had arrived at Berlevaag. She had, she added, engaged an old man with a wheelbarrow to have them conveyed from the harbor to the house.

But what goods, Babette? the ladies asked. Why, Mesdames, Babette replied, the ingredients for the birthday dinner. Praise be to God, they had all arrived in good condition from Paris.

By this time Babette, like the bottled demon of the fairy tale, had swelled and grown to such dimensions that her mistresses felt small before her. They now saw the French dinner coming upon them, a thing of incalculable nature and range. But they had never in their life broken a promise; they gave themselves into their cook's hands.

All the same when Martine saw a barrow load of bottles wheeled into the kitchen, she stood still. She touched the bottles and lifted up one. "What is there in this bottle, Babette?" she asked in a low voice. "Not wine?" "Wine, Madame!" Babette answered. "No, Madame. It is a Clos Vougeot 1846!" After a moment she added: "From Philippe, in Rue Montorgueil!" Martine had never suspected that wines could have names to them, and was put to silence.

Late in the evening she opened the door to a ring, and was once 85 more faced with the wheelbarrow, this time with a red-haired sailor-boy behind it, as if the old man had by this time been worn out. The youth grinned at her as he lifted a big, undefinable object from the barrow. In the light of the lamp it looked like some greenish-black stone, but when set down on the kitchen floor it suddenly shot out a snake-like head and moved it slightly from side to side. Martine had seen pictures of tortoises, and had even as a child owned a pet tortoise, but this thing was monstrous in size and terrible to behold. She backed out of the kitchen without a word.

She dared not tell her sister what she had seen. She passed an almost sleepless night; she thought of her father and felt that on his very birthday she and her sister were lending his house to a witches' sabbath. When at last she fell asleep she had a terrible dream, in which she saw Babette poisoning the old Brothers and Sisters, Philippa and herself.

Early in the morning she got up, put on her gray cloak and went out in the dark street. She walked from house to house, opened her heart to her Brothers and Sisters, and confessed her guilt. She and Philippa, she said, had meant no harm; they had granted their servant a prayer and had not foreseen what might come of it. Now she could not tell what, on her father's birthday, her guests would be given to eat or drink. She did not actually mention the turtle, but it was present in her face and voice.

The old people, as has already been told, had all known Martine and Philippa as little girls; they had seen them cry bitterly over a broken doll. Martine's tears brought tears into their own eyes. They gathered in the afternoon and talked the problem over.

Before they again parted they promised one another that for their little sisters' sake they would, on the great day, be silent upon all matters of food and drink. Nothing that might be set before them, be it even frogs or snails, should wring a word from their lips.

"Even so," said a white-bearded Brother, "the tongue is a little member and boasteth great things. The tongue can no man tame; it is an unruly evil, full of deadly poison.[2] On the day of our master we will cleanse our tongues of all taste and purify them of all delight or disgust of the senses, keeping and preserving them for the higher things of praise and thanksgiving."

So few things ever happened in the quiet existence of the Berlevaag brotherhood that they were at this moment deeply moved and ele-

[2]See James 3:9.

vated. They shook hands on their vow, and it was to them as if they were doing so before the face of their Master.

VIII. THE HYMAN

On Sunday morning it began to snow. The white flakes fell fast and thick; the small windowpanes of the yellow house became pasted with snow.

Early in the day a groom from Fossum brought the two sisters a note. Old Mrs. Loewenhielm still resided in her country house. She was now ninety years old and stone-deaf, and she had lost all sense of smell or taste. But she had been one of the Dean's first supporters, and neither her infirmity nor the sledge journey would keep her from doing honor to his memory. Now, she wrote, her nephew, General Lorens Loewenhielm, had unexpectedly come on a visit; he had spoken with deep veneration of the Dean, and she begged permission to bring him with her. It would do him good, for the dear boy seemed to be in somewhat low spirits.

Martine and Philippa at this remembered the young officer and his visits; it relieved their present anxiety to talk of old happy days. They wrote back that General Loewenhielm would be welcome. They also called in Babette to inform her that they would now be twelve for dinner; they added that their latest guest had lived in Paris for several years. Babette seemed pleased with the news, and assured them that there would be food enough.

The hostesses made their little preparations in the sitting room. 95 They dared not set foot in the kitchen, for Babette had mysteriously nosed out a cook's mate from a ship in the harbor—the same boy, Martine realized, who had brought in the turtle—to assist her in the kitchen and to wait at table, and now the dark woman and the red-haired boy, like some witch with her familiar spirit, had taken possession of these regions. The ladies could not tell what fires had been burning or what cauldrons bubbling there from before daybreak.

Table linen and plate had been magically mangled[3] and polished, glasses and decanters brought, Babette only knew from where. The

[3]Ironed.

Dean's house did not possess twelve dining-room chairs; the long horsehair-covered sofa had been moved from the parlor to the dining room, and the parlor, ever sparsely furnished, now looked strangely bare and big without it.

Martine and Philippa did their best to embellish the domain left to them. Whatever troubles might be in wait for their guests, in any case they should not be cold; all day the sisters fed the towering old stove with birch-knots. They hung a garland of juniper round their father's portrait on the wall, and placed candlesticks on their mother's small working table beneath it; they burned juniper-twigs to make the room smell nice. The while they wondered if in this weather the sledge from Fossum would get through. In the end they put on their old black best frocks and their confirmation gold crosses. They sat down, folded their hands in their laps and committed themselves unto God.

The old Brothers and Sisters arrived in small groups and entered the room slowly and solemnly.

This low room with its bare floor and scanty furniture was dear to the Dean's disciples. Outside its windows lay the great world. Seen from in here the great world in its winter-whiteness was ever prettily bordered in pink, blue and red by the row of hyacinths on the window-sills. And in summer, when the windows were open, the great world had a softly moving frame of white muslin curtains to it.

Tonight the guests were met on the doorstep with warmth and 100 sweet smell, and they were looking into the face of their beloved Master, wreathed with evergreen. Their hearts like their numb fingers thawed.

One very old Brother, after a few moments' silence, in his trembling voice struck up one of the Master's own hymns:

"Jerusalem, my happy home
name ever dear to me . . ."

One by one the other voices fell in, thin quivering women's voices, ancient seafaring Brothers' deep growls, and above them all Philippa's clear soprano, a little worn with age but still angelic. Unwittingly the choir had seized one another's hands. They sang the hymn to the end, but could not bear to cease and joined in another:

"Take not thought for food or raiment
careful one, so anxiously . . ."

The mistresses of the house somewhat reassured by it, the words of the third verse:

"Wouldst thou give a stone, a reptile
to thy pleading child for food? . . ."

went straight to Martine's heart and inspired her with hope.

In the middle of this hymn sledge bells were heard outside; the guests from Fossum had arrived.

Martine and Philippa went to receive them and saw them into the parlor. Mrs. Loewenhielm with age had become quite small, her face colorless like parchment, and very still. By her side General Loewenhielm, tall, broad and ruddy, in his bright uniform, his breast covered with decorations, strutted and shone like an ornamental bird, a golden pheasant or a peacock, in this sedate party of black crows and jackdaws.

IX. GENERAL LOEWENHIELM

General Loewenhielm had been driving from Fossum to Berlevaag in a strange mood. He had not visited this part of the country for thirty years. He had come now to get a rest from his busy life at Court, and he had found no rest. The old house of Fossum was peaceful enough and seemed somehow pathetically small after the Tuileries and the Winter Palace.[4] But it held one disquieting figure: young Lieutenant Loewenhielm walked in its rooms.

General Loewenhielm saw the handsome, slim figure pass close by him. And as he passed the boy gave the elder man a short glance and

[4]Royal palaces in Paris and St. Petersburg.

a smile, the haughty, arrogant smile which youth gives to age. The General might have smiled back, kindly and a little sadly, as age smiles at youth, if it had not been that he was really in no mood to smile; he was, as his aunt had written, in low spirits.

General Loewenhielm had obtained everything that he had striven for in life and was admired and envied by everyone. Only he himself knew of a queer fact, which jarred with his prosperous existence: that he was not perfectly happy. Something was wrong somewhere, and he carefully felt his mental self all over, as one feels a finger over to determine the place of a deep-seated, invisible thorn.

He was in high favor with royalty, he had done well in his calling, he had friends everywhere. The thorn sat in none of these places.

His wife was a brilliant woman and still good-looking. Perhaps she 110 neglected her own house a little for her visits and parties; she changed her servants every three months and the General's meals at home were served unpunctually. The General, who valued good food highly in life, here felt a slight bitterness against the lady, and secretly blamed her for the indigestion from which he sometimes suffered. Still the thorn was not here either.

Nay, but an absurd thing had lately been happening to General Loewenhielm: he would find himself worrying about his immortal soul. Did he have any reason for doing so? He was a moral person, loyal to his king, his wife and his friends, an example to everybody. But there were moments when it seemed to him that the world was not a moral, but a mystic, concern. He looked into the mirror, examined the row of decorations on his breast and sighed to himself: "Vanity, vanity, all is vanity!"[5]

The strange meeting at Fossum had compelled him to make out the balance-sheet of his life.

Young Lorens Loewenhielm had attracted dreams and fancies as a flower attracts bees and butterflies. He had fought to free himself of them; he had fled and they had followed. He had been scared of the Huldre of the family legend and had declined her invitation to come into the mountain; he had firmly refused the gift of second sight.

[5]See Ecclesiastes 1:2.

The elderly Lorens Loewenhielm found himself wishing that one little dream would come his way, and a gray moth of dusk look him up before nightfall. He found himself longing for the faculty of second sight, as a blind man will long for the normal faculty of vision.

Can the sum of a row of victories in many years and in many countries be a defeat? General Loewenhielm had fulfilled Lieutenant Loewenhielm's wishes and had more than satisfied his ambitions. It might be held that he had gained the whole world.[6] And it had come to this, that the stately, worldly-wise older man now turned toward the naïve young figure to ask him, gravely, even bitterly, in what he had profited? Somewhere something had been lost.

When Mrs. Loewenhielm had told her nephew of the Dean's anniversary and he had made up his mind to go with her to Berlevaag, his decision had not been an ordinary acceptance of a dinner invitation.

He would, he resolved, tonight make up his account with young Lorens Loewenhielm, who had felt himself to be a shy and sorry figure in the house of the Dean, and who in the end had shaken its dust off his riding boots. He would let the youth prove to him, once and for all, that thirty-one years ago he had made the right choice. The low rooms, the haddock and the glass of water on the table before him should all be called in to bear evidence that in their milieu the existence of Lorens Loewenhielm would very soon have become sheer misery.

He let his mind stray far away. In Paris he had once won a *concours hippique*[7] and had been feted by high French cavalry officers, princes and dukes among them. A dinner had been given in his honor at the finest restaurant of the city. Opposite him at table was a noble lady, a famous beauty whom he had long been courting. In the midst of dinner she had lifted her dark velvet eyes above the rim of her champagne glass and without words had promised to make him happy. In the sledge he now all of a sudden remembered that he had then, for a second, seen Martine's face before him and had rejected it. For a while he listened to the tinkling of the sledge bells, then he smiled a little as

---

[6] See Luke 9:25.
[7] Horse show (French).

he reflected how he would tonight come to dominate the conversation round that same table by which young Lorens Loewenhielm had sat mute.

Large snowflakes fell densely; behind the sledge the tracks were wiped out quickly. General Loewenhielm sat immovable by the side of his aunt, his chin sunk in the high fur collar of his coat.

X. BABETTE'S DINNER

As Babette's red-haired familiar opened the door to the dining room, and the guests slowly crossed the threshold, they let go one another's hands and became silent. But the silence was sweet, for in spirit they still held hands and were still singing. 120

Babette had set a row of candles down the middle of the table; the small flames shone on the black coats and frocks and on the one scarlet uniform, and were reflected in clear, moist eyes.

General Loewenhielm saw Martine's face in the candlelight as he had seen it when the two parted, thirty years ago. What traces would thirty years of Berlevaag life have left on it? The golden hair was now streaked with silver; the flower-like face had slowly been turned into alabaster. But how serene was the forehead, how quietly trustful the eyes, how pure and sweet the mouth, as if no hasty word had ever passed its lips.

When all were seated, the eldest member of the congregation said grace in the Dean's own words:

"May my food my body maintain,
   may my body my soul sustain,
   may my soul in deed and word
   give thanks for all things to the Lord."

At the word of "food" the guests, with their old heads bent over their folded hands, remembered how they had vowed not to utter a word about the subject, and in their hearts they reinforced the vow: they would not even give it a thought! They were sitting down to a meal, well, so had people done at the wedding of Cana.[8] And grace has chosen to manifest itself there, in the very wine, as fully as anywhere.

Babette's boy filled a small glass before each of the party. They 125 lifted it to their lips gravely, in confirmation of their resolution.

General Loewenhielm, somewhat suspicious of his wine, took a sip of it, startled, raised the glass first to his nose and then to his eyes, and sat it down bewildered. "This is very strange!" he thought. "Amontillado! And the finest Amontillado that I have ever tasted." After a moment, in order to test his senses, he took a small spoonful of his soup, took a second spoonful and laid down his spoon. "This is exceedingly strange!" he said to himself. "For surely I am eating turtle-soup—and what turtle-soup!" He was seized by a queer kind of panic and emptied his glass.

Usually in Berlevaag people did not speak much while they were eating. But somehow this evening tongues had been loosened. An old Brother told the story of his first meeting with the Dean. Another went through that sermon which sixty years ago had brought about his conversion. An aged woman, the one to whom Martine had first confided her distress, reminded her friends how in all afflictions any Brother or Sister was ready to share the burden of any other.

General Loewenhielm, who was to dominate the conversation of the dinner table, related how the Dean's collection of sermons was a favorite book of the Queen's. But as a new dish was served he was silenced. "Incredible!" he told himself. "It is Blinis Demidoff!"[9] He looked round at his fellow-diners. They were all quietly eating their Blinis Demidoff without any sign of either surprise or approval, as if they had been doing so every day for thirty years.

A Sister on the other side of the table opened on the subject of strange happenings which had taken place while the Dean was still amongst his children, and which one might venture to call miracles. Did they remember, she asked, the time when he had promised a Christmas sermon in the village the other side of the fjord? For a fort-

[8] Jesus turned water into wine at a wedding in Cana (See John 2:1–11).
[9] Buckwheat pancakes with caviar and sour cream.

night the weather had been so bad that no skipper or fisherman would risk the crossing. The villagers were giving up hope, but the Dean told them that if no boat would take him, he would come to them walking upon the waves. And behold! Three days before Christmas the storm stopped, hard frost set in, and the fjord froze from shore to shore—and this was a thing which had not happened within the memory of man!

The boy once more filled the glasses. This time the Brothers and Sisters knew that what they were given to drink was not wine, for it sparkled. It must be some kind of lemonade. The lemonade agreed with their exalted state of mind and seemed to lift them off the ground, into a higher and purer sphere. 130

General Loewenhielm again set down his glass, turned to his neighbor on the right and said to him: "But surely this is a Veuve Cliquot[1] 1860?" His neighbor looked at him kindly, smiled at him and made a remark about the weather.

Babette's boy had his instructions; he filled the glasses of the Brotherhood only once, but he refilled the General's glass as soon as it was emptied. The General emptied it quickly time after time. For how is a man of sense to behave when he cannot trust his senses? It is better to be drunk than mad.

Most often the people in Berlevaag during the course of a good meal would come to feel a little heavy. Tonight it was not so. The *convives*[2] grew lighter in weight and lighter of heart the more they ate and drank. They no longer needed to remind themselves of their vow. It was, they realized, when man has not only altogether forgotten but has firmly renounced all ideas of food and drink that he eats and drinks in the right spirit.

General Loewenhielm stopped eating and sat immovable. Once more he was carried back to that dinner in Paris of which he had thought in the sledge. An incredibly recherché and palatable dish had been served there; he had asked its name from his fellow diner, Colonel Galliffet, and the Colonel had smilingly told him that it was named

[1]Veuve Clicquot was (and is) a brand of premium champagne.
[2]Dinner guests, fellow diners (French).

"Cailles en Sarcophage."[3] He had further told him that the dish had been invented by the chef of the very café in which they were dining, a person known all over Paris as the greatest culinary genius of the age, and—most surprisingly—a woman! "And indeed," said Colonel Galliffet, "this woman is now turning a dinner at the Café Anglais into a kind of love affair—into a love affair of the noble and romantic category in which one no longer distinguishes between bodily and spiritual appetite or satiety! I have, before now, fought a duel for the sake of a fair lady. For no woman in all Paris, my young friend, would I more willingly shed my blood!" General Loewenhielm turned to his neighbor on the left and said to him: "But this is Cailles en Sarcophage!" The neighbor, who had been listening to the description of a miracle, looked at him absent-mindedly, then nodded his head and answered: "Yes, Yes, certainly. What else would it be?"

From the Master's miracles the talk round the table had turned to the smaller miracles of kindliness and helpfulness daily performed by his daughters. The old Brother who had first struck up the hymn quoted the Dean's saying: "The only things which we may take with us from our life on earth are those which we have given away!" The guests smiled—what nabobs would not the poor, simple maidens become in the next world!

General Loewenhielm no longer wondered at anything. When a few minutes later he saw grapes, peaches and fresh figs before him, he laughed to his neighbor across the table and remarked: "Beautiful grapes!" His neighbor replied: " 'And they came onto the brook of Eshcol, and cut down a branch with one cluster of grapes. And they bare it two upon a staff.' "[4]

Then the General felt that the time had come to make a speech. He rose and stood up very straight.

Nobody else at the dinner table had stood up to speak. The old people lifted their eyes to the face above them in high, happy expectation. They were used to seeing sailors and vagabonds dead drunk

[3]Quail in puff pastry with foie gras and truffle sauce.
[4]See Numbers 13:23.

with the crass gin of the country, but they did not recognize in a warrior and courtier the intoxication brought about by the noblest wine of the world.

XI. GENERAL LOEWENHIELM'S SPEECH

"Mercy and truth, my friends, have met together," said the General. "Righteousness and bliss shall kiss one another."

He spoke in a clear voice which had been trained in drill grounds 140 and had echoed sweetly in royal halls, and yet he was speaking in a manner so new to himself and so strangely moving that after his first sentence he had to make a pause. For he was in the habit of forming his speeches with care, conscious of his purpose, but here, in the midst of the Dean's simple congregation, it was as if the whole figure of General Loewenhielm, his breast covered with decorations, were but a mouthpiece for a message which meant to be brought forth.

"Man, my friends," said General Loewenhielm, "is frail and foolish. We have all of us been told that grace is to be found in the universe. But in our human foolishness and short-sightedness we imagine divine grace to be finite. For this reason we tremble . . ." Never till now had the General stated that he trembled; he was genuinely surprised and even shocked at hearing his own voice proclaim the fact. "We tremble before making our choice in life, and after having made it again tremble in fear of having chosen wrong. But the moment comes when our eyes are opened, and we see and realize that grace is infinite. Grace, my friends, demands nothing from us but that we shall await it with confidence and acknowledge it in gratitude. Grace, brothers, makes no conditions and singles out none of us in particular; grace takes us all to its bosom and proclaims general amnesty. See! that which we have chosen is given us, and that which we have refused is, also and at the same time, granted us. Ay, that which we have rejected is poured upon us abundantly. For mercy and truth have met together, and righteousness and bliss have kissed one another!"

The Brothers and Sisters had not altogether understood the General's speech, but his collected and inspired face and the sound of well-known and cherished words had seized and moved all hearts. In this way, after thirty-one years, General Loewenhielm succeeded in dominating the conversation at the Dean's dinner table.

Of what happened later in the evening nothing definite can here be stated. None of the guests later on had any clear remembrance of it. They only knew that the rooms had been filled with a heavenly light, as if a number of small halos had blended into one glorious radiance. Taciturn old people received the gift of tongues; ears that for years had been almost deaf were opened to it. Time itself had merged into eternity. Long after midnight the windows of the house shone like gold, and golden song flowed out into the winter air.

The two old women who had once slandered each other now in their hearts went back a long way, past the evil period in which they had been stuck, to those days of their early girlhood when together they had been preparing for confirmation and hand in hand had filled the roads round Berlevaag with singing. A Brother in the congregation gave another a knock in the ribs, like a rough caress between boys, and cried out: "You cheated me on that timber, you old scoundrel!" The Brother thus addressed almost collapsed in a heavenly burst of laughter, but tears ran from his eyes. "Yes, I did so, beloved Brother," he answered. "I did so." Skipper Halvorsen and Madam Oppegaarden suddenly found themselves close together in a corner and gave one another that long, long kiss, for which the secret uncertain love affair of their youth had never left them time.

The old Dean's flock were humble people. When later in life they thought of this evening it never occurred to any of them that they might have been exalted by their own merit. They realized that the infinite grace of which General Loewenhielm had spoken had been allotted to them, and they did not even wonder at the fact, for it had been but the fulfillment of an ever-present hope. The vain illusions of this earth had dissolved before their eyes like smoke, and they had seen the universe as it really is. They had been given one hour of the millennium.

Old Mrs. Loewenhielm was the first to leave. Her nephew accompanied her, and their hostesses lighted them out. While Philippa was helping the old lady into her many wraps, the General seized Martine's hand and held it for a long time without a word. At last he said:

"I have been with you every day of my life. You know, do you not, that it has been so?"

"Yes," said Martine, "I know that it has been so."

"And," he continued, "I shall be with you every day that is left to me. Every evening I shall sit down, if not in the flesh, which means nothing, in spirit, which is all, to dine with you, just like tonight. For tonight I have learned, dear sister, that in this world anything is possible."

"Yes, it is so, dear brother," said Martine. "In this world anything is possible." 150

Upon this they parted.

When at last the company broke up it had ceased to snow. The town and the mountains lay in white, unearthly splendor and the sky was bright with thousands of stars. In the street the snow was lying so deep that it had become difficult to walk. The guests from the yellow house wavered on their feet, staggered, sat down abruptly or fell forward on their knees and hands and were covered with snow, as if they had indeed had their sins washed white as wool, and in this regained innocent attire were gamboling like little lambs. It was, to each of them, blissful to have become as a small child; it was also a blessed joke to watch old Brothers and Sisters, who had been taking themselves so seriously, in this kind of celestial second childhood. They stumbled and got up, walked on or stood still, bodily as well as spiritually hand in hand, at moments performing the great chain of a beatified *lanciers*.[5]

"Bless you, bless you, bless you," like an echo of the harmony of the spheres rang on all sides.

Martine and Philippa stood for a long time on the stone steps outside the house. They did not feel the cold. "The stars have come nearer," said Philippa.

"They will come every night," said Martine quietly. "Quite possibly it will never snow again." 155

In this, however, she was mistaken. An hour later it again began to snow, and such a heavy snowfall had never been known in Berlevaag. The next morning people could hardly push open their doors against

[5]Traditional Danish dance.

the tall snowdrifts. The windows of the houses were so thickly covered with snow, it was told for years afterwards, that many good citizens of the town did not realize that daybreak had come, but slept on till late in the afternoon.

XII. THE GREAT ARTIST

When Martine and Philippa locked the door they remembered Babette. A little wave of tenderness and pity swept through them: Babette alone had had no share in the bliss of the evening.

So they went out into the kitchen, and Martine said to Babette: "It was quite a nice dinner, Babette."

Their hearts suddenly filled with gratitude. They realized that none of their guests had said a single word about the food. Indeed, try as they might, they could not themselves remember any of the dishes which had been served. Martine bethought herself of the turtle. It had not appeared at all, and now seemed very vague and far away; it was quite possible that it had been nothing but a nightmare.

Babette sat on the chopping block, surrounded by more black and greasy pots and pans than her mistresses had ever seen in their life. She was as white and as deadly exhausted as on the night when she first appeared and had fainted on their doorstep.

After a long time she looked straight at them and said: "I was once cook at the Café Anglais."

Martine said again: "They all thought that it was a nice dinner." And when Babette did not answer a word she added: "We will all remember this evening when you have gone back to Paris, Babette."

Babette said: "I am not going back to Paris."

"You are not going back to Paris?" Martine exclaimed.

"No," said Babette. "What will I do in Paris? They have all gone. I have lost them all, Mesdames."

The sisters' thoughts went to Monsieur Hersant and his son, and they said: "Oh, my poor Babette."

"Yes, they have all gone," said Babette. "The Duke of Morny, the Duke of Decazes, Prince Narishkine, General Galliffet, Aurélian Scholl, Paul Daru, the Princesse Pauline! All!"

The strange names and titles of people lost to Babette faintly confused the two ladies, but there was such an infinite perspective of tragedy in her announcement that in their responsive state of mind they felt her losses as their own, and their eyes filled with tears.

At the end of another long silence Babette suddenly smiled slightly at them and said: "And how would I go back to Paris, Mesdames? I have no money."

"No money?" the sisters cried as with one mouth. 170

"No," said Babette.

"But the ten thousand francs?" the sisters asked in a horrified gasp.

"The ten thousand francs have been spent, Mesdames," said Babette.

The sisters sat down. For a full minute they could not speak.

"But ten thousand francs?" Martine slowly whispered. 175

"What will you, Mesdames," said Babette with great dignity. "A dinner for twelve at the Café Anglais would cost ten thousand francs."

The ladies still did not find a word to say. The piece of news was incomprehensible to them, but then many things tonight in one way or another had been beyond comprehension.

Martine remembered a tale told by a friend of her father's who had been a missionary in Africa. He had saved the life of an old chief's favorite wife, and to show his gratitude the chief had treated him to a rich meal. Only long afterwards the missionary learned from his own black servant that what he had partaken of was a small fat grandchild of the chief's, cooked in honor of the great Christian medicine man. She shuddered.

But Philippa's heart was melting in her bosom. It seemed that an unforgettable evening was to be finished off with an unforgettable proof of human loyalty and self-sacrifice.

"Dear Babette," she said softly, "you ought not to have given away all 180 you had for our sake."

Babette gave her mistress a deep glance, a strange glance. Was there not pity, even scorn, at the bottom of it?

"For your sake?" she replied. "No. For my own."

She rose from the chopping block and stood up before the two sisters.

"I am a great artist!" she said.

She waited a moment and then repeated: "I am a great artist, 185 Mesdames."

Again for a long time there was deep silence in the kitchen.

Then Martine said: "So you will be poor now all your life, Babette?"

"Poor?" said Babette. She smiled as if to herself. "No, I shall never be poor. I told you that I am a great artist. A great artist, Mesdames, is never poor. We have something, Mesdames, of which other people know nothing."

While the elder sister found nothing more to say, in Philippa's heart deep, forgotten chords vibrated. For she had heard, before now, long ago, of the Café Anglais. She had heard, before now, long ago, the names on Babette's tragic list. She rose and took a step toward her servant.

"But all those people whom you have mentioned," she said, "those 190 princes and great people of Paris whom you named, Babette? You yourself fought against them. You were a Communard! The General you named had your husband and son shot! How can you grieve over them?"

Babette's dark eyes met Philippa's.

"Yes," she said, "I was a Communard. Thanks be to God, I was a Communard! And those people whom I named, Mesdames, were evil and cruel. They let the people of Paris starve; they oppressed and wronged the poor. Thanks be to God, I stood upon a barricade; I loaded the gun for my menfolk! But all the same, Mesdames, I shall not go back to Paris, now that those people of whom I have spoken are no longer there."

She stood immovable, lost in thought.

"You see, Mesdames," she said, at last, "those people belonged to me, they were mine. They had been brought up and trained, with greater expense than you, my little ladies, could ever imagine or believe, to understand what a great artist I am. I could make them happy. When I did my very best I could make them perfectly happy."

She paused for a moment. 195

"It was like that with Monsieur Papin too," she said.

"With Monsieur Papin?" Philippa asked.

"Yes, with your Monsieur Papin, my poor lady," said Babette. "He told me so himself: 'It is terrible and unbearable to an artist,' he said, 'to be encouraged to do, to be applauded for doing, his second best.' He said: 'Through all the world there goes one long cry from the heart of the artist: Give me leave to do my utmost!'"

Philippa went up to Babette and put her arms round her. She felt the cook's body like a marble monument against her own, but she herself shook and trembled from head to foot.

For a while she could not speak. Then she whispered: 200

"Yet this is not the end! I feel, Babette, that this is not the end. In Paradise you will be the great artist that God meant you to be! Ah!" she added, the tears streaming down her cheeks. "Ah, how you will enchant the angels!"

STUDY QUESTIONS

1. How would you describe the relationship between Babette and the two sisters? Point to excerpts from the story that support your interpretation of their relationship.

2. Dinesen's story is structured by CONTRASTS, which she reconciles in the end. Trace one set of opposites throughout the story, pointing to passages that apply.

3. In addition to thematic contrasts Dinesen uses METAPHORS and SIMILES to show comparisons and contrasts. Which similes and metaphors did you find most effective? Why?

4. One of Dinsen's THEMES is silence. Names the kinds of silence you recognize in this story (for example, awed, shocked, grave, customary, repressive). What is the effect of Dinesen's use of so many kinds of silence?

5. *For Writing.* Write a short story in which food plays a significant role. Use contrasts that you reconcile in the end. Also, like Dinesen, use similes and metaphors.

AMITAI ETZIONI { *The Fast-Food Factories:*
McJobs Are Bad for Kids

AMITAI ETZIONI (b. 1929) was born in Cologne, Germany, and relocated
to Palestine in the 1930s to escape Nazi persecution. He earned his PhD in
sociology from the University of California, Berkeley, in 1958 and taught at
Columbia University for twenty years. After serving in the Carter administration as a senior advisor on domestic affairs from 1979 to 1980, Etzioni
returned to academia at George Washington University, where he now also
directs the Institute for Communitarian Policy Studies. In 1990 he founded
the Communitarian Network, a nonprofit, nonpartisan organization that
works toward the goal of a more ethical society. Etzioni has written more
than twenty books, including *From Empire to Community: A New Approach
to International Relations* (2004) and *Security First: For a Muscular, Moral
Foreign Policy* (2007).

In the following opinion piece, first published in the *Washington Post* in
1986, Etzioni argues that fast-food jobs are not good for teenagers—not
just because they don't provide educational benefits in their own right but
because they cause students to waste time that would be better spent in
school. As you read his argument, consider the persuasiveness of his logic
and evidence. Does he convince you?

═══════════════

MCDONALD'S IS BAD FOR YOUR kids. I do not kids mean the flat patties
and the white-flour buns; I refer to the jobs teenagers undertake, mass-
producing these choice items.

As many as two-thirds of America's high-school juniors and seniors
now hold down part-time paying jobs, according to studies. Many of

these are in fast-food chains, of which McDonald's is the pioneer, trendsetter and symbol.

At first, such jobs may seem right out of the Founding Fathers' educational manual for how to bring up self-reliant, work-ethic-driven, productive youngsters. But in fact, these jobs undermine school attendance and involvement, impart few skills that will be useful in later life, and simultaneously skew the values of teenagers—especially their ideas about the worth of a dollar.

It has been a long-standing American tradition that youngsters ought to get paying jobs. In folklore, few pursuits are more deeply revered than the newspaper route and the sidewalk lemonade stand. Here the youngsters are to learn how sweet are the fruits of labor and self-discipline (papers are delivered early in the morning, rain or shine) and the ways of trade (if you price your lemonade too high or too low . . .).

Roy Rogers, Baskin Robbins, Kentucky Fried Chicken, et al., may at 5 first seem nothing but a vast extension of the lemonade stand. They provide very large numbers of teen jobs, provide regular employment, pay quite well compared to many other teen jobs and, in the modern equivalent of toiling over a hot stove, test one's stamina.

Closer examination, however, finds the McDonald's kind of job highly uneducational in several ways. Far from providing opportunities for entrepreneurship (the lemonade stand) or self-discipline, self-supervision and self-scheduling (the paper route), most teen jobs these days are highly structured—what social scientists call "highly routinized."

True, you still have to have the gumption to get yourself over to the hamburger stand, but once you don the prescribed uniform, your task is spelled out in minute detail. The franchise prescribes the shape of the coffee cups; the weight, size, shape and color of the patties; and the texture of the napkins (if any). Fresh coffee is to be made every *eight* minutes. And so on. There is no room for initiative, creativity or even elementary rearrangements. These are breeding grounds for robots working for yesterday's assembly lines, not tomorrow's high-tech posts.

There are very few studies of the matter. One is a 1984 study by Ivan

Charner and Bryan Shore Fraser. It relies mainly on what teenagers write in response to questionnaires rather than actual observations of fast-food jobs. The authors argue that the employees develop many skills, such as how to operate a food-preparation machine and a cash register. However, little attention is paid to how long it takes to acquire such a skill, or what its significance is. What does it matter if you spend 20 minutes learning to use a cash register and then "operate" it? What "skill" have you acquired? It is a long way from learning to work with a lathe or carpenter tools in the olden days or to program computers in the modern age.

A 1980 study by A. V. Harrell and P. W. Wirtz found that, among those students who worked at least 25 hours per week while in school, their unemployment rate four years later was half of that of seniors who did not work. This is an impressive statistic. It must be seen, though, together with the finding that many who begin as part-time employees in fast-food chains drop out of high school and are gobbled up in the world of low-skill jobs.

Some say that while these jobs are rather unsuited for college-bound, white, middle-class youngsters, they are "ideal" for lower-class, "non-academic," minority youngsters. Indeed, minorities are "over-represented" in these jobs (21 percent of fast-food employees). While it is true that these places provide income, work, and even some training to such youngsters, they also tend to perpetuate their disadvantaged status. They provide no career ladders and few marketable skills, and they undermine school attendance and involvement.

The hours are often long. Among those 14 to 17, a third of fast-food employees (including some school dropouts) labor *more* than 30 hours per week, according to the Charner-Fraser study. Only 20 percent work 15 hours or less. The rest: between 15 and 30 hours. Often the restaurants close late, and after closing one must clean up and tally up. In affluent Montgomery County, where child labor would not seem to be a widespread economic necessity, 24 percent of the seniors at Walt Whitman High School in 1985 worked as much as five to seven days a week; 27 percent, three to five. There is just no way such amounts of work will not interfere with school work, especially homework. In an informal survey published in the most recent Walt Whitman yearbook,

10

58 percent of the seniors acknowledged that their jobs interfere with their school work.

The Charner-Fraser study sees merit in learning teamwork and working under supervision. The authors have a point here. However, it must be noted that such learning is not automatically educational or wholesome. For example, much of the supervision in fast-food places leans toward teaching one the wrong kinds of compliance: blind obedience, or shared alienation with the "boss."

Supervision is often both tight and woefully inappropriate. Today, fast-food chains and other such places of work (record shops, bowling alleys) keep costs down by having teens supervise teens, often with no adult on the premises. There is no father or mother figure with which to identify, to emulate, to provide a role model and guidance. The work-culture varies from one place to another: Sometimes it is a tightly run shop (must keep the cash registers ringing); sometimes a rather loose pot party interrupted by customers. However, only rarely is there a master to learn from, or much worth learning. Indeed, far from being places where solid adult work values are being transmitted, these are places where all too often delinquent teen values dominate. Typically, when my son Oren was dishing out ice cream for Baskin Robbins in upper Manhattan, his fellow teen-workers considered him a sucker for not helping himself to the till. Most youngsters felt they were entitled to $50 severance "pay" on their last day on the job.

The pay, oddly, is the part of the teen work-world which is most difficult to evaluate. The lemonade stand or paper route money was for your allowance. In the old days, apprentices learning a trade from a master contributed most, if not all, of their income to their parents' household. Today, the teen pay may be low by adult standards, but it is often, especially in the middle class, spent largely or wholly by the teens. That is, the youngsters live free at home ("after all, they are high school kids"), and are left with very substantial sums of money.

Where this money goes is not quite clear. Some use it to support them- 15 selves, especially among the poor. More middle-class kids set some money aside to help pay for college, or save it for a major purchase— often a car. But large amounts seem to flow to pay for an early introduction into the most trite aspects of American consumerism: flimsy punk clothes, trinkets and whatever else is the last fast-moving teen craze.

One may say that this is only fair and square; they are being good American consumers, working and spending their money on what turns them on. At least, a cynic might add, these funds do not go into illicit drugs and booze. On the other hand, an educator might bemoan that these young, yet unformed individuals, so early in life are driven to buy objects of no intrinsic educational, cultural or social merit, learn so quickly the dubious merit of keeping up with the Joneses in ever-changing fads promoted by mass merchandising.

Many teens find the instant reward of money, and the youth status symbols it buys, much more alluring than credits in calculus courses, European history, or foreign languages. No wonder quite a few would rather skip school—and certainly homework—and instead work longer at a Burger King. Thus, most teen work these days is not providing early lessons in work ethic; it fosters escape from school and responsibilities, quick gratification and a short cut to the consumeristic aspects of adult life.

Thus, ironically, we must add youth *employment,* not merely unemployment, to our list of social problems. And, like many other social ills, the unfortunate aspects of teen work resist easy correction. Sure, it would be much better if corporations that employ teens would do so in conjunction with high schools and school districts. Educators could help define what is the proper amount of gainful work (not more than "X" hours per school week); how late kids may be employed on school nights (not later than 9 p.m.), encourage employer understanding during exam periods, and insist on proper supervision. However, corporations are extremely unlikely to accept such an approach which, in effect, would curb their ability to draw on a major source of cheap labor. And, in these *laissez faire*[1] days, Congress is quite disinclined to pass new social legislation forcing corporations to be more attentive to the education needs of the minors they so readily employ.

Schools might extend their own work-study programs (starting

---

[1]Literally, let [the people] do [as they choose] (French), the doctrine that opposes governmental regulation of economic affairs.

their own franchises?!) but, without corporate help, these are unlikely to amount to much. Luckily, few schools (less than 10 percent) provide any credit for such work experience. But schools that do should insist that they will provide credit for work only if it meets their educational standards; only if they are consulted on matters such as supervision and on-the-job training; and only if their representatives are allowed to inspect the places of employment. School counselors should guide the youngsters only to those places of work that are willing to pay attention to educational elements of these jobs.

Parents who are still willing to take their role seriously may encour- 20
age their youngsters to seek jobs at places that are proper work settings and insist that fast-food chains and other franchises shape up or not employ *their* kids. Also an agreement should be reached with the youngsters that a significant share of teen earnings should be dedicated to the family, or saved for agreed-upon items.

Above all, parents should look at teen employment not as automatically educational. It is an activity—like sports—that can be turned *into* an educational opportunity. But it can also easily be abused. Youngsters must learn to balance the quest for income with the needs to keep growing and pursue other endeavors which do not pay off instantly—above all education.

Go back to school.

STUDY QUESTIONS

1. According to Etzioni, why is working in the fast-food industry bad for teenagers? Who does he CLAIM is over-represented in these jobs? Why?

2. Evaluate the EVIDENCE that Etzioni uses to support his ARGUMENT. Which evidence seems to be the most effective? The least effective? Why?

3. What objections to his argument does Etzioni anticipate? How effectively does he refute these objections? Explain.

4. *For Writing.* What kinds of employment—for instance, summer jobs, after-school jobs, work-study jobs—have you held? Drawing on your own experience and taking into consideration Etzioni's argument against "McJobs," write an essay in which you argue that one (or more) kind of work is good for teenagers.

MELISSA A. GOLDTHWAITE { *Three Courses, Provence*

MELISSA A. GOLDTHWAITE (b. 1972) grew up in New England and now lives outside of Philadelphia, when she is not in New Hampshire or France. She is professor of English at Saint Joseph's University, where she teaches courses in creative writing (food writing, nature writing, poetry writing, and creative nonfiction) and rhetoric. She has written or edited a number of books, many of them collaboratively: *The Norton Reader, The Norton Pocket Book of Writing by Students, The St. Martin's Guide to Teaching Writing, Surveying the Literary Landscapes of Terry Tempest Williams*, and others.

In "Three Courses, Provence," Goldthwaite uses the form of a photographic triptych to show three courses of a French meal: *entrée* (appetizer), *plat principal* (main course), and *dessert*. This photo series, like other photos of food, encourages the viewer to see food as art. Who is the artist? the person who cooked the food? plated it? the photographer? What is it about the photographs or their subjects that makes it art?

All photos by Melissa A. Goldthwaite.

STUDY QUESTIONS

1. Choose one of the three photos in the triptych to ANALYZE. Consider the effects of the colors, textures, arrangements, and other elements (such as what is included within the frame, the photographer's position in relation to the food, etc.).

2. Now consider all three photos. Do you see any visual THEMES? What elements provide clues that these photos were taken of the same meal?

3. Do these photos tell you anything about the place in which this meal was served? Do they tell you anything about the person who prepared the food? the person who ate it?

4. *For Writing.* Take a photo of the next meal you eat at a restaurant— whether it's a several-course meal, a tray of food from a fast-food restaurant, or a pizza. Write a visual ANALYSIS of your photograph. Has the food been presented to create a particular visual effect? Is there anything besides food within the frame of the photograph? Is the lighting effective? What are the dominant colors and textures?

Food and Identity

ANTHONY BOURDAIN {   *Food Is Good*

ANTHONY BOURDAIN (b. 1956) was born in New York City. He
attended Vassar College and, in 1978, graduated from the Culinary
Institute of America. He is a well-known chef and television personality,
hosting *Anthony Bourdain: No Reservations* on the Travel Channel. He
has written several nonfiction books about food, including *The Nasty
Bits*, *Kitchen Confidential*, *A Cook's Tour*, and *Anthony Bourdain's Les
Halles Cookbook*. He has also written two crime novels: *Gone Bamboo*
and *Bone in the Throat*.

In this excerpt from Bourdain's memoir *Kitchen Confidential:
Adventures in the Culinary Underbelly* (2000), the author begins with
the moment he discovered that eating wasn't merely "like filling up at
a gas station," a realization that came when he first tasted vichyssoise,
a cold soup, on a family cruise to Europe. He goes on to share the
experiences that helped him understand the power of food and become
a more adventurous eater.

───────────

MY FIRST INDICATION THAT FOOD was something other than a substance one stuffed in one's face when hungry—like filling up at a gas
station—came after fourth-grade elementary school. It was on a family
vacation to Europe, on the *Queen Mary*, in the cabin-class dining room.
There's a picture somewhere: my mother in her Jackie O sunglasses, my
younger brother and I in our painfully cute cruisewear, boarding the
big Cunard[1] ocean liner, all of us excited about our first transatlantic
voyage, our first trip to my father's ancestral homeland, France.

───────────

[1]British-American ocean liner company.

It was the soup.

It was *cold*.

This was something of a discovery for a curious fourth-grader whose entire experience of soup to this point had consisted of Campbell's cream of tomato and chicken noodle. I'd eaten in restaurants before, sure, but this was the first food I really noticed. It was the first food I enjoyed and, more important, remembered enjoying. I asked our patient British waiter what this delightfully cool, tasty liquid was.

"Vichyssoise," came the reply, a word that to this day—even though 5 it's now a tired old warhorse of a menu selection and one I've prepared thousands of times—still has a magical ring to it. I remember everything about the experience: the way our waiter ladled it from a silver tureen into my bowl, the crunch of tiny chopped chives he spooned on as garnish, the rich, creamy taste of leek and potato, the pleasurable shock, the surprise that it was cold.

I don't remember much else about the passage across the Atlantic. I saw *Boeing Boeing* with Jerry Lewis and Tony Curtis in the *Queen's* movie theater, and a Bardot flick.[2] The old liner shuddered and groaned and vibrated terribly the whole way—barnacles on the hull was the official explanation—and from New York to Cherbourg, it was like riding atop a giant lawnmower. My brother and I quickly became bored, and spent much of our time in the "Teen Lounge," listening to "House of the Rising Sun"[3] on the jukebox, or watching the water slosh around like a contained tidal wave in the below-deck salt-water pool.

But that cold soup stayed with me. It resonated, waking me up, making me aware of my tongue, and in some way, preparing me for future events.

My second pre-epiphany in my long climb to chefdom also came during that first trip to France. After docking, my mother, brother and I stayed with cousins in the small seaside town of Cherbourg, a bleak, chilly resort area in Normandy, on the English Channel. The sky was almost always cloudy; the water was inhospitably cold. All the neigh-

[2]That is, a movie starring French actress Brigitte Bardot (b. 1934).
[3]Folk song recorded as a pop hit by the English band The Animals in 1964.

borhood kids thought I knew Steve McQueen and John Wayne personally—as an American, it was assumed we were all pals, that we hung out together on the range, riding horses and gunning down miscreants—so I enjoyed a certain celebrity right away. The beaches, while no good for swimming, were studded with old Nazi blockhouses and gun emplacements, many still bearing visible bullet scars and the scorch of flamethrowers, and there were tunnels under the dunes—all very cool for a little kid to explore. My little French friends were, I was astonished to find, allowed to have a cigarette on Sunday, were given watered *vin ordinaire*[4] at the dinner table, and best of all, they owned Velo Solex motorbikes. *This* was the way to raise kids, I recall thinking, unhappy that my mother did not agree.

So for my first few weeks in France, I explored underground passageways, looking for dead Nazis, played miniature golf, sneaked cigarettes, read a lot of Tintin and Asterix comics, scooted around on my friends' motorbikes and absorbed little life-lessons from observations that, for instance, the family friend Monsieur Dupont brought his mistress to some meals and his wife to others, his extended brood of children apparently indifferent to the switch.

I was largely unimpressed by the food.   10

The butter tasted strangely "cheesy" to my undeveloped palate. The milk—a staple, no, a mandatory ritual in '60s American kiddie life— was undrinkable here. Lunch seemed always to consist of sandwich au jambon or croque-monsieur.[5] Centuries of French cuisine had yet to make an impression. What I noticed about food, French style, was what they *didn't* have.

After a few weeks of this, we took a night train to Paris, where we met up with my father, and a spanking new Rover Sedan Mark III, our touring car. In Paris, we stayed at the Hôtel Lutétia, then a large, slightly shabby old pile on Boulevard Haussmann. The menu selections for my brother and me expanded somewhat, to include steak-frites and steak haché (hamburger). We did all the predictable touristy things: climbed the Tour Eiffel, picnicked in the Bois de Boulogne,

[4]Inexpensive red table wine; literally, ordinary wine (French).
[5]Respectively, ham sandwich and grilled ham and cheese (French).

marched past the Great Works at the Louvre, pushed toy sailboats around the fountain in the Jardin de Luxembourg—none of it much fun for a nine-year-old with an already developing criminal bent. My principal interest at this time was adding to my collection of English translations of Tintin adventures. Hergé's crisply drafted tales of drug-smuggling, ancient temples, and strange and faraway places and cultures were *real* exotica for me. I prevailed on my poor parents to buy hundreds of dollars-worth of these stories at W. H. Smith, the English bookstore, just to keep me from whining about the deprivations of France. With my little short-shorts a permanent affront, I was quickly becoming a sullen, moody, difficult little bastard. I fought constantly with my brother, carped about everything, and was in every possible way a drag on my mother's Glorious Expedition.

My parents did their best. They took us everywhere, from restaurant to restaurant, cringing, no doubt, every time we insisted on steak haché (with ketchup, no less) and a "Coca." They endured silently my gripes about cheesy butter, the seemingly endless amusement I took in advertisements for a popular soft drink of the time, Pschitt. "I want shit! I want shit!" They managed to ignore the eye-rolling and fidgeting when they spoke French, tried to encourage me to find something, anything, to enjoy.

And there came a time when, finally, they *didn't* take the kids along.

I remember it well, because it was such a slap in the face. It was a 15 wake-up call that food could be important, a challenge to my natural belligerence. By being denied, a door opened.

The town's name was Vienne. We'd driven miles and miles of road to get there. My brother and I were fresh out of Tintins and cranky as hell. The French countryside, with its graceful, tree-lined roads, hedgerows, tilled fields and picture-book villages provided little distraction. My folks had by now endured weeks of relentless complaining through many tense and increasingly unpleasant meals. They'd dutifully ordered our steak haché, crudités variées,[6] sandwich au jambon and the like long enough. They'd put up with our grousing that the beds were too hard, the pillows too soft, the neck-rolls and toilets and plumbing too weird.

---

[6]Mixed raw vegetables (French).

They'd even allowed us a little watered wine, as it was clearly the French thing to do—but also, I think, to shut us up. They'd taken my brother and me, the two Ugliest Little Americans, everywhere.

Vienne was different.

They pulled the gleaming new Rover into the parking lot of a restaurant called, rather promisingly, La Pyramide, handed us what was apparently a hoarded stash of Tintins . . . *and then left us in the car!*

It was a hard blow. Little brother and I were left in that car for over three hours, an eternity for two miserable kids already bored out of their minds. I had plenty of time to wonder: *What could be so great inside those walls?* They were eating in there. I knew that. And it was certainly a Big Deal; even at a witless age nine, I could recognize the nervous anticipation, the excitement, the near-reverence with which my beleaguered parents had approached this hour. And I had the Vichyssoise Incident still fresh in my mind. Food, it appeared, could be *important*. It could be an event. It had secrets.

I know now, of course, that La Pyramide, even in 1966, was the center of the culinary universe. Bocuse, Troisgros,[7] *everybody* had done their time there, making their bones under the legendarily fearsome proprietor, Ferdinand Point. Point was the Grand Master of cuisine at the time, and La Pyramide was Mecca for foodies. This was a pilgrimage for my earnestly francophile parents. In some small way, I got that through my tiny, empty skull in the back of the sweltering parked car, even then.

Things changed. *I* changed after that.

First of all, I was furious. Spite, always a great motivating force in my life, caused me to become suddenly adventurous where food was concerned. I decided then and there to outdo my foodie parents. At the same time, I could gross out my still uninitiated little brother. I'd show *them* who the gourmet was!

Brains? Stinky, runny cheeses that smelled like dead man's feet? Horsemeat? Sweetbreads? Bring it on!! Whatever had the most shock value became my meal of choice. For the rest of that summer, and in the summers that followed, I ate *everything*. I scooped gooey Vacherin,

[7]Paul Bocuse (b. 1926) and Jean (b. 1926) and Pierre (b. 1928) Troisgros, prominent French chefs.

learned to love the cheesy, rich Normandy butter, especially slathered on baguettes and dipped in bitter hot chocolate. I sneaked red wine whenever possible, tried fritures—tiny whole fish, fried and eaten with persillade—loving that I was eating heads, eyes, bones and all. I ate ray in beurre noisette, saucisson à l'ail, tripes, rognons de veau (kidneys), boudin noir that squirted blood down my chin.

And I had my first oyster.

Now, *this* was a truly significant event. I remember it like I remem- 25 ber losing my virginity—and in many ways, more fondly.

August of that first summer was spent in La Teste sur Mer, a tiny oyster village on the Bassin d'Arcachon in the Gironde (Southwest France). We stayed with my aunt, Tante Jeanne, and my uncle, Oncle Gustav, in the same red tile-roofed, white stuccoed house where my father had summered as a boy. My Tante Jeanne was a frumpy, bespectacled, slightly smelly old woman, my Oncle Gustav, a geezer in coveralls and beret who smoked hand-rolled cigarettes until they disappeared onto the tip of his tongue. Little had changed about La Teste in the years since my father had vacationed there. The neighbors were still all oyster fishermen. Their families still raised rabbits and grew tomatoes in their backyards. Houses had two kitchens, an inside one and an outdoor "fish kitchen." There was a hand pump for drinking water from a well, and an outhouse by the rear of the garden. Lizards and snails were everywhere. The main tourist attractions were the nearby Dune of Pyla (Europe's Largest Sand Dune!) and the nearby resort town of Arcachon, where the French flocked in unison for *Les Grandes Vacances*.[8] Television was a Big Event. At seven o'clock, when the two national stations would come on the air, my Oncle Gustav would solemnly emerge from his room with a key chained to his hip and ceremoniously unlock the cabinet doors that covered the screen.

My brother and I were happier here. There was more to do. The beaches were warm, and closer in climate to what we knew back home, with the added attraction of the ubiquitous Nazi blockhouses. There were lizards to hunt down and exterminate with readily available

---

[8]The long vacation (French), usually July and August, when many French people take their vacations from work and school.

pétards, firecrackers which one could buy legally (!) over-the-counter. There was a forest within walking distance where an actual hermit lived, and my brother and I spent hours there, spying on him from the underbrush. By now I could read and enjoy comic books in French and of course I was eating—*really* eating. Murky brown soupe de poisson, tomato salad, moules marinières, poulet basquaise (we were only a few miles from the Basque country). We made day trips to Cap Ferret, a wild, deserted and breathtakingly magnificent Atlantic beach with big rolling waves, taking along baguettes and saucissons and wheels of cheese, wine and Evian (bottled water was at that time unheard of back home). A few miles west was Lac Cazeaux, a fresh-water lake where my brother and I could rent *pédalo* watercraft and pedal our way around the deep. We ate gaufres, delicious hot waffles, covered in whipped cream and powdered sugar. The two hot songs of that summer on the Cazeaux jukebox were "Whiter Shade of Pale" by Procol Harum, and "These Boots Were Made for Walkin" by Nancy Sinatra. The French played those two songs over and over again, the music punctuated by the sonic booms from French air force jets which would swoop over the lake on their way to a nearby bombing range. With all the rock and roll, good stuff to eat and high-explosives at hand, I was reasonably happy.

So, when our neighbor, Monsieur Saint-Jour, the oyster fisherman, invited my family out on his *penas* (oyster boat), I was enthusiastic.

At six in the morning, we boarded Monsieur Saint-Jour's small wooden vessel with our picnic baskets and our sensible footwear. He was a crusty old bastard, dressed like my uncle in ancient denim coveralls, espadrilles and beret. He had a leathery, tanned and wind-blown face, hollow cheeks, and the tiny broken blood vessels on nose and cheeks that everyone seemed to have from drinking so much of the local Bordeaux. He hadn't fully briefed his guests on what was involved in these daily travails. We put-putted out to a buoy marking his underwater oyster *parc*, a fenced-off section of bay bottom, and we sat . . . and sat . . . and sat, in the roaring August sun, waiting for the tide to go out. The idea was to float the boat over the stockaded fence walls, then sit there until the boat slowly sank with the water level, until it rested on the *bassin* floor. At this point, Monsieur Saint-Jour, and his guests presumably, would rake the oysters, collect a few good specimens for sale in port, and remove any parasites that might be endangering his crop.

There was, I recall, still about two feet of water left to go before the hull of the boat settled on dry ground and we could walk about the *parc*. We'd already polished off the Brie and baguettes and downed the Evian, but I was still hungry, and characteristically said so. 30

Monsieur Saint-Jour, on hearing this—as if challenging his American passengers—inquired in his thick Girondais accent, if any of us would care to try an oyster.

My parents hesitated. I doubt they'd realized they might have actually to *eat* one of the raw, slimy things we were currently floating over. My little brother recoiled in horror.

But I, in the proudest moment of my young life, stood up smartly, grinning with defiance, and volunteered to be the first.

And in that unforgettably sweet moment in my personal history, that one moment still more alive for me than so many of the other "firsts" which followed—first pussy, first joint, first day in high school, first published book, or any other thing—I attained glory. Monsieur Saint-Jour beckoned me over to the gunwale, where he leaned over, reached down until his head nearly disappeared underwater, and emerged holding a single silt-encrusted oyster, huge and irregularly shaped, in his rough, clawlike fist. With a snubby, rust-covered oyster knife, he popped the thing open and handed it to me, everyone watching now, my little brother shrinking away from this glistening, vaguely sexual-looking object, still dripping and nearly alive.

I took it in my hand, tilted the shell back into my mouth as instructed by the by now beaming Monsieur Saint-Jour, and with one bite and a slurp, wolfed it down. It tasted of seawater . . . of brine and flesh . . . and somehow . . . of the future. 35

Everything was different now. Everything.

I'd not only survived—I'd *enjoyed*.

This, I knew, was the magic I had until now been only dimly and spitefully aware of. I was hooked. My parents' shudders, my little brother's expression of unrestrained revulsion and amazement only reinforced the sense that I had, somehow, become a man. I had had an *adventure*, tasted forbidden fruit, and everything that followed in my life—the food, the long and often stupid and self-destructive chase for *the next thing*, whether it was drugs or sex or some other new sensation—would all stem from this moment.

I'd learned something. Viscerally, instinctively, spiritually—even in some small, precursive way, sexually—and there was no turning back. The genie was out of the bottle. My life as a cook, and as a chef, had begun.

Food had *power*. 40

⚡ It could inspire, astonish, shock, excite, delight and *impress*. It had the power to please me . . . and others. This was valuable information.

For the rest of that summer, and in later summers, I'd often slip off by myself to the little stands by the port, where one could buy brown paper bags of unwashed, black-covered oysters by the dozen. After a few lessons from my new soul-mate, blood brother and bestest buddy, Monsieur Saint-Jour—who was now sharing his after-work bowls of sugared *vin ordinaire* with me too—I could easily open the oysters by myself, coming in from behind with the knife and popping the hinge like it was Aladdin's cave.

I'd sit in the garden among the tomatoes and the lizards and eat my oysters and drink Kronenbourgs (France was a wonderland for under-age drinkers), happily reading *Modesty Blaise* and the *Katzenjammer Kids* and the lovely hard-bound *bandes dessinées*[9] in French, until the pictures swam in front of my eyes, smoking the occasional pilfered Gitane. And I still associate the taste of oysters with those heady, won-derful days of illicit late-afternoon buzzes. The smell of French ciga-rettes, the taste of beer, that unforgettable feeling of doing something I shouldn't be doing.

I had, as yet, no plans to cook professionally. But I frequently look back at my life, searching for that fork in the road, trying to figure out where, exactly, I *went bad* and became a thrill-seeking, pleasure-hungry sensualist, always looking to shock, amuse, terrify and manip-ulate, seeking to fill that empty spot in my soul with something new.

I like to think it was Monsieur Saint-Jour's fault. But of course, it was me all along. 45

[9]Comic books (French).

STUDY QUESTIONS

1. List the experiences Bourdain recounts that most affected his childhood relationship with food. Which experience was most memorable to you as reader?

2. In this MEMOIR, Bourdain often COMPARES AND CONTRASTS his responses to specific foods with the responses of his family members. Explain the differences in Bourdain's and his parents' and brother's responses. What do those differences show about Bourdain?

3. Bourdain is known for his unapologetically direct, sometimes bawdy writing and speaking style. How would you characterize his ETHOS? What passages in this excerpt best EXEMPLIFY this ethos

4. *For Writing.* Think back to your most important childhood memories of food—of tasting something new. Write a four- to five-page MEMOIR in which you describe several early experiences with food, and reflect on what your response to those experiences says about you as a person.

SUZANNE BRITT { *That Lean and Hungry Look*

SUZANNE BRITT was born in Winston-Salem, North Carolina. She
received her BA from Salem College and her MA from Washington
University; a poet and essayist, she currently teaches at Meredith College.
Her poetry has appeared in many literary magazines, and her essays have
been published in *Newsweek*, the *New York Times*, the *Boston Globe*,
Newsday, and other publications. She has written four books: *Show and
Tell* (1982), *Skinny People Are Dull and Crunchy Like Carrots* (1982),
A Writer's Rhetoric (1988), and *Images: A Centennial Journey* (1991).

In this personal essay, written when she taught English at North Carolina
State University, Britt takes a humorous look at the differences between
overweight and thin people. She offers a gently pointed rebuttal to society's
classification of overweight people, suggesting a new stereotype for thin
people. As you read, consider how Britt uses humor to simultaneously
soften and sharpen her attack on society's rejection of obesity.

CAESAR WAS RIGHT. THIN PEOPLE need watching.[1] I've been watching them for most of my adult life, and I don't like what I see. When
these narrow fellows spring at me, I quiver to my toes. Thin people
come in all personalities, most of them menacing. You've got your
"together" thin person, your mechanical thin person, your conde-
scending thin person, your tsk-tsk thin person, your efficiency-expert
thin person. All of them are dangerous.

In the first place, thin people aren't fun. They don't know how to

---

[1]In Shakespeare's *Julius Caesar*, Caesar says, "Yon Cassius has a lean and hungry look. /
He thinks too much. Such men are dangerous" (1.2.195–6).

goof off, at least in the best, fat sense of the word. They've always got to be adoing. Give them a coffee break, and they'll jog around the block. Supply them with a quiet evening at home, and they'll fix the screen door and lick S&H green stamps.[2] They say things like "there aren't enough hours in the day." Fat people never say that. Fat people think the day is too damn long already.

Thin people make me tired. They've got speedy little metabolisms that cause them to bustle briskly. They're forever rubbing their bony hands together and eying new problems to "tackle." I like to surround myself with sluggish, inert, easygoing fat people, the kind who believe that if you clean it up today, it'll just get dirty again tomorrow.

Some people say the business about the jolly fat person is a myth, that all of us chubbies are neurotic, sick, sad people. I disagree. Fat people may not be chortling all day long, but they're a hell of a lot *nicer* than the wizened and shriveled. Thin people turn surly, mean and hard at a young age because they never learn the value of a hot-fudge sundae for easing tension. Thin people don't like gooey soft things because they themselves are neither gooey nor soft. They are crunchy and dull, like carrots. They go straight to the heart of the matter while fat people let things stay all blurry and hazy and vague, the way things actually are. Thin people want to face the truth. Fat people know there is no truth. One of my thin friends is always staring at complex, unsolvable problems and saying "The key thing is . . ." Fat people never say that. They know there isn't any such thing as the key thing about anything.

Thin people believe in logic. Fat people see all sides. The sides fat people see are rounded blobs, usually gray, always nebulous and truly not worth worrying about. But the thin person persists. "If you consume more calories than you burn," says one of my thin friends, "You will gain weight. It's that simple." Fat people always grin when they hear statements like that. They know better.

Fat people realize that life is illogical and unfair. They know very well that God is not in his heaven and all is not right with the world. If

---

[2] Trading stamps that were issued by retail merchants when items were purchased. They could later be redeemed for merchandise from a Green Stamps catalog.

God was up there, fat people could have two doughnuts and a big orange drink anytime they wanted it.

Thin people have a long list of logical things they are always spouting off to me. They hold up one finger at a time as they reel off these things, so I won't lose track. They speak slowly as if to a young child. The list is long and full of holes. It contains tidbits like "get a grip on yourself," "cigarettes kill," "cholesterol clogs," "fit as a fiddle," "ducks in a row," "organize" and "sound fiscal management." Phrases like that.

They think these 2,000-point plans lead to happiness. Fat people know happiness is elusive at best and even if they could get the kind thin people talk about, they wouldn't want it. Wisely, fat people see that such programs are too dull, too hard, too off the mark. They are never better than a whole cheesecake.

Fat people know all about the mystery of life. They are the ones acquainted with the night, with luck, with fate, with playing it by ear. One thin person I know once suggested that we arrange all the parts of a jigsaw puzzle into groups according to size, shape and color. He figured this would cut the time needed to complete the puzzle by at least 50 per cent. I said I wouldn't do it. One, I like to muddle through. Two, what good would it do to finish early? Three, the jigsaw puzzle isn't the important thing. The important thing is the fun of four people (one thin person included) sitting around a card table, working a jigsaw puzzle. My thin friend had no use for my list. Instead of joining us, he went outside and mulched the boxwoods. The three remaining fat people finished the puzzle and made chocolate, double-fudged brownies to celebrate.

The main problem with thin people is they oppress. Their good intentions, bony torsos, tight ships, neat corners, cerebral machinations and pat solutions loom like dark clouds over the loose, comfortable, spread-out, soft world of the fat. Long after fat people have removed their coats and shoes and put their feet up on the coffee table, thin people are still sitting on the edge of the sofa, looking neat as a pin, discussing rutabagas. Fat people are heavily into fits of laughter, slapping their thighs and whooping it up, while thin people are still politely waiting for the punch line.

Thin people are downers. They like math and morality and reasoned

10

evaluation of the limitations of human beings. They have their skinny little acts together. They expound, prognose, probe and prick.

Fat people are convivial. They will like you even if you're irregular and have acne. They will come up with a good reason why you never wrote the great American novel. They will cry in your beer with you. They will put your name in the pot. They will let you off the hook. Fat people will gab, giggle, guffaw, gallumph, gyrate and gossip. They are generous, giving and gallant. They are gluttonous and goodly and great. What you want when you're down is soft and jiggly, not muscled and stable. Fat people know this. Fat people have plenty of room. Fat people will take you in.

STUDY QUESTIONS

1. Explain the value of the hot fudge sundae, according to Britt.

2. Britt begins her essay by dividing people into two kinds: overweight and thin. Then she makes further divisions. List them and explain how Britt classifies each one.

3. In COMPARING overweight and thin people, Britt explains what society thinks about one group and then CONTRASTS them with the other. Identify two contrasting characteristics Britt uses. Do you agree or disagree with her descriptions? What do you think was Britt's point in making the comparison? How literally are we meant to take her descriptions? Explain.

4. *For Writing.* Choose a fairly broad subject (food, movies, vacations, etc.) that can easily be broken into different distinguishable groups. Write a DIVISION AND CLASSIFICATION essay that gives multiple examples and arrives at a conclusion about the groups in the final paragraph.

LAURA FRASER { *Why I Stopped Being*
a Vegetarian

LAURA FRASER (b. 1961), a longtime resident of San Francisco, is a
journalist and author who often writes about food. She has contributed to
periodicals such as *Mother Jones, Bon Appétit,* and the *New York Times
Magazine* and has worked as a contributing editor at *More, Health,* and *Good
Housekeeping.* Her books include *Losing It: False Hopes and Fat Profits in
the Diet Industry* (1998) and *An Italian Affair* (2002). Fraser has also
taught writing at the University of California, Berkeley School of Journalism.

In this selection, Fraser mixes a lighthearted tone with serious social commentary as she explains why she gave up vegetarianism. After listing her
own unorthodox reasons for becoming a vegetarian, she enumerates the
many logical reasons people become vegetarian. Consider how effectively
Fraser marries tone with content. To what audience would this essay
appeal? Why?

UNTIL A FEW MONTHS AGO, I had been a vegetarian for 15 years. Like
most people who call themselves vegetarians (somewhere between 4
and 10 percent of us, depending on the definition; only 1 percent of
Americans are vegans, eating no animal products at all), I wasn't strict
about it. I ate dairy products and eggs, as well as fish. That made me a
pesco-ovo-lacto-vegetarian, which isn't a category you can choose for
special meals on airlines.

About a year ago, in Italy, it dawned on me that a little pancetta was
really good in pasta, too. After failing to convince myself that pancetta
was a vegetable, I became a pesco-ovo-lacto-pancetta-vegetarian, with

a "Don't Ask, Don't Tell" policy about chicken broth. It was a slippery slope from there.

Nevertheless, for most of those 15 years, hardly a piece of animal flesh crossed my lips. Over the course of that time, many people asked me why I became a vegetarian. I came up with vague answers: my health, the environment, the impracticality and heartlessness of killing animals for food when we can survive perfectly well on soy burgers. It was political, it was emotional and it made me special, not to mention slightly morally superior to all those bloodthirsty carnivores out there.

The truth is, I became a vegetarian in college for two reasons. One was that meat was more expensive than lentils, and I was broke, or broke enough to choose to spend my limited budget on other classes of ingestibles. The other was that I was not a lesbian.

This is not to say that all lesbians are carnivores; in fact, there's 5 probably a higher percentage of vegetarians among lesbians than most other groups. But there was a fair amount of political pressure to be something in those days. Since, as a privileged white girl from suburban Denver, I couldn't really identify with any oppressed minority group, I was faced with becoming a lesbian in order to prove my political mettle. I had to decide between meat and men, and for better or worse, I became a vegetarian.

The identity stuck, even though the political imperative for my label faded. It wasn't an identity that ever really fit: My friends thought it odd that such an otherwise hedonistic woman should have that one ascetic streak. It was against my nature, they said. But by then, I'd started to believe the other arguments about vegetarianism.

First was health. There's a lot of evidence that vegetarians live longer, have lower cholesterol levels and are thinner than meat-eaters. This is somewhat hard to believe, since for the first few years of not eating meat, I was basically a cheesetarian. Try leafing through some of those vegetarian recipe books from the early '80s: You added three cups of grated cheddar to everything but the granola. Then vegetarianism went through that mathematical phase where you had to figure out which proteins you had to combine with which in order to get a complete protein. Since many nutritionists will tell you people don't need that much protein anyway, I gave up, going for days and days without so much as contemplating beans or tofu.

For whatever haphazard combination of proteins I ate, being a vegetarian did seem to have a stunning effect on my cholesterol level. This, of course, could be genetic. But when I had a very involved physical exam once at the Cooper Institute for Aerobic Fitness in Dallas, my total cholesterol level was a super-low 135, and my ratio of HDL (good) cholesterol to LDL (evil) was so impressive that the doctor drawled, "Even if you had heart disease, you would be reversing it." This good news, far from reassuring me that I could well afford a few barbecued ribs now and then, spurred me on in my vegetarianism, mainly because my cholesterol numbers effectively inoculated me against the doctor's advice that I also needed to lose 15 pounds.

"Why?" I asked. "Don't you lose weight to lower your cholesterol?"

He couldn't argue with that. Whether or not vegetarians are leaner 10 than carnivores, in my case I was happy to more than make up the calories with carbohydrates, which, perhaps not coincidentally, I always craved.

After the health rationale came the animal rights one. Like most vegetarians, I cracked Peter Singer's[1] philosophical treatise on animal rights, and bought his utilitarian line that if you don't have to kill animals, and it potentially causes suffering, you shouldn't do it. (Singer, now at Princeton, has recently come under attack for saying that if a human being's incapacitated life causes more suffering than good, it is OK to kill him.)

It's hard to know where to stop with utilitarianism. Do I need a cashmere sweater more than those little shorn goats need to be warm themselves? Do animals really suffer if they have happy, frolicking lives before a quick and painless end? Won't free-range do?

My animal rights philosophy had a lot of holes from the start. First of all, I excluded fish from the animal kingdom—not only because fish taste delicious grilled with a little butter and garlic, but also because they make it a lot easier to be a vegetarian when you go out to restaurants. Now that's utilitarian. Besides, as soon as you start spending

[1]Australian philosopher (b. 1946) and author of *Animal Liberation* (1975).

167

your time fretting about the arguments that crowd the inner pens of animal rights philosophy—do fish think?—then you know you're experiencing a real protein deficiency.

I rationalized the fish thing by telling myself I would eat anything I would kill myself. I had been fly-fishing with my dad and figured a few seconds of flopping around was outweighed by the merits of trout almondine. (Notice that I, not the fish, was doing the figuring.) But who was I kidding? If I were hungry enough, I'd kill a cow in a heartbeat. I'd practically kill a cow just for a great pair of shoes.

Which brings me to the leather exception. As long as other people 15 are eating cow, I decided, I might as well recycle the byproducts and diminish the harm by wearing leather jackets and shoes. When everyone stopped eating meat, I'd stop buying leather jackets and shoes. In the meantime, better stock up.

Then there's the environmental rationale. There is no doubt, as Frances Moore Lappe first pointed out in her 1971 book *Food First*, that there is a huge loss of protein resources going from grain to meat, and that some animals, especially cattle and Americans, use up piggish amounts of wafer, grain and crop land.

But the problem really isn't meat, but too much meat—over-grazing, over-fishing and over-consumption. If Americans just ate less meat—like driving cars less often—the problem could be alleviated without giving up meat entirely. That approach has worked for centuries, and continues to work in Europe.

All my deep vegetarian questioning was silenced one day when a friend ordered roasted rosemary chicken for two. I thought I'd try "just a bite," and then I was ripping into it like a starving hyena. Roasted chicken, I realized, is wonderful. Meat is good.

From a culinary point of view, that's obvious. Consider that most vegetarians live in America and England, places tourists do not visit for the food. You don't find vegetarians in France, and rarely in Italy. Enough said.

As for health, if nutritionists are always telling you to "listen to your 20 body," mine was definitely shouting for more meat. One roasted bird unleashed 15 years' worth of cravings. All of a sudden I felt like I had a bass note playing in my body to balance out all those soprano carbohydrates. Forget about winning the low-cholesterol Olympics. For the first time in a long time, I felt satisfied.

As a vegetarian, not only had I denied myself something I truly enjoyed, I had been anti-social. How many times had I made a hostess uncomfortable by refusing the main course at a dinner party, lamely saying I'd "eat around it"? How often did my vegetarianism cause other people to go to extra trouble to make something special for me to eat, and why did it never occur to me that that was selfish? How about the time, in a small town in Italy, when the chef had presented me with a plate of very special local sausage, since I was the American guest— and I had refused it, to the mortification of my Italian friends? Or when a then-boyfriend, standing in the meat section of the grocery store, forlornly told a friend, "If only I had a girlfriend who ate meat"? If eating is a socially conscious act, you have to be conscious of the society of your fellow homo sapiens along with the animals. And we humans, as it happens, are omnivores.

STUDY QUESTIONS

1. What were Fraser's two initial reasons for becoming a vegetarian in college?

2. Identify the steps in Fraser's PROCESS ANALYSIS of formulating her vegetarian philosophy—and then rejecting it. Be sure to include the points at which she thinks of reasons for changing her behavior.

3. How does Fraser employ humor when discussing a topic that is, for some people, extremely serious? Does her humor strengthen or weaken her ARGUMENT? Explain.

4. *For Writing.* Write an essay in which you defend your food choices using logical reasoning (and, if you like, humor). You do not need to focus on the debate between vegetarianism and meat-eating; rather, you might consider a college student's steady diet of pizza, for instance, or some other food choice that you know well.

JILL McCORKLE { *Her Chee-to Heart*

JILL McCORKLE (b. 1958) was born in Lumberton, North Carolina. She has degrees from University of North Carolina at Chapel Hill and Hollins College; she currently teaches in the creative writing MFA program at North Carolina State. Including her first two books, which came out on the same day, McCorkle has published several novels and collections of short stories, many of which have been named *New York Times* notable books. Her work has been published in *Allure*, *The Atlantic*, *Ploughshares*, *Oxford American*, *Southern Review*, and other publications.

"Her Chee-to Heart" originally appeared in *Allure* in 1996. In this humorous essay, McCorkle describes herself as a "junk-food junkie" and uses lists, product brand names, and rhetorical questions create a lighthearted tone. Note the way McCorkle links the consumption of junk food to feelings of happiness. Are your experiences similar to hers? What would be your perfect day of eating? Why?

IF I COULD HAVE A perfect day of eating, this would be it: I'd begin with pancakes and sausage patties drenched in Log Cabin syrup. Then I'd visit my grandmother's kitchen, where my sister and I used to watch ravenously as Gramma made her famous pound cake (a real pound cake—a pound of butter, a pound of sugar, egg after egg after egg swirled in Swans Down cake flour), We'd each slurp batter off the mixer whisks and then split what was left in the red-and-white Pyrex bowl. My grandmother also made chicken and pastry (her pastry was more like dumplings) and homemade biscuits (the secret ingredient is lard), which might be dipped in redeye gravy or covered in butter and Karo syrup (doughboys) and eaten as dessert. She made homemade apple pies (the fruit part of our diet) fried in Crisco and filled with sugar.

If I couldn't have homemade food, then I would settle for what could be bought. A foot-long hot dog at the B&R Drive-In, for example; french fries limp with grease and salt from the bowling alley; a barbecue sandwich (Carolina style—chopped fine and spiced up with hot sauce); a triple-chocolate milk shake from Tastee Freez. Banana splits and hot-fudge sundaes. Maybe a frozen Zero candy bar or a Milky Way, a Little Debbie snack cake and a moon pie, too.

I am a junk-food junkie and always have been. My college roommate and my husband both blame me for their slides into high-fat, preservative-filled meals, like the frozen Mexican TV dinners that my roommate and I ate all the way through college, or the microwavable burritos I now stash at the back of my freezer for desperate moments (desperate meaning a craving for Tex-Mex or a need to drive a nail and not being able to find a hammer). Forget meals, anyway; the truly good treats for a junk-food junkie get served up in between: colorful Ben & Jerry's pints, natural in an ethical way (the money goes to good places, at least) that makes me feel healthy; names—Chubby Hubby, Chunky Monkey, Wavy Gravy—that make me laugh. Good Humor is what it's all about and has been since childhood: kids trained to respond to the ringing of a bell, to chase alongside trucks in neighborhood streets like so many pups for a Nutty Buddy. Ice cream is near the top of any junk-food junkie's list to be sure, but I haven't even begun to mention the Chee-tos, the Pecan Sandies.

There's something about unnatural food colors that has always attracted me. What tastes or looks better than the frosting on grocery-store-bakery birthday cakes? Hot pink or blue roses that melt in your mouth. The fluorescent brilliance of a crunchy Chee-to. Not too long ago my children (ages four and seven) were eating at a friend's. They were served a lovely meal of homemade macaroni and cheese, white, the way something without any additives and preservatives should be. I was on the other side of the room, helpless to defend myself when I heard my daughter say, "But my mom's macaroni and cheese is bright orange." Well? What can I say? I also love that fuchsia-colored sweet-and-sour sauce that you often find on Chinese food buffets.

At the last big dinner party we had, my husband bought Yodels to throw out on the dessert table along with a fresh-fruit concoction, which had taken me forever to cut up, and little cheesecakes. At the end of the night, there was not a Yodel in sight, but very few people had openly indulged. These scrumptious lunch-box treats (creme-filled chocolate rolls, 140 calories and 8 grams of fat each, which means, of course, that they are good) had instead been slyly tucked away into pockets and purses for the ride home. Yodels, Twinkies, Hostess Sno Balls. They make people nostalgic for elementary school, those wonderful years when we were advised to eat beef and pork. Children thriving on sloppy joes and Saturday T-bones. Pork chops with applesauce. Sausage gravy over homemade biscuits. A good green vegetable in the South, where I grew up, was a green-bean casserole in which the beans were camouflaged in Campbell's cream of mushroom soup and canned fried onion rings. All the recipes in my favorite cookbooks begin with Campbell's cream-of-something soup.

I was enamored of a boy named Michael in the first grade who licked Kool-Aid powder from his palm whenever the teacher wasn't looking. He moved away before the end of the year, and yet thirty-one years later, I still remember him with a fond mixture of repulsion at the sticky red saliva that graced his notebook paper and admiration for the open ease with which he indulged his habit. I loved Pixy Stix straws, which, let's face it, were nothing more than dry Kool-Aid mix poured right into your mouth. SweeTarts. Jawbreakers. Firecrackers. Mary Janes. Any item that I was told was *very* bad for my teeth.

Maybe it's an oral-gratification thing. I'm sure that's why I smoked for fifteen years. When I quit nine years ago, I rediscovered my taste buds. I found flavors I had forgotten all about: Sugar Babies and Raisin-ets, that thick mashed-potato gravy that is the *real* secret ingredient at Kentucky Fried Chicken. I found flavors I had never had before, such as cheese blintzes and latkes smothered in sour cream. I found that wonderful, all-natural, fortified cereal Quaker 100% Natural Granola Oats, Honey & Raisins. I need oral participation, oral gratification.

Despite what they will tell you on television, a little stick of Juicy Fruit is not going to get you there if you've been lighting up for years. But M&M's? Junior Mints? Those diablo-style peanuts thoroughly doused with cayenne pepper? Now, that's chewing satisfaction. A Coke (or Diet Coke for the figure-minded; Jolt Cola for the desperate-to-start-the-day-minded) chaser.

I could do a taste test. I can recognize all the sodas. The soda wanna-bes. I drink a good two to three cups of coffee when I get up, and by the time I drive the kids to school, I've switched over to Diet Coke. People say, "Doesn't it keep you awake?" I wish! During one of my pregnancies I lost all taste for Coke. I couldn't believe it. I'd been drinking Coke for as long as I could remember. It was so sad; filling myself up on Hawaiian Punch (which is very good in its own right), Pop-Tarts, and ice cream, ice cream, ice cream. But I missed the Coke cans rolling around under the seat of my car. I missed the whoosh and zap of buying a Coke from a vending machine. And one day, like magic, it returned, this desire, like an old love resurfacing.

There are ways a junk-food junkie can feel less guilty about all this food, if indeed you ever do feel guilty. Did I mention caffeine? It's like air—essential for full enjoyment. And it burns calories. If that doesn't work, there are always things like the NordicTrack where I hang my clothes at the end of the day and the Suzanne Somers ThighMaster I keep in my closet for decoration.

Besides, I consider myself a purist; I don't like substitute things— 10 like these new clear sodas. Who cares? I went into the all-natural health-food grocery store not long ago only to discover that there are a lot of things in this world that are foreign to me. The produce section had products you might find growing in a neglected basement. There were name brands I'd never heard of; certainly they don't buy airtime on television. There were cereals without colored marshmallows or prizes in the box. They boasted of having no sugar (as if this were good). It did not take me long to get back to the familiar aisles of the Super Stop & Shop, the red-and-white Campbell's soup labels, the chip-and-cookie aisle (nothing there sweetened with fruit juice or carob imitating chocolate), and the candy bars at the checkout.

One of my fondest junk-food memories is of a rare snow day in Lumberton, North Carolina, when I was in the sixth grade, a wonderful age at which, though I liked boys, they were not nearly as exciting as the ice cream store nearby that served up an oversize cone called a Kitchen Sink. But that day, I sat with a couple of friends in the back of the Kwik Pik (the South's version of the convenience store) and ate raw chocolate-chip-cookie dough while drinking Eagle Brand sweetened condensed milk straight from the can. My friends and I waddled home feeling sick but warmly nourished, our stomachs coated and glowing with sugar. I mean, really, there is no cake or cookie on earth that tastes as good as dough or batter.

My favorite food in the eighth grade was Slim Jim sausages. For the uninformed, these are the miniature pepperoni sticks usually found near the register of convenience stores, where you might also find the beef jerky and pickled eggs. When I was growing up, there was usually a big jar of pickled pig's feet too, but this was not a treat that ever caught my eye. No, I lived on Slim Jims, spicy and chewy. I kept them with me at all times, getting a good chew while at cheerleading practices. They reminded me of being an even younger kid and getting a little bit of raw, salty country ham from my grandmother and chewing it all day like a piece of gum. (Sorry, Juicy Fruit; failed again.)

My husband, a doctor whose specialty is infectious diseases, is certain that I have been host to many parasites. Maybe, but what I'm certain that I have been host to are the junk-food parasites who refuse to admit that they indulge, but they do. Just put out a bowl of pistachios and check out the red fingertips leaving; chips, M&M's. Ah, M&M's. It was a sad day long ago when they retired the red ones. I had spent years being entertained by a pack; segregate and then integrate, close your eyes and guess which color. I was thrilled when the red ones returned, and now blue! Lovely blue M&M's. I love the pastel ones at Easter, along with those Cadbury eggs, and my own personal favorite: malted Easter eggs. These are actually Whoppers (malted-milk balls) covered in a speckled candy shell. Sometimes they are called robin eggs and sometimes simply malteds, but a Whopper is a Whopper is a Whopper. I like to bite one in half and then suck in. When the air is pulled out of a Whopper, what's left is more like a Milk Dud.

Of course there is also the Whopper from Burger King. Once, after a Friday night high-school football game, I sat down at a table with a bag of food that looked similar to those of all the guys on the team. I had a Whopper with everything, large fries, an apple pie, and a chocolate shake. Our cheerleading adviser told me that I wouldn't always be able to do that.

Thank God I didn't know she was right. It would have ruined the 15 next four years as I continued to down cream-filled Krispy Kreme doughnuts and my own special high-protein omelette that was filled with mayonnaise and cheese. I loved Funyuns, too, except that nobody wanted to sit next to me on the bus when I ate them.

After all these years, I've made some adjustments. I now buy Hebrew National for things like hot dogs and bologna. I figure the kosher laws probably serve me well in this particular purchase, and try as I might to dissuade them, my children love bologna with an absolute passion. They can smell the reject turkey substitute from fifty paces. They don't like *real* mac and cheese. They like the microwave kind. My niece (at age four) once invited me into her playhouse for lunch. She said, "Would you like a Diet Coke while I cook lunch in the microwave?" So maybe it's a family thing. Maybe it's the potassium benzoate.

I would love a Diet Coke and a cream horn right about now. Some salt-and-vinegar chips. Onion dip and Ruffles. S'mores. I like to get in bed to read with a stash of something close by. I have found that I am especially drawn to things with a high polyglycerol-ester-of-fatty-acids content. It makes me feel *happy*. I think maybe this is die key to a true junk-food junkie's hearts happiness. Just as Proust[1] bit into his little madeleine and had a flood of memories, I bite into my Devil Dog, my Ring Ding, Twinkie, Ho Ho, Yodel. I bite into my Hostess Sno Ball and retreat to a world where the only worry is what to ask

---

[1]Marcel Proust (1871–1922), French writer whose best-known work, *In Search of Lost Time* (often called *Remembrance of Things Past*, 1913–27), includes a scene in which a small cake called a *madeleine* induces involuntary memories.

your mother to put in your lunch box the next day or which pieces of candy you will select at the Kwik Pik on your way home from school. Ahead of you are the wasteland years; a pack of cigarettes, some Clearasil pads, a tube of Blistex, and breath spray. But for now, reach back to those purer, those sugar-filled, melt-in-your-mouth, forever-a-kid years. Who cares if there is a little polysorbate 60 and some diglycerides, some carrageenan, some Red 40 and Blue I, some agar-agar? I have a dream that somewhere out there in the grown-up, low-fat world there is a boy named Michael licking his lips and getting all the fumaric acid that he can.

STUDY QUESTIONS

1. Does McCorkle hint at any differences between her childhood eating habits and those of her adult years? Why do you think she devotes more of this essay to what she ate as a child than to what she eats as adult (though some of that food might be the same)?

2. McCorkle writes a DESCRIPTIVE humorous essay. What strategies or literary elements make this essay funny?

3. McCorkle uses many FRAGMENTS in this essay. Locate those fragments. Do you find them effective? Why?

4. *For Writing.* Write a PERSONAL ESSAY about your own "perfect day of eating." Consider what TONE you will use—for example, humorous, reflective, angry, or poignant. Use literary devices such as METAPHOR, SIMILE, IMAGERY, IRONY, HYPERBOLE, and/or repetition to highlight your chosen tone.

MICHEL DE MONTAIGNE 〔 *Of Cannibals*

MICHEL DE MONTAIGNE (1533–1592), one of France's most influential essayists, was born near Bordeaux, France, to a wealthy family. As a child he was addressed exclusively in Latin and received a thorough education from a private tutor; at age six he was enrolled in an elite boarding school in Bordeaux. Montaigne went on to study and then practice law before becoming a courtier to King Charles IX from 1561 to 1563. When a dear friend, the poet Étienne de la Boétie, died in 1563, Montaigne began writing essays to fill the void left by Boétie's death. He retired to his home in 1571, where he began writing in earnest; he ultimately spent almost ten years writing in isolation. The result of this self-imposed solitude was *Essais* (1580), Montaigne's collection of short essays on various topics.

In one of his best-known essays, "Of Cannibals," Montaigne compares and contrasts Europeans with natives of the New World and finds that the former are lacking, arguing that cannibalism is preferable to the morality of higher cultures. Noting that we call barbaric anything that is culturally unfamiliar, Montaigne systematically attacks the characterization of the peoples of the New World as uncivilized. As you read, consider whether his argument could apply equally well to today's society.

WHEN KING PYRRHUS INVADED ITALY,[1] having viewed and considered the order of the army the Romans sent out to meet him; I know not, said he, what kind of barbarians (for so the Greeks called all other nations) these may be; but the disposition of this army that I see has nothing of barbarism in it. As much said the Greeks of that which

---

[1]King of Epirus (312–272 BCE), in northern Greece, who defeated the Romans in 279 BCE.

Flaminius[2] brought into their country; and Philip, beholding from an eminence the order and distribution of the Roman camp formed in his kingdom by Publius Sulpicius Galba, spake to the same effect. By which it appears how cautious men ought to be of taking things upon trust from vulgar opinion, and that we are to judge by the eye of reason, and not from common report.

I long had a man in my house that lived ten or twelve years in the New World, discovered in these latter days, and in that part of it where Villegaignon[3] landed, which he called Antarctic France. This discovery of so vast a country seems to be of very great consideration. I cannot be sure, that hereafter there may not be another, so many wiser men than we having been deceived in this. I am afraid our eyes are bigger than our bellies, and that we have more curiosity than capacity; for we grasp at all, but catch nothing but wind.

Plato brings in Solon,[4] telling a story that he had heard from the priests of Sais in Egypt, that of old, and before the Deluge, there was a great island called Atlantis, situate directly at the mouth of the straits of Gibraltar, which contained more countries than both Africa and Asia put together; and that the kings of that country, who not only possessed that Isle, but extended their dominion so far into the continent that they had a country of Africa as far as Egypt, and extending in Europe to Tuscany, attempted to encroach even upon Asia, and to subjugate all the nations that border upon the Mediterranean Sea, as far as the Black Sea; and to that effect overran all Spain, the Gauls, and Italy, so far as to penetrate into Greece, where the Athenians stopped them: but that some time after, both the Athenians, and they and their island, were swallowed by the Flood.

It is very likely that this extreme irruption and inundation of water

---

[2]Titus Quinctius Flaminius (c. 228–174 BCE), Roman general who defeated Philip V of Macedonia (238–179 BCE) in 197 BCE. *Publius Sulpicius Galba*: Roman general of the same period.

[3]Nicolas Durand de Villegaignon (1510–71), French explorer who landed in present-day Rio de Janeiro in 1555.

[4]Greek politician (c. 638–558 BCE) featured in Plato's dialogues. *Sais*: Ancient Egyptian city, now known as Sa el-Hagar.

made wonderful changes and alterations in the habitations of the earth, as 'tis said that the sea then divided Sicily from Italy:

> These lands, they say, formerly with violence and vast desolation convulsed, burst asunder, where before both were one country.[5]

Cyprus from Syria, the isle of Negropont from the continent of 5
Boeotia, and elsewhere united lands that were separate before, by filling up the channel betwixt them with sand and mud:

> The long-time sterile marsh, adapted for ships, feeds neighboring cities, and feels the heavy plough.[6]

But there is no great appearance that this isle was this New World so lately discovered: for that almost touched upon Spain, and it were an incredible effect of an inundation, to have tumbled back so prodigious a mass, above twelve hundred leagues: besides that our modern navigators have already almost discovered it to be no island, but terra firma, and continent with the East Indies on the one side, and with the lands under the two poles on the other side; or, if it be separate from them, it is by so narrow a strait and channel, that it none the more deserves the name of an island for that.

It should seem, that in this great body, there are two sorts of motions, the one natural and the other febrific, as there are in ours. When I consider the impression that our river of Dordogne has made in my time on the right bank of its descent, and that in twenty years it has gained so much, and undermined the foundations of so many houses, I perceive it to be an extraordinary agitation: for had it always followed this course, or were hereafter to do it, the aspect of the world would be totally changed. But rivers alter their course, sometimes beating against the one side, and sometimes the other, and sometimes quietly keeping the channel. I do not speak of sudden inundations, the causes of which everybody understands. In Medoc, by the seashore, the Sieur d'Arsac, my brother, sees an estate he had there, buried under the

[5]Virgil's *Aeneid* 3.414.
[6]Horace, *De Arte Poetica*, 5.65.

sands which the sea vomits before it: where the tops of some houses are yet to be seen, and where his rents and domains are converted into pitiful barren pasturage. The inhabitants of this place affirm, that of late years the sea has driven so vehemently upon them, that they have lost above four leagues of land. These sands are her harbingers: and we now see great heaps of moving sand, that march half a league before her, and occupy the land.

The other testimony from antiquity, to which some would apply this discovery of the New World, is in Aristotle; at least, if that little book of Unheard-of Miracles[7] be his. He there tells us, that certain Carthaginians, having crossed the Atlantic Sea without the Straits of Gibraltar, and sailed a very long time, discovered at last a great and fruitful island, all covered over with wood, and watered with several broad and deep rivers, far remote from all terra firma; and that they, and others after them, allured by the goodness and fertility of the soil, went thither with their wives and children, and began to plant a colony. But the senate of Carthage perceiving their people by little and little to diminish, issued out an express prohibition, that none, upon pain of death, should transport themselves thither; and also drove out these new inhabitants; fearing, 'tis said, lest in process of time they should so multiply as to supplant themselves and ruin their state. But this relation of Aristotle no more agrees with our new-found lands than the other.

This man that I had was a plain ignorant fellow, and therefore the more likely to tell truth: for your better-bred sort of men are much more curious in their observation, 'tis true, and discover a great deal more; but then they gloss upon it, and to give the greater weight to what they deliver, and allure your belief, they cannot forbear a little to alter the story; they never represent things to you simply as they are, but rather as they appeared to them, or as they would have them appear to you, and to gain the reputation of men of judgment, and the better to induce your faith, are willing to help out the business with something more than is really true, of their own invention. Now in this case, we should either have a man of irreproachable veracity, or so simple that he has not wherewithal to contrive, and to give a color of truth

---

[7]Book falsely attributed to Aristotle.

to false relations, and who can have no ends in forging an untruth. Such a one was mine; and besides, he has at divers times brought to me several seamen and merchants who at the same time went the same voyage. I shall therefore content myself with his information, without inquiring what the cosmographers say to the business. We should have topographers to trace out to us the particular places where they have been; but for having had this advantage over us, to have seen the Holy Land, they would have the privilege, forsooth, to tell us stories of all the other parts of the world beside. I would have every one write what he knows, and as much as he knows, but no more; and that not in this only but in all other subjects; for such a person may have some particular knowledge and experience of the nature of such a river, or such a fountain, who, as to other things, knows no more than what everybody does, and yet to give a currency to his little pittance of learning, will undertake to write the whole body of physics: a vice from which great inconveniences derive their original.

Now, to return to my subject, I find that there is nothing barbarous and savage in this nation,[8] by anything that I can gather, excepting, that every one gives the title of barbarism to everything that is not in use in his own country. As, indeed, we have no other level of truth and reason than the example and idea of the opinions and customs of the place wherein we live: there is always the perfect religion, there the perfect government, there the most exact and accomplished usage of all things. They are savages at the same rate that we say fruits are wild, which nature produces of herself and by her own ordinary progress; whereas, in truth, we ought rather to call those wild whose natures we have changed by our artifice and diverted from the common order. In those, the genuine, most useful, and natural virtues and properties are vigorous and sprightly, which we have helped to degenerate in these, by accommodating them to the pleasure of our own corrupted palate. And yet for all this, our taste confesses a flavor and delicacy excellent even to emulation of the best of ours, in several fruits wherein those countries abound without art or culture. Neither is it reasonable that

[8]Brazil.

art should gain the pre-eminence of our great and powerful mother nature. We have so surcharged her with the additional ornaments and graces we have added to the beauty and riches of her own works by our inventions, that we have almost smothered her; yet in other places, where she shines in her own purity and proper lustre, she marvellously baffles and disgraces all our vain and frivolous attempts:

> And the ivy grows best spontaneously, the arbutus best in solitary caves; and the birds sing more sweetly without art.[9]

Our utmost endeavors cannot arrive at so much as to imitate the nest of the least of birds, its contexture, beauty, and convenience: not so much as the web of a poor spider.

All things, says Plato, are produced either by nature, by fortune, or by art; the greatest and most beautiful by the one or the other of the former, the least and the most imperfect by the last.

These nations then seem to me to be so far barbarous, as having received but very little form and fashion from art and human invention, and consequently to be not much remote from their original simplicity. The laws of nature, however, govern them still, not as yet much vitiated with any mixture of ours: but 'tis in such purity, that I am sometimes troubled we were not sooner acquainted with these people, and that they were not discovered in those better times, where there were men much more able to judge of them than we are. I am sorry that Lycurgus[1] and Plato had no knowledge of them; for to my apprehension, what we now see in those nations, does not only surpass all the pictures with which the poets have adorned the golden age, and all their inventions in feigning a happy state of man, but, moreover, the fancy and even the wish and desire of philosophy itself; so native and so pure a simplicity, as we by experience see to be in them, could never enter into their imagination, nor could they ever believe that human society could have been maintained with so little artifice and human

---

[9]Propertius, *Elegies* 1.2 10–12.
[1]Spartan lawgiver (c. 800–c. 730 BCE).

patchwork. I should tell Plato that it is a nation wherein there is no manner of traffic, no knowledge of letters, no science of numbers, no name of magistrate or political superiority; no use of service, riches or poverty, no contracts, no successions, no dividends, no properties, no employments, but those of leisure, no respect of kindred, but common, no clothing, no agriculture, no metal, no use of corn or wine; the very words that signify lying, treachery, dissimulation, avarice, envy, detraction, pardon, never heard of. How much would he find his imaginary Republic short of his perfection?

> Men not far removed from the gods.[2]
> These manners nature first inculcated.[3]

As to the rest, they live in a country very pleasant and temperate, so that, as my witness informed me, 'tis rare to hear of a sick person, and they moreover assure me, that they never saw any of the natives, either paralytic, blear-eyed, toothless, or crooked with age. The situation of their country is along the sea-shore, enclosed on the other side towards the land, with great and high mountains, having about a hundred leagues in breadth between. They have great store of fish and flesh, that have no resemblance to those of ours; which they eat without any other cookery, than plain boiling, roasting, and broiling. The first that rode a horse thither, though in several other voyages he had contracted an acquaintance and familiarity with them, put them into so terrible a fright, with his centaur appearance, that they killed him with their arrows before they could come to discover who he was. Their buildings are very long, and of capacity to hold two or three hundred people, made of the barks of tall trees, reared with one end upon the ground, and leaning to and supporting one another at the top, like some of our barns, of which the covering hangs down to the very ground, and serves for the side walls. They have wood so hard, that they cut with it, and make their swords of it, and their grills of it to broil their meat. Their beds are of cotton, hung swinging from the roof, like our seamen's hammocks, every

[2]Seneca's *Epistles* 90.
[3]Virgil, *Georgics* 2.20.

man his own, for the wives lie apart from their husbands. They rise with the sun, and so soon as they are up, eat for all day, for they have no more meals but that; they do not then drink, as Suidas[4] reports of some other people of the East that never drank at their meals; but drink very often all day after, and sometimes to a rousing pitch. Their drink is made of a certain root, and is of the color of our claret, and they never drink it but lukewarm. It will not keep above two or three days; it has a somewhat sharp, brisk taste, is nothing heady, but very comfortable to the stomach; laxative to strangers, but a very pleasant beverage to such as are accustomed to it. They make use, instead of bread, of a certain white compound, like coriander seeds; I have tasted of it; the taste is sweet and a little flat. The whole day is spent in dancing. Their young men go a-hunting after wild beasts with bows and arrows; one part of their women are employed in preparing their drink the while, which is their chief employment. One of their old men, in the morning before they fall to eating, preaches to the whole family, walking from the one end of the house to the other, and several times repeating the same sentence, till he has finished the round, for their houses are at least a hundred yards long. Valor towards their enemies and love towards their wives, are the two heads of his discourse, never failing in the close, to put them in mind, that 'tis their wives who provide them their drink warm and well seasoned. The fashion of their beds, ropes, swords, and of the wooden bracelets they tie about their wrists, when they go to fight, and of the great canes, bored hollow at one end, by the sound of which they keep the cadence of their dances, are to be seen in several places, and amongst others, at my house. They shave all over, and much more neatly than we, without other razor than one of wood or stone. They believe in the immortality of the soul, and that those who have merited well of the gods are lodged in that part of heaven where the sun rises, and the accursed in the west.

They have I know not what kind of priests and prophets, who very rarely present themselves to the people, having their abode in the mountains. At their arrival, there is a great feast, and solemn assembly of many villages: each house, as I have described, makes a village, and they are

---

[4]Apocryphal name of the author of an ancient Byzantine encyclopedia.

about a French league[5] distant from one another. This prophet declaims to them in public, exhorting them to virtue and their duty: but all their ethics are comprised in these two articles, resolution in war, and affection to their wives. He also prophesies to them events to come, and the issues they are to expect from their enterprises, and prompts them to or diverts them from war: but let him look to't; for if he fail in his divination, and anything happen otherwise than he has foretold, he is cut into a thousand pieces, if he be caught, and condemned for a false prophet: for that reason, if any of them has been mistaken, he is no more heard of.

Divination is a gift of God, and therefore to abuse it, ought to be a punishable imposture. Amongst the Scythians,[6] where their diviners failed in the promised effect, they were laid, bound hand and foot, upon carts loaded with firs and bavins,[7] and drawn by oxen, on which they were burned to death. Such as only meddle with things subject to the conduct of human capacity, are excusable in doing the best they can: but those other fellows that come to delude us with assurances of an extraordinary faculty, beyond our understanding, ought they not to be punished, when they do not make good the effect of their promise, and for the temerity of their imposture?

They have continual war with the nations that live further within the mainland, beyond their mountains, to which they go naked, and without other arms than their bows and wooden swords, fashioned at one end like the head of our javelins. The obstinacy of their battles is wonderful, and they never end without great effusion of blood: for as to running away, they know not what it is. Every one for a trophy brings home the head of an enemy he has killed, which he fixes over the door of his house. After having a long time treated their prisoners very well, and given them all the regales they can think of, he to whom the prisoner belongs, invites a great assembly of his friends. They being come, he ties a rope to one of the arms of the prisoner, of which, at a distance, out of his reach, he holds the one end himself, and gives to the friend he loves best the other arm to hold after the same manner; which being done,

[5]About two-and-a-half miles.
[6]Ancient Iranian nomads.
[7]Bundles of brushwood.

they two, in the presence of all the assembly, despatch him with their swords. After that, they roast him, eat him amongst them, and send some chops to their absent friends. They do not do this, as some think, for nourishment, as the Scythians anciently did, but as a representation of an extreme revenge; as will appear by this: that having observed the Portuguese, who were in league with their enemies, to inflict another sort of death upon any of them they took prisoners, which was to set them up to the girdle in the earth, to shoot at the remaining part till it was stuck full of arrows, and then to hang them, they thought those people of the other world (as being men who had sown the knowledge of a great many vices amongst their neighbors, and who were much greater masters in all sorts of mischief than they) did not exercise this sort of revenge without a meaning, and that it must needs be more painful than theirs, they began to leave their old way, and to follow this. I am not sorry that we should here take notice of the barbarous horror of so cruel an action, but that, seeing so clearly into their faults, we should be so blind to our own. I conceive there is more barbarity in eating a man alive, than when he is dead; in tearing a body limb from limb by racks and torments, that is yet in perfect sense; in roasting it by degrees; in causing it to be bitten and worried by dogs and swine (as we have not only read, but lately seen, not amongst inveterate and mortal enemies, but among neighbors and fellow-citizens, and, which is worse, under color of piety and religion), than to roast and eat him after he is dead.

Chrysippus and Zeno, the two heads of the Stoic sect, were of opinion that there was no hurt in making use of our dead carcasses, in what way soever for our necessity, and in feeding upon them too; as our own ancestors, who being besieged by Caesar in the city Alexia, resolved to sustain the famine of the siege with the bodies of their old men, women, and other persons who were incapable of bearing arms:

The Gascons (as fame reports), lived with meats of such sorts.[8]

And the physicians make no bones of employing it to all sorts of use, either to apply it outwardly; or to give it inwardly for the health of the

[8]Juvenal, *Satires* 15.93–94.

patient. But there never was any opinion so irregular, as to excuse treachery, disloyalty, tyranny, and cruelty, which are our familiar vices. We may then call these people barbarous, in respect to the rules of reason: but not in respect to ourselves, who in all sorts of barbarity exceed them. Their wars are throughout noble and generous, and carry as much excuse and fair pretence, as that human malady is capable of; having with them no other foundation than the sole jealousy of valor. Their disputes are not for the conquest of new lands, for these they already possess are so fruitful by nature, as to supply them without labor or concern, with all things necessary, in such abundance that they have no need to enlarge their borders. And they are, moreover, happy in this, that they only covet so much as their natural necessities require: all beyond that is superfluous to them: men of the same age call one another generally brothers, those who are younger, children; and the old men are fathers to all. These leave to their heirs in common the full possession of goods, without any manner of division, or other title than what nature bestows upon her creatures, in bringing them into the world. If their neighbors pass over the mountains to assault them, and obtain a victory, all the victors gain by it is glory only, and the advantage of having proved themselves the better in valor and virtue: for they never meddle with the goods of the conquered, but presently return into their own country, where they have no want of anything necessary, nor of this greatest of all goods, to know happily how to enjoy their condition and to be content. And those in turn do the same; they demand of their prisoners no other ransom, than acknowledgment that they are overcome: but there is not one found in an age, who will not rather choose to die than make such a confession, or either by word or look recede from the entire grandeur of an invincible courage. There is not a man amongst them who had not rather be killed and eaten, than so much as to open his mouth to entreat he may not. They use them with all liberality and freedom, to the end their lives may be so much the dearer to them; but frequently entertain them with menaces of their approaching death, of the torments they are to suffer, of the preparations making in order to it, of the mangling their limbs, and of the feast that is to be made, where their carcass is to be the only dish. All which they do, to no other end, but only to extort some gentle or submissive word from them, or to frighten them so as to make them run away, to obtain this advantage that they were terrified, and that their constancy was shaken; and indeed, if rightly taken, it is in this point only that a true victory consists:

No victory is complete, which the conquered do not admit to be so.[9]

The Hungarians, a very warlike people, never pretend further than to reduce the enemy to their discretion; for having forced this confession from them, they let them go without injury or ransom, excepting, at the most, to make them engage their word never to bear arms against them again. We have sufficient advantages over our enemies that are borrowed and not truly our own; it is the quality of a porter, and no effect of virtue, to have stronger arms and legs; it is a dead and corporeal quality to set in array; 'tis a turn of fortune to make our enemy stumble, or to dazzle him with the light of the sun; 'tis a trick of science and art, and that may happen in a mean base fellow, to be a good fencer. The estimate and value of a man consist in the heart and in the will: there his true honor lies. Valor is stability, not of legs and arms, but of the courage and the soul; it does not lie in the goodness of our horse or our arms: but in our own. He that falls obstinate in his courage—

If he falls, he fights from his knee;[1]

—he who, for any danger of imminent death, abates nothing of his assurance; who, dying, yet darts at his enemy a fierce and disdainful look, is overcome not by us, but by fortune; he is killed, not conquered; the most valiant are sometimes the most unfortunate. There are defeats more triumphant than victories. Never could those four sister victories, the fairest the sun ever beheld, of Salamis, Plataea, Mycale, and Sicily, venture to oppose all their united glories, to the single glory of the discomfiture of King Leonidas and his men, at the pass of Thermopylae.[2] Whoever ran

[9]Claudian, *Panegyric on the Sixth Consulate of Honorius* 248–49.

[1]Seneca's *Of Providence*.

[2]References are to the second Persian invasion of Greece and the battle against Carthaginian forces in Sicily, 480–479 BCE. The Battle of Thermopylae was the only one the Greeks lost.

with a more glorious desire and greater ambition, to the winning, than
Captain Iscolas to the certain loss of a battle? Who could have found
out a more subtle invention to secure his safety, than he did to assure
his destruction? He was set to defend a certain pass of Peloponnesus
against the Arcadians, which, considering the nature of the place and
the inequality of forces, finding it utterly impossible for him to do, and
seeing that all who were presented to the enemy, must certainly be left
upon the place; and on the other side, reputing it unworthy of his own
virtue and magnanimity and of the Lacedaemonian[3] name to fail in any
part of his duty, he chose a mean betwixt these two extremes after
this manner; the youngest and most active of his men, he preserved
for the service and defence of their country, and sent them back; and
with the rest, whose loss would be of less consideration, he resolved to
make good the pass, and with the death of them, to make the enemy
buy their entry as dear as possibly he could; as it fell out, for being
presently environed on all sides by the Arcadians, after having made a
great slaughter of the enemy, he and his were all cut in pieces. Is there
any trophy dedicated to the conquerors which was not much more due
to these who were overcome? The part that true conquering is to play,
lies in the encounter, not in the coming off; and the honor of valor consists in fighting, not in subduing.

But to return to my story: these prisoners are so far from discover- 20
ing the least weakness, for all the terrors that can be represented to
them, that, on the contrary, during the two or three months they are
kept, they always appear with a cheerful countenance; importune their
masters to make haste to bring them to the test, defy, rail at them, and
reproach them with cowardice, and the number of battles they have
lost against those of their country. I have a song made by one of these
prisoners, wherein he bids them come all, and dine upon him, and welcome, for they shall withal eat their own fathers and grandfathers,
whose flesh has served to feed and nourish him. Those muscles, says
he, this flesh and these veins, are your own; poor silly souls as you
are, you little think that the substance of your ancestors' limbs is here
yet; notice what you eat, and you will find in it the taste of your own

[3]That is, Spartan.

flesh: in which song there is to be observed an invention that nothing relishes of the barbarian. Those that paint these people dying after this manner, represent the prisoner spitting in the faces of his executioners and making wry mouths at them. And, tis most certain, that to the very last gasp, they never cease to brave and defy them both in word and gesture. In plain truth, these men are very savage in comparison of us; of necessity, they must either be absolutely so or else we are savages; for there is a vast difference betwixt their manners and ours.

The men there have several wives, and so much the greater number, by how much they have the greater reputation for valor. And it is one very remarkable feature in their marriages, that the same jealousy our wives have to hinder and divert us from the friendship and familiarity of other women, those employ to promote their husbands' desires, and to procure them many spouses; for being above all things solicitous of their husbands' honor, 'tis their chiefest care to seek out, and to bring in the most companions they can, forasmuch as it is a testimony of the husbands' virtue. Most of our ladies will cry out, that 'tis monstrous; whereas in truth it is not so, but a truly matrimonial virtue, and of the highest form. In the Bible, Sarah, with Leah and Rachel, the two wives of Jacob, gave the most beautiful of their handmaids to their husbands;[4] Livia preferred the passions of Augustus[5] to her own interest; and the wife of King Deiotarus, Stratonice,[6] did not only give up a fair young maid that served her to her husband's embraces, but moreover carefully brought up the children he had by her, and assisted them in the succession to their father's crown.

And that it may not be supposed, that all this is done by a simple and servile obligation to their common practice, or by any authoritative impression of their ancient custom, without judgment or reasoning, and from having a soul so stupid that it cannot contrive what else to do, I must here give you some touches of their sufficiency in point of understanding. Besides what I repeated to you before, which was one

---

[4]See Genesis 10 for Sarah's story, Genesis 30 for Leah and Rachel's.

[5]Livia Drusilla (58 BCE–29 CE), wife of Augustus (63 BCE–14 CE), emperor of Rome.

[6]The childless Stratonice raised the children of her husband, Galatian King Deiotarus, as her own.

of their songs of war, I have another, a love-song, that begins thus: "Stay, adder, stay, that by thy pattern my sister may draw the fashion and work of a rich ribbon, that I may present to my beloved, by which means thy beauty and the excellent order of thy scales shall for ever be preferred before all other serpents." Wherein the first couplet, "Stay, adder," &c.,[7] makes the burden of the song. Now I have conversed enough with poetry to judge thus much: that not only there is nothing barbarous in this invention, but, moreover, that it is perfectly Anacreontic. To which may be added, that their language is soft, of a pleasing accent, and something bordering upon the Greek termination.[8]

Three of these people, not foreseeing how dear their knowledge of the corruptions of this part of the world will one day cost their happiness and repose, and that the effect of this commerce will be their ruin, as I presuppose it is in a very fair way (miserable men to suffer themselves to be deluded with desire of novelty and to have left the serenity of their own heaven to come so far to gaze at ours!), were at Rouen at the time that the late King Charles IX[9] was there. The king himself talked to them a good while, and they were made to see our fashions, our pomp, and the form of a great city. After which, some one asked their opinion, and would know of them, what of all the things they had seen they found most to be admired? To which they made answer, three things, of which I have forgotten the third, and am troubled at it, but two I yet remember. They said, that in the first place they thought it very strange that so many tall men, wearing beards, strong, and well armed, who were about the king ('tis like they meant the Swiss of the guard), should submit to obey a child, and that they did not rather choose out one amongst themselves to command. Secondly (they have a way of speaking in their language to call men the half of one another), that they had observed that there were amongst us men full and crammed with all manner of commodities, whilst, in the meantime, their halves were begging at their doors, lean and half-starved with hunger and poverty; and they thought it strange that these neces-

---

[7]Archaic expression of "and so forth" (Latin). Contemporary writers use "etc."
[8]Case ending.
[9]French king (1550–74), who ascended to the throne at age ten.

sitous halves were able to suffer so great an inequality and injustice, and that they did not take the others by the throats, or set fire to their houses.

I talked to one of them a great while together, but I had so ill an interpreter, and one who was so perplexed by his own ignorance to apprehend my meaning, that I could get nothing out of him of any moment. Asking him what advantage he reaped from the superiority he had amongst his own people (for he was a captain, and our mariners called him king), he told me, to march at the head of them to war. Demanding of him further how many men he had to follow him, he showed me a space of ground, to signify as many as could march in such a compass, which might be four or five thousand men; and putting the question to him whether or no his authority expired with the war, he told me this remained: that when he went to visit the villages of his dependence, they planed him paths through the thick of their woods, by which he might pass at his ease. All this does not sound very ill, and the last was not at all amiss, for they wear no breeches.

STUDY QUESTIONS

1. Why does Montaigne think that "barbaric" cannibals are superior to "civ-ilized" Europeans?

2. How does Montaigne use COMPARISON AND CONTRAST to make his ARGUMENT? How effective are his comparisons?

3. Montaigne's many allusions may seem confusing to the modern reader. How do you think the author's contemporary reader would have taken them? What contemporary allusions might you substitute to make Montaigne's essay resonate with a reader today?

4. *For Writing.* Write an essay in which you argue for the relevance of Montaigne's "Of Cannibals" in today's society. How could you recast the roles of "cannibals" and "Europeans" for a contemporary reader? What lessons from Montaigne, if any, are applicable to contemporary culture?

Food and Culture

WENDELL BERRY { *The Pleasures of Eating*

WENDELL BERRY (b. 1934) is a farmer and prolific writer of fiction, poetry, and essays, having written more than fifty books. He often writes about sustainability and the importance of a connection to one's local community. Berry has demonstrated such a connection to place not only in his writing but also by living and working on the same farm in Kentucky for more than forty years.

"The Pleasures of Eating" appeared in Berry's 1990 essay collection *What Are People For?* In this essay, Berry provides guidelines for eating responsibly, including trying to participate in food production by growing at least some of one's own food; preparing one's own meals; buying locally produced food; dealing directly with local food producers; and learning about farming, gardening, industrial food production, and the life histories of what one eats. Berry links such awareness and practices not only to health, environmental, and economic concerns, but also to pleasure—to eating with gratitude, understanding, and enjoyment. As you read Berry's essay consider how much you know about where your food comes from and whether you can not only learn more about food production but also take more pleasure in eating.

MANY TIMES, AFTER I HAVE finished a lecture on the decline of American farming and rural life, someone in the audience has asked, "What can city people do?"

"Eat responsibly," I have usually answered. Of course, I have tried to explain what I meant by that, but afterwards I have invariably felt that there was more to be said than I had been able to say. Now I would like to attempt a better explanation.

I begin with the proposition that eating is an agricultural act. Eating ends the annual drama of the food economy that begins with planting and birth. Most eaters, however, are no longer aware that this is true. They think of food as an agricultural product, perhaps, but they do not think of themselves as participants in agriculture. They think of themselves as "consumers." If they think beyond that, they recognize that they are passive consumers. They buy what they want—or what they have been persuaded to want—within the limits of what they can get. They pay, mostly without protest, what they are charged. And they mostly ignore certain critical questions about the quality and the cost of what they are sold: How fresh is it? How pure or clean is it, how free of dangerous chemicals? How far was it transported, and what did transportation add to the cost? How much did manufacturing or packaging or advertising add to the cost? When the food product has been manufactured or "processed" or "precooked," how has that affected its quality or price or nutritional value?

Most urban shoppers would tell you that food is produced on farms. But most of them do not know what farms, or what kinds of farms, or where the farms are, or what knowledge or skills are involved in farming. They apparently have little doubt that farms will continue to produce, but they do not know how or over what obstacles. For them, then, food is pretty much an abstract idea—something they do not know or imagine—until it appears on the grocery shelf or on the table.

The specialization of production induces specialization of con- 5
sumption. Patrons of the entertainment industry, for example, entertain themselves less and less and have become more and more passively dependent on commercial suppliers. This is certainly true also of patrons of the food industry, who have tended more and more to be *mere* consumers—passive, uncritical, and dependent. Indeed, this sort of consumption may be said to be one of the chief goals of industrial production. The food industrialists have by now persuaded millions of consumers to prefer food that is already prepared. They will grow, deliver, and cook your food for you and (just like your mother) beg you to eat it. That they do not yet offer to insert it, prechewed, into

your mouth is only because they have found no profitable way to do so. We may rest assured that they would be glad to find such a way. The ideal industrial food consumer would be strapped to a table with a tube running from the food factory directly into his or her stomach.

Perhaps I exaggerate, but not by much. The industrial eater is, in fact, one who does not know that eating is an agricultural act, who no longer knows or imagines the connections between eating and the land, and who is therefore necessarily passive and uncritical—in short, a victim. When food, in the minds of eaters, is no longer associated with farming and with the land, then the eaters are suffering a kind of cultural amnesia that is misleading and dangerous. The current version of the "dream home" of the future involves "effortless" shopping from a list of available goods on a television monitor and heating precooked food by remote control. Of course, this implies and depends on, a perfect ignorance of the history of the food that is consumed. It requires that the citizenry should give up their hereditary and sensible aversion to buying a pig in a poke. It wishes to make the selling of pigs in pokes an honorable and glamorous activity. The dreamer in this dream home will perforce know nothing about the kind or quality of this food, or where it came from, or how it was produced and prepared, or what ingredients, additives, and residues it contains—unless, that is, the dreamer undertakes a close and constant study of the food industry, in which case he or she might as well wake up and play an active and responsible part in the economy of food.

There is, then, a politics of food that, like any politics, involves our freedom. We still (sometimes) remember that we cannot be free if our minds and voices are controlled by someone else. But we have neglected to understand that we cannot be free if our food and its sources are controlled by someone else. The condition of the passive consumer of food is not a democratic condition. One reason to eat responsibly is to live free.

But if there is a food politics, there are also a food esthetics and a food ethics, neither of which is dissociated from politics. Like industrial sex, industrial eating has become a degraded, poor, and paltry thing. Our kitchens and other eating places more and more resemble filling stations, as our homes more and more resemble motels. "Life is not very interesting," we seem to have decided. "Let its satisfactions be minimal, perfunctory, and fast." We hurry through our meals to go to work and hurry through our work in order to "recreate" ourselves in the evenings and on weekends and vacations. And then we hurry, with the greatest possible speed and noise and violence, through our recreation—for what? To eat the billionth hamburger at some fast-food joint hellbent on increasing the "quality" of our life? And all this is carried out in a remarkable obliviousness to the causes and effects, the possibilities and the purposes, of the life of the body in this world.

One will find this obliviousness represented in virgin purity in the advertisements of the food industry, in which food wears as much makeup as the actors. If one gained one's whole knowledge of food from these advertisements (as some presumably do), one would not know that the various edibles were ever living creatures, or that they all come from the soil, or that they were produced by work. The passive American consumer, sitting down to a meal of pre-prepared or fast food, confronts a platter covered with inert, anonymous substances that have been processed, dyed, breaded, sauced, gravied, ground, pulped, strained, blended, prettified, and sanitized beyond resemblance to any part of any creature that ever lived. The products of nature and agriculture have been made, to all appearances, the products of industry. Both eater and eaten are thus in exile from biological reality. And the result is a kind of solitude, unprecedented in human experience, in which the eater may think of eating as, first, a purely commercial transaction between him and a supplier and then as a purely appetitive transaction between him and his food.

And this peculiar specialization of the act of eating is, again, of obvi- 10
ous benefit to the food industry, which has good reasons to obscure the connection between food and farming. It would not do for the consumer to know that the hamburger she is eating came from a steer who spent much of his life standing deep in his own excrement in a feedlot, helping to pollute the local streams, or that the calf that yielded the veal cutlet on her plate spent its life in a box in which it did not have room to turn around. And, though her sympathy for the slaw might be less tender, she should not be encouraged to meditate on the hygienic and biological implications of mile-square fields of cabbage,

for vegetables grown in huge monocultures are dependent on toxic chemicals—just as animals in close confinement are dependent on antibiotics and other drugs.

The consumer, that is to say, must be kept from discovering that, in the food industry—as in any other industry—the overriding concerns are not quality and health, but volume and price. For decades now the entire industrial food economy, from the large farms and feedlots to the chains of supermarkets and fast-food restaurants, has been obsessed with volume. It has relentlessly increased scale in order to increase volume in order (presumably) to reduce costs. But as scale increases, diversity declines; as diversity declines, so does health; as health declines, the dependence on drugs and chemicals necessarily increases. As capital replaces labor, it does so by substituting machines, drugs, and chemicals for human workers and for the natural health and fertility of the soil. The food is produced by any means or any shortcut that will increase profits. And the business of the cosmeticians of advertising is to persuade the consumer that food so produced is good, tasty, healthful, and a guarantee of marital fidelity and long life.

It is possible, then, to be liberated from the husbandry and wifery of the old household food economy. But one can be thus liberated only by entering a trap (unless one sees ignorance and helplessness as the signs of privilege, as many people apparently do). The trap is the ideal of industrialism: a walled city surrounded by valves that let merchandise in but no consciousness out. How does one escape this trap? Only voluntarily, the same way that one went in: by restoring one's consciousness of what is involved in eating; by reclaiming responsibility for one's own part in the food economy. One might begin with the illuminating principle of Sir Albert Howard's *The Soil and Health*, that we should understand "the whole problem of health in soil, plant, animal, and man as one great subject." Eaters, that is, must understand that eating takes place inescapably in the world, that it is inescapably an agricultural act, and that how we eat determines, to a considerable extent, how the world is used. This is a simple way of describing a relationship that is inexpressibly complex. To eat responsibly is to understand and enact, so far as one can, this complex relationship. What can one do? Here is a list, probably not definitive:

1. Participate in food production to the extent that you can. If you have a yard or even just a porch box or a pot in a sunny window, grow something to eat in it. Make a little compost of your kitchen scraps and use it for fertilizer. Only by growing some food for yourself can you become acquainted with the beautiful energy cycle that revolves from soil to seed to flower to fruit to food to offal to decay, and around again. You will be fully responsible for any food that you grow for yourself, and you will know all about it. You will appreciate it fully, having known it all its life.

2. Prepare your own food. This means reviving in your own mind and life the arts of kitchen and household. This should enable you to eat more cheaply, and it will give you a measure of "quality control": you will have some reliable knowledge of what has been added to the food you eat.

3. Learn the origins of the food you buy, and buy the food that is 15 produced closest to your home. The idea that every locality should be, as much as possible, the source of its own food makes several kinds of sense. The locally produced food supply is the most secure, the freshest, and the easiest for local consumers to know about and to influence.

4. Whenever possible, deal directly with a local farmer, gardener, or orchardist. All the reasons listed for the previous suggestion apply here. In addition, by such dealing you eliminate the whole pack of merchants, transporters, processors, packagers, and advertisers who thrive at the expense of both producers and consumers.

5. Learn, in self-defense, as much as you can of the economy and technology of industrial food production. What is added to food that is not food, and what do you pay for these additions?

6. Learn what is involved in the *best* farming and gardening.

7. Learn as much as you can, by direct observation and experience if possible, of the life histories of the food species.

The last suggestion seems particularly important to me. Many people 20 are now as much estranged from the lives of domestic plants and animals (except for flowers and dogs and cats) as they are from the lives of the wild ones. This is regrettable, for these domestic creatures are in diverse ways attractive; there is much pleasure in knowing them. And farming, animal husbandry, horticulture, and gardening, at their best, are complex and comely arts; there is much pleasure in knowing them, too.

It follows that there is great *dis*pleasure in knowing about a food economy that degrades and abuses those arts and those plants and animals and the soil from which they come. For anyone who does know something of the modern history of food, eating away from home can be a chore. My own inclination is to eat seafood instead of red meat or poultry when I am traveling. Though I am by no means a vegetarian, I dislike the thought that some animal has been made miserable in order to feed me. If I am going to eat meat, I want it to be from an animal that has lived a pleasant, uncrowded life outdoors, on bountiful pasture, with good water nearby and trees for shade. And I am getting almost as fussy about food plants. I like to eat vegetables and fruits that I know have lived happily and healthy in good soil, not the products of the huge, bechemicaled factory-fields that I have seen, for example, in the Central Valley of California. The industrial farm is said to have been patterned on the factory production line. In practice, it looks more like a concentration camp.

The pleasure of eating should be an *extensive* pleasure, not that of the mere gourmet. People who know the garden in which their vegetables have grown and know that the garden is healthy will remember the beauty of the growing plants, perhaps in the dewy first light of morning when gardens are at their best. Such a memory involves itself with the food and is one of the pleasures of eating. The knowledge of the good health of the garden relieves and frees and comforts the eater. The same goes for eating meat. The thought of the good pasture and of the calf contentedly grazing flavors the steak. Some, I know, will think it bloodthirsty or worse to eat a fellow creature you have known all its life. On the contrary, I think it means that you eat with understanding and with gratitude. A significant part of the pleasure of eating is in one's accurate consciousness of the lives and the world from which food comes. The pleasure of eating, then, may be the best available standard of our health. And this pleasure, I think, is pretty fully available to the urban consumer who will make the necessary effort.

I mentioned earlier the politics, esthetics, and ethics of food. But to speak of the pleasure of eating is to go beyond those categories. Eating with the fullest pleasure—pleasure, that is, that does not depend on ignorance—is perhaps the profoundest enactment of our connection with the world. In this pleasure we experience and celebrate our dependence and our gratitude, for we are living from mystery, from creatures we did not make and powers we cannot comprehend. When I think of the meaning of food, I always remember these lines by the poet William Carlos Williams, which seem to me merely honest:

> There is nothing to eat,
> seek it where you will,
> but the body of the Lord.
> The blessed plants
> and the sea, yield it
> to the imagination
> intact.

STUDY QUESTIONS

1. In this EXPOSITORY ESSAY, Berry seeks to explain the ways in which eating is an agricultural act. What, to Berry, are the differences between a passive consumer and a person who actively eats responsibly?

2. Throughout his essay, Berry uses COMPARISONS. For example, he compares eating places to filling stations and homes to motels (paragraph 8). Make a list of the **comparisons** Berry makes. Which ones do you find most effective? Why?

3. Berry often uses the word "pleasure" in relation to eating. What do you think his DEFINITION of that word would be? That is, what—to Berry—makes an act of eating pleasurable? How does his definition of pleasure compare with yours?

4. *For Writing.* Berry provides a list of seven elements that, for him, make up responsible eating practices. Make your own list of seven elements for doing something responsibly (for example, dating, shopping, or driving). Turn your list into an essay on that topic.

BARBARA KINGSOLVER { *Lily's Chickens*

BARBARA KINGSOLVER (b. 1955) writes fiction, nonfiction, and
poetry, much of which is influenced by her interest in science and
the environment. In 1977 she earned a BS in biology from DePauw
University in Indiana, and she later received a Master's degree in ecology
and evolutionary biology from the University of Arizona. A native of
rural Kentucky, she lived in Arizona for two decades, and she has also
lived in England, France, and the Canary Islands. Kingsolver now lives
on a farm in Virginia, where she and her family grow and raise much of
their own food and do their best to eat locally, a practice she has written
about in her nonfiction book *Animal, Vegetable, Miracle* (2007).

"Lily's Chickens" appeared in Kingsolver's 2002 nonfiction collection
Small Wonder. In this essay, Kingsolver contemplates the environmental
effects of the industrial food system and discusses her choice to grow some
of her food in her garden and to procure much of her other food locally. She
also considers the way her five-year-old daughter raises chickens—and the
benefits of self-provisioning. As you read this selection, notice the ways
Kingsolver embeds both facts and personal stories to bolster her argument.

MY DAUGHTER IS IN LOVE. She's only five years old, but this is real.
Her beau is shorter than she is, by a wide margin, and she couldn't
care less. He has dark eyes, a loud voice, and a tendency to crow. He
also has five girlfriends, but Lily doesn't care about that, either. She
loves them all: Mr. Doodle, Jess, Bess, Mrs. Zebra, Pixie, and Kiwi.
They're chickens. Lily likes to sit on an overturned bucket and sing to
them in the afternoons. She has them eating out of her hand.

It began with coveting our neighbor's chickens. Lily would volunteer to collect the eggs, and then she offered to move in with them. Not the neighbors, the chickens. She said if she could have some of her own, she would be the happiest girl on earth. What parent could resist this bait? Our life style could accommodate a laying flock; my husband and I had kept poultry before, so we knew it was a project we could manage, and a responsibility Lily could handle largely by herself. I understood how much that meant to her when I heard her tell her grandmother, "They're going to be just *my* chickens, Grandma. Not even one of them will be my sister's." To be five years old and have some other life form entirely under your control—not counting goldfish or parents—is a majestic state of affairs.

So her dutiful father built a smart little coop right next to our large garden enclosure, and I called a teenage friend who might, I suspected, have some excess baggage in the chicken department. She raises championship show chickens, and she culls her flock tightly. At this time of year she'd be eyeing her young birds through their juvenile molt to be sure every feather conformed to the gospel according to the chicken-breeds handbook, which is titled, I swear, *The Standard of Perfection.* I asked if she had a few feather-challenged children that wanted adoption, and she happily obliged. She even had an adorable little bantam rooster that would have caused any respectable chicken-show judge to keel over—the love child of a Rose-comb and a Wyandotte. I didn't ask how it happened.

In Lily's eyes *this* guy, whom she named Mr. Doodle, was the standard of perfection. We collected him and a motley harem of sweet little hens in a crate and brought them home. They began to scratch around contentedly right away, and Lily could hardly bear to close her eyes at night on the pride she felt at poultry ownership. Every day after feeding them she would sit on her overturned bucket and chat with them about the important things. She could do this for an hour, easily, while I worked nearby in the garden. We discovered that they loved to eat the weeds I pulled, and the grasshoppers I caught red-handed eating my peppers. We wondered, would they even eat the nasty green hornworms that are the bane of my tomato plants? *Darling,* replied Mrs. Zebra, licking her non-lips, *that was to die for.*

I soon became so invested in pleasing the hens, along with Lily, that I would let a fresh green pigweed grow an extra day or two to get some size on before pulling it. And now, instead of carefully dusting my tomato plants with Bacillus spores (a handy bacterium that gives caterpillars a fatal bellyache), I allow the hornworms to reach heroic sizes, just for the fun of throwing the chickens into conniptions. Growing hens alongside my vegetables, and hornworms and pig- weeds as part of the plan, has drawn me more deeply into the organic cycle of my gardening that is its own fascinating reward.

Watching Mr. Doodle's emergent maturity has also given me, for the first time in my life, an appreciation for machismo. At first he didn't know what to do with all these girls; to him they were just com- petition for food. Whenever I tossed them a juicy bug, he would dis- play the manners of a teenage boy on a first date at a hamburger joint, rushing to scarf down the whole thing, then looking up a little sheep- ishly to ask, "Oh, did you want some?" But as hormones nudged him toward his rooster imperatives, he began to strut with a new eye toward his coopmates. Now he rushes up to the caterpillar with a valiant air, picking it up in his beak and flogging it repeatedly against the ground until the clear and present danger of caterpillar attack has passed. Then he cocks his head and gently approaches Jess or Bess with a throaty little pickup line, dropping the defeated morsel at her feet. He doles out the food equitably, herds his dizzy-headed girls to the roost when it's time for bed, and uses an impressive vocabulary to address their specific needs: A low, monotonous cluck calls them to the grub; a higher-pitched chatter tells them a fierce terrestrial carnivore (our dog) is staring balefully through the chicken-wire pen; a quiet, descending croak warns "Heads up!" when the ominous shadow of an owl or hawk passes overhead. Or a dove, or a bumblebee—OK, this isn't rocket science. But he does his job. There is something very touching about Mr. Doodle when he stretches up onto his toes, shimmies his golden-feather shawl, throws back his little head, and cries—as Alexander Haig[1] did in that brief moment when he thought he was president—"As of now, I *am* in control!"

With the coop built and chickens installed, all we had to do now was wait for our flock to pass through puberty and begin to give us our daily eggs. We were warned it might take a while because they would be upset by the move and would need time for emotional adjustment. I was skeptical about this putative pain and suffering; it is hard to put much stock in the emotional life of a creature with the I.Q. of an eggplant. Seems to me you put a chicken in a box, and she looks around and says, "Gee, life is a box." You take her out, she looks around and says, "Gee, it's sunny here." But sure enough, they took their time. Lily began each day with high hopes, marching out to the coop with cup of corn in one hand and my twenty-year-old wire egg-basket in the other. She insisted that her dad build five nest boxes in case they all suddenly got the urge at once. She fluffed up the straw in all five nests, nervous as a bride preparing her boudoir.

I was looking forward to the eggs, too. To anyone who has eaten an egg just a few hours' remove from the hen, those white ones in the store have the charisma of day-old bread. I looked forward to organizing my family's meals around the pleasures of quiches, Spanish tortillas, and soufflés, with a cupboard that never goes bare. We don't go to the grocery very often; our garden produces a good deal of what we eat, and in some seasons nearly all of it. This is not exactly a hobby. It's more along the lines of religion, something we believe in the way families believe in patriotism and loving thy neighbor as thyself. If our food ethic seems an unusual orthodoxy to set alongside those other two, it probably shouldn't. We consider them to be connected.

Globally speaking, I belong to the 20 percent of the world's population—and chances are you do, too—that uses 67 percent of the planet's resources and generates 75 percent of its pollution and waste. This doesn't make me proud. U.S. citizens by ourselves, comprising just 5 percent of the world's people, use a quarter of its fuels. An aver-

---

[1]American politician (1924–2010); as secretary of state under President Ronald Reagan, Haig briefly assumed control of the administration following the assassination attempt on the president while Vice President George H. W. Bush hurried back to Washington.

age American gobbles up the goods that would support thirty citizens of India. Much of the money we pay for our fuels goes to support regimes that treat their people—particularly their women—in ways that make me shudder. I'm a critic of this shameful contract, and of wasteful consumption, on general principles. Since it's nonsensical, plus embarrassing, to be an outspoken critic of things you do yourself, I set myself long ago to the task of consuming less. I never got to India, but in various stages of my free-wheeling youth I tried out living in a tent, in a commune, and in Europe, before eventually determining that I could only ever hope to dent the salacious appetites of my homeland and make us a more perfect union by living *inside* this amazing beast, poking at its belly from the inside with my one little life and the small, pointed sword of my pen. So this is where I feed my family and try to live lightly on the land.

The Union of Concerned Scientists notes that there are two main areas where U.S. citizens take a hoggish bite of the world's limited resources and fuels. First is transportation. Anybody would guess this. I'm lucky, since I can commute from bedroom to office in my fuzzy slippers, by way of the coffeepot in the kitchen. We get the kids to school via bus and carpool and organize our errands so trips to town are minimized. I have lived some years of my adulthood without a car (it's easier in Europe), though for now I have one. I hope soon to trade it in for one of those electric-hybrid station wagons that gets forty-eight miles per gallon. Ironically, my interests in conservation and the personal act as political have led me into a career that garners me hundreds of invitations a year to burn jet fuel in order to spread my gospel. I solve this dilemma, imperfectly, by sticking mostly to recycled paper as the medium of that gospel and turning down ninety-nine invitations out of a hundred, taking only the trips that somehow promise me a story whose telling will have been worth its purchase. So in the realm of transporting myself, so long as I can avoid the wild-goose chase of a book tour, I can live within fairly modest means.

Gas-guzzling area number two, and this may surprise you, is our diet. Americans have a taste for food that's been seeded, fertilized, harvested, processed, and packaged in grossly energy-expensive ways and then shipped, often refrigerated, for so many miles it might as well be green cheese from the moon. Even if you walk or bike to the store, if you come home with bananas from Ecuador, tomatoes from Holland, cheese from France, and artichokes from California, you have guzzled some serious gas. This extravagance that most of us take for granted is a stunning energy boondoggle: Transporting 5 calories' worth of strawberry from California to New York costs 435 calories of fossil fuel. The global grocery store may turn out to be the last great losing proposition of our species.

Most Americans are entangled in a car dependency not of our own making, but nobody *has* to eat foods out of season from Rio de Janeiro. It's a decision we remake daily, and an unnecessary kind of consumption that I decided some time ago to try to expunge from my life. I had a head start because I grew up among farmers and have found since then that you can't take the country out of the girl. Wherever I've lived, I've gardened, even when the only dirt I owned was a planter box on an apartment balcony. I've grown food through good times and bad, busy and slow, richer and poorer—especially poorer. When people protest that gardening is an expensive hobby, I suggest they go through their garden catalogs and throw out the ones that offer footwear and sundials. Seeds cost pennies apiece or less. For years I've grown much of what my family eats and tried to attend to the sources of the rest. As I began to understand the energy crime of food transportation, I tried to attend even harder, eliminating any foods grown on the dark side of the moon. I began asking after the processes that brought each item to my door: what people had worked where, for slave wages and with deadly pesticides; what places had been deforested; what species were being driven extinct for my cup of coffee or banana bread. It doesn't taste so good when you think about what died going into it.

Responsible eating is not so impossible as it seems. I was encouraged in my quest by *This Organic Life*, a compelling book by Joan Dye Gussow that tells how, and more important *why*, she aspired to and achieved vegetable self-sufficiency. She does it in her small backyard in upstate New York, challenging me to make better use of my luxuries of larger space and milder clime. Sure enough, she's right. In the year since I started counting, I've found I need never put a vegetable on my table that has traveled more than an hour or so from its home ground to ours.

I should explain that I do this in the *places* where I live, because I am not I, but we. My husband and I met in our late thirties; he had already grown deep roots in a farming community in southern Appalachia. I had roots of my own, plus a kid, in my little rancho outside Tucson, Arizona. So our marriage is a more conspicuous compromise than most: We all live out the school year in the Southwest and spend the summer growing season in Appalachia. By turns we work two very different farms, both of which we share with other families who inhabit them year-round so nothing has to lie very fallow or stand empty. Eventually, when we've fulfilled all our premarital obligations, we'll settle in one place. Until then I blow some of the parsimony of my daily bedroom-slipper commute on one whopper of an annual round trip, but it's a fine life for a gardener. In the mild winters of Tucson, where we get regular freezes but no snow, we grow the cool-weather crops that can take a little frost: broccoli, peas, spinach, lettuce, Chinese vegetables, garlic, artichokes. And in the verdant southern summers, we raise everything else: corn, peppers, green beans, tomatoes, eggplants, too much zucchini, and never enough of the staples (potatoes, dried beans) that carry us through the year. Most of whatever else I need comes from the local growers I meet at farmers' markets. Our family has arrived, as any sentient people would, at a strong preference for the breads and pasta we make ourselves, so I'm always searching out proximate sources of organic flour. Just by reading labels, I have discovered I can buy milk that comes from organic dairies only a few counties away; in season I can often get it from my neighbors, in exchange for vegetables; and I've become captivated by the alchemy of creating my own cheese and butter. (Butter is a sport; cheese is an art.) Wine-making remains well beyond my powers, but fortunately good wine is made in both Arizona and Virginia, and in the latter state I am especially glad to support some neighbors in a crashing tobacco-based economy who are trying to hold on to their farms by converting them to vineyards. Somewhere near you, I'm sure, is a farmer who desperately needs your support, for one of a thousand reasons that are pulling the wool out of the proud but unraveling traditions of family farming.

I am trying to learn about this complicated web as I go, and I'm in 15
no position to judge anyone else's personal habits, believe me. My life is riddled with energy inconsistencies: We try hard to conserve, but I've found no way as yet to rear and support my family without a car, a computer, the occasional airplane flight, a teenager's bathroom equipped with a hair dryer, et cetera. I'm no Henry D. Thoreau. (And just for the record, for all his glorification of his bean patch, Henry is known habitually to have gone next door to eat Mrs. Ralph W. Emerson's cooking.) Occasional infusions of root beer are apparently necessary to my family's continued life, along with a brand of vegetable chips made in Uniondale, New York. And there's no use in my trying to fib about it, either, for it's always when I have just these items in the grocery cart, and my hair up in the wackiest of slapdash ponytails, that some kind person in the checkout line will declare, "Oh, Ms. Kingsolver, I just love your work!"

Our quest is only to be thoughtful and simplify our needs, step by step. In the way of imported goods, I try to stick to nonperishables that are less fuel-costly to ship; rice, flour, and coffee are good examples. Just as simply as I could buy coffee and spices from the grocery, I can order them through a collective in Fort Wayne, Indiana, that gives my money directly to cooperative farmers in Africa and Central America who are growing these crops without damaging their tropical habitat. We struggled with the notion of giving up coffee altogether until we learned from ornithologist friends who study migratory birds being lost to habitat destruction, that there is a coffee-cultivation practice that helps rather than hurts. Any coffee labeled "shade grown"—now available in most North American markets—was grown under rain-forest canopy on a farm that is holding a piece of jungle intact, providing subsistence for its human inhabitants and its birds.

I understand the power implicit in these choices. That I have such choices at all is a phenomenal privilege in a world where so many go hungry, even as our nation uses food as a political weapon, embargoing grain shipments to places such as Nicaragua and Iraq. I find both security and humility in feeding myself as best I can, and learning to live within the constraints of my climate and seasons. I like the challenge of organizing our meals as my grandmothers did, starting with the question of season and which cup is at the moment running over. I love to trade recipes with my gardening friends, and join in their cheerful competition to see who can come up with the most ways to conceal the i.d. of a zucchini squash.

If we are blessed with an abundance of choices about food, we are surely also obliged to consider the responsibility implicit in our choices. There has never been a more important time to think about where our food comes from. We could make for ourselves a safer nation, overnight, simply by giving more support to our local food economies and learning ways of eating and living around a table that reflects the calendar. Our families, of course, will never need to be as beholden to the seasons as the Native Americans who called February by the name "Hungry Month," and I'm grateful for that. But we can try to live close enough to the land's ordinary time that we notice when something is out of place and special. My grandfather Kingsolver used to tell me with a light in his eyes about the boxcar that came through Kentucky on the L&N line when he was a boy—only once a year, at Christmas—carrying oysters and oranges from the coast. Throughout my own childhood, every year at Christmastime while an endless burden of wants burgeoned around everybody else, my grandfather wanted only two things: a bowl of oyster soup and an orange. The depth of his pleasure in that meal was so tangible, even to a child, that my memory of it fills me with wonder at how deeply fulfillment can blossom from a cultivated ground of restraint.

I remember this as I struggle—along with most parents I know—to make clear distinctions between love and indulgence in raising my children. I honestly believe that material glut can rob a child of certain kinds of satisfaction—though deprivation is no picnic, either. And so our family indulges in exotic treats on big occasions. A box of Portuguese clementines one Christmas is still on Lily's catalog of favorite memories, and a wild turkey we got from Canada one Thanksgiving remains on my own. We enjoy these kinds of things spectacularly because at our house they're rare.

And yes, we eat some animals, in careful deference to the reasons 20
for avoiding doing so. I don't really feel, as some have told me, that it's
a sin to eat anything with a face, nor do I believe it's possible to live by
that rule unless one maintains a certain degree of purposeful ignorance. Butterflies and bees and locusts all have faces, and they die like
lambs to the slaughter (and in greater numbers) whenever a field of
vegetable food is sprayed or harvested. Faceless? Not the birds that
eat the poisoned insects, the bunnies sliced beneath the plow, the
foxes displaced from the forest-turned-to-organic-wheat-field, and so
on. If the argument is that meat comes from *higher orders* of life than
those creatures, I wonder how the artificial, glassy-eyed construct of a
bovine life gets to weigh more than the wiles of a fox or the virtuosity of
a songbird. Myself, I love wild lives at least as much as tame ones, and
eating costs lives. Even organic farmers kill crop predators in ways that
aren't pretty, so a vegetable diet doesn't provide quite the sparkling
karma one might wish. Most soybeans grown in this country are gene-
tically engineered in ways that are anathema to biodiversity. So drinking soy milk, however wholesome it may be, doesn't save animals.

No, it's the other savings that compel me most toward a vegetable-
based diet—the ones revealed by simple math. A pound of cow or hog
flesh costs about ten pounds of plant matter to produce. So a field of
grain that would feed a hundred people, when fed instead to cows or
pigs that are *then* fed to people, fills the bellies of only ten of them; the
other ninety, I guess, will just have to go hungry. That, in a nutshell,
is how it's presently shaking down with the world, the world's arable
land, and the world's hamburger eaters.

Some years ago our family took a trip across the Midwest to visit
relatives in Iowa, and for thousands of miles along the way we saw
virtually no animal life except feedlots full of cattle—surely the most
unappetizing sight and smell I've encountered in my life (and my life
includes some years of intimacy with diaper pails). And we saw almost
no plant life but the endless fields of corn and soybeans required to
feed those pathetic penned beasts. Our kids kept asking, mile after
mile, "What used to be here?" It led to long discussions of America's
vanished prairie, Mexico's vanished forests, and the diversity of spe-

cies in the South American rain forests that are now being extinguished to make way for more cattle graze. We also talked about a vanishing American culture: During the last half century or so, each passing year has seen about half a million more people move away from farms (including all of my children's grandparents or great-grandparents). The lively web of farmhouses, schoolhouses, pasture lands, woodlots, livestock barns, poultry coops, and tilled fields that once constituted America's breadbasket has been replaced with a meat-fattening monoculture. When we got home our daughter announced firmly, "I'm never going to eat a cow again."

When your ten-year-old calls your conscience to order, you show up: She *hasn't* eaten a cow since, and neither have we. It's an industry I no longer want to get tangled up in, even at the level of the ninety-nine-cent exchange. Each and every quarter pound of hamburger is handed across the counter after the following productions costs, which I've searched out precisely: 100 gallons of water, 1.2 pounds of grain, a cup of gasoline, greenhouse-gas emissions equivalent to those produced by a six-mile drive in your average car, and the loss of 1.25 pounds of topsoil, every inch of which took five hundred years for the microbes and earthworms to build. How can all this cost less than a dollar, and who is supposed to pay for the rest of it? If I were a cow, right here is where I'd go mad.

Thus our family parted ways with all animal flesh wrought from feedlots. But for some farmers on certain land, assuming that they don't have the option of turning their acreage into a national park (and that people will keep wanting to eat), the most ecologically sound use of it is to let free-range animals turn its grass and weeds into edible flesh, rather than turning it every year under the plow. We also have neighbors who raise organic beef for their family on hardly more than the byproducts of other things they grow. It's quite possible to raise animals sustainably, and we support the grass-based farmers around us by purchasing their chickens and eggs.

Or we did, that is, until Lily got her chickens. The next time a 25 roasted bird showed up on our table she grew wide-eyed, set down her fork, and asked, "Mama . . . is that . . . Mr. Doodle?"

I reassured her a dozen times that I would *never* cook Mr. Doodle; this was just some chicken *we didn't know*. But a lesson had come home to, well, roost. All of us sooner or later must learn to look our food in the face. If we're willing to eat an animal, it's probably only responsible to accept the truth of its living provenance rather than pretending it's a "product" from a frozen-foods shelf with its gizzard in a paper envelope. I've been straight with my kids ever since the first one leveled me with her eye and said, "Mom, no offense, but I think *you're* the Tooth Fairy." So at dinner that night we talked about the biology, ethics, and occasional heartbreaks of eating food. I told Lily that when I was a girl growing up among creatures I would someday have to eat, my mother had promised we would never butcher anything that had a first name. Thereafter I was always told from the outset which animals I could name. I offered Lily the same deal.

So she made her peace with the consumption of her beloveds' nameless relatives. We still weren't sure, though, how we'd fare when it came to eating their direct descendants. We'd allowed that next spring she might let a hen incubate and hatch out a few new chicks (Lily quickly decided on the precise number she wanted and, significantly, their names), but we stressed that we weren't in this business to raise ten thousand pets. Understood, said Lily. So we waited a week, then two, while Jess, Bess, and company worked through their putative emotional trauma and settled in to laying. We wondered, How will it go? When our darling five-year-old pantheist, who believes that even stuffed animals have souls, goes out there with the egg basket one day and comes back with eggs, how will we explain to her that she can't name those babes, because we're going to scramble them?

Here is how it went: She returned triumphantly that morning with one unbelievably small brown egg in her basket, planted her feet on the kitchen tile, and shouted at the top of her lungs, "Attention, everybody, I have an announcement: FREE BREAKFAST."

We agreed that the first one was hers. I cooked it to her very exact specifications, and she ate it with gusto. We admired the deep red-orange color of the yolk, from the beta-carotenes in those tasty green weeds. Lily could hardly wait for the day when all of us would sit down to a free breakfast, courtesy of her friends. I wish that every child could feel so proud, and every family could share the grace of our table.

•   ○   •

I think a lot about those thirty citizens of India who, it's said, could   30
live on the average American's stuff. I wonder if I could build a life of contentment on their material lot, and then I look around my house and wonder what they'd make of mine. My closet would clothe more than half of them, and my books—good Lord—could open a library branch in New Delhi. Our family's musical instruments would outfit an entire (if very weird) village band, featuring electric guitars, violin, eclectic percussion section, and a really dusty clarinet. We have more stuff than we need; there is no question of our being perfect. I'm not even sure what "perfect" means in this discussion. I'm not trying to persuade my family to evaporate and live on air. We're here, we're alive, it's the only one we get, as far as I know, so I am keenly inclined to take hold of life by its *huevos*. As a dinner guest I gratefully eat just about anything that's set before me, because graciousness among friends is dearer to me than any other agenda. I'm not up for a guilt trip, just an adventure in bearable lightness. I approach our efforts at simplicity as a novice approaches her order, aspiring to a lifetime of deepening understanding, discipline, serenity, and joy. Likening voluntary simplicity to a religion is neither hyperbole nor sacrilege. Some people look around and declare the root of all evil to be sex or blasphemy, and so they aspire to be pious and chaste. Where I look for evil I'm more likely to see degradations of human and natural life, an immoral gap between rich and poor, a ravaged earth. At the root of these I see greed and overconsumption by the powerful minority. I was born to that caste, but I can aspire to waste not and want less.

I'm skeptical of evangelism, so I'm not going to have a tent revival here. But if you've come with me this far, you are in some sense a fellow traveler, and I'm glad for your company. In this congregation we don't confess or sit around chanting "we are not worthy"; we just do what we can and trust that the effort matters. Of all the ways we consume, food is a sensible one to attend to. Eating is a genuine need, continuous from our first day to our last, amounting over time to our most significant statement of what we are made of and what we have chosen to make of our connection to home ground. We can hardly choose *not* to eat, but we have to choose *how*, and our choices can have astounding consequences. Consider this: The average food item set before a U.S. consumer traveled 1,300 miles to get there. If Mr. Average eats ten or so items a day (and most of us eat more), in a year's time his food will have conquered five million miles by land, sea, and air. Picture a truck loaded with apples and oranges and iceberg lettuce rumbling to the moon and back ten times a year, all just for you. Multiply that by the number of Americans who like to eat—picture that flotilla of 285 million trucks on their way to the moon—and tell me you don't think it's time to revise this scenario.

Obviously, if you live in Manhattan, your child can't have chickens. But I'll wager you're within walking distance of a farmer's market where you can make the acquaintance of some farmers and buy what's in season. (I have friends in Manhattan who actually garden—on rooftops, and in neighborhood community plots.) In recent years nearly three thousand green markets have sprung up across the country, giving more than a hundred thousand farmers a place to sell their freshly harvested, usually organic produce to a regular customer base. In some seven hundred communities, both rural and urban (including inner-city New York), thousands of Americans are supporting their local food economies by signing up with Community-Supported Agriculture, a system that lets farmers get paid at planting time for produce that they then deliver weekly to their subscribers until year's end. Thousands of other communities have food co-operatives that specialize at least in organic goods, if not local ones, and promote commodities (such as bulk flours, cereals, oils, and spices) that minimize energy costs for packaging and shipping. Wherever you are, if you have a grocery store, you'll find something in there that is in season and hasn't spent half its life in a boxcar. The way to find out is to *ask*. If every U.S. consumer would earmark just ten dollars a month for local items, the consequences would be huge.

I realize there are deep, traditional divisions of class between white bread and whole wheat. I grew up among many people who would feel uncomfortable saying the word *organic* out loud. But I know I am witnessing a reordering of tradition when some of my rural Virginia neighbors who've heretofore grown, and chewed, tobacco become comfortable saying (and growing) "Chardonnay" and "Merlot grape." A dear friend of mine who has gardened for over six decades using the fertilizers and pesticides recommended by her farming father and husband, while they lived, confided to me not long ago that she'd secretly gone organic. (Her tomatoes that summer were some of her best ever.) It's clear that this movement is reaching across class lines, when farmers' markets redeem more than $100 million in food stamps each year. Community food-security initiatives in many areas are also working to link organic farmers with food banks and school lunch programs. Growing and eating are both infused with new politics.

Before anyone rules out eating locally and organically because it seems expensive, I'd ask him or her to figure in the costs paid *outside* the store: the health costs, the land costs, the big environmental Visa bill that sooner or later comes due. It's easy to notice that organic vegetables cost more than their chemically reared equivalents, but that difference is rarely the one consumers take home. A meal prepared at home from whole, chemical-free ingredients costs just pennies on the dollar paid for the highly processed agribusiness products that most Americans eat at restaurants or heat up in the microwave nearly every day. For every dollar we send to a farmer, fisherman, or rancher, we send between three and four to the shippers, processors, packagers, retailers, and advertisers. And there are countless other costs for that kind of food. Our history of overtaking the autonomy and economies of small countries with our large corporations, the wars and campaigns we wage to maintain our fossil-fuel dependency—these have finally brought us costs beyond our wildest fears. Cancer is expensive, too, as are topsoil loss and species extinction. The costs of global warming will bring us eventually to our knees. When I have to explain to my kids someday that, yes, back at the turn of the century we *did* know we were starting to cause catastrophic changes in the planet's climate that might end their lives prematurely, do I have to tell them we just couldn't be bothered to alter our convenience-food habits?

It doesn't, in principle, take more time to buy a local peach than 35 a world-weary banana, and cooking from whole ingredients is not prohibitively time-consuming, either. As a working mother I am possessive of my time; I have to log in hours on my job—about forty a week—my spouse does the same, and our kids require of us the usual amount of kid-attention. But sometimes our family outings involve picking apples. I can peel the fruit and cook it into pies, jam, and purees for flavoring yogurt while I listen to the news on the radio or hear about my kids' day at school. Like many busy families, we cook in quantity on the weekends and freeze portions for easy midweek dinners. And we've befriended some fascinating microbes that will stay up all night in our kitchen making yogurt, feta, neufchatel, and sourdough bread without adult supervision. (I think copulation is involved, but we're open-minded.) Gardening is the best way I know to stay fit and trim, so during garden season, when it's up to me to make the earth move, I don't waste hours at the gym. Eating this way requires organization and skills more than time. Our great-grandmas did all this, and they may not have had other employment, but they did have to skin hogs for shoe leather, cut stove wood, sew everybody's clothes, and make the soap to wash them. Sheesh. My kitchen's on Easy Street.

It seems to me that giving up junk foods and jet-lagged vegetables is something like giving up smoking: It takes some discipline at first, but in the long run it's hard to see the minus sign in the equation. If there's anyone left who still thinks eating organically is a bland, granola-crunching affair, he or she must have missed the boat back around midmorning in the Age of Aquarius. The movement has grown up. Most Europeans think we're fools to eat some of the tasteless gunk that passes for food in our supermarkets. The Italians who pioneered Slow Food have forged a conscientious movement for preserving farms and the culture of unique, sustainable foods, but their starting point was pure epicurean disgust with fast food and watery, transported vegetables. Now that I've gotten into local eating I can't quit, because I've inadvertently raised children who are horrified by the taste of a store-bought tomato. Health is an issue, too: My growing girls don't need the hormones and toxins that lace American food in regulated quantities (the allowable doses are more about economic feasibility than about proven safety). But that is only part of the picture. Objecting to irresponsible agriculture for reasons of your personal health is a bit like objecting to having a nuclear power plant in your backyard for reasons of your view. My own two children are the smallest part of the iceberg. The millions of children in sub-Saharan Africa and other places now facing famine and historically unprecedented climatic extremes because of global warming—they are the rest of the iceberg.

Developing an intimate relationship with the processes that feed my family has brought me surprising personal rewards. I've tasted heirloom vegetables with poetic names—Mortgage Lifter tomato, Moon and Stars watermelon—whose flavors most never will know because they turn to pulp and vinegar in a boxcar. I've learned how to look a doe-goat right in the weird horizontal pupil of her big brown eye, sit down and extract her milk, and make feta cheese. (Step 1 is the hardest.) I've learned that with an unbreakable jar and the right music, a gang of kids can render butter from cream in eleven minutes flat. I've discovered a kind of citrus tree that withstands below-zero temperatures, almost extinct today but commonly grown by farm wives a hundred years ago. I've learned that the best-tasting vegetables on God's green earth are the ones our garden-wise foremothers bred for consumption, not hard travel. And I seem to be raising kids who like healthy food. When Lily streaks through the crowd at the farmer's market shouting, "Mama, look, they have *broccoli*, let's get a *lot!*"—well, heads do turn. Women have asked me, "How do you get one like that?"

I'm not going to tell you it's a done deal. If there were a bin of Twinkies at the farmer's market, the broccoli would go to rot. Once upon a time, when I had my first baby, I believed that if I took care not to train her to the bad habits of sugar, salt, and fat, she would grow up not wanting those things. That delusion lasted exactly one year, until someone put a chocolate-frosted birthday confection in front of my sugar-free child and—how can I say this delicately?—she put her face in the cake. We humans crave sugar, fat, and salt because we evolved through thousands of years in which these dietary components were desperately scarce; those members of the tribe who most successfully glutted on them, when they found them, would store up the body fat to live through lean times and bear offspring. And now we've organized the whole enchilada around those latent biochemical passions—an early hominid's dream come true, a health-conscious mom's nightmare.

If my cupboards were full of junk food, it would vanish, with no help from mice. We have our moments of abandon—Halloween, I've learned, is inescapable without a religious conversion—but most of the time my kids get other treats they've come to love. Few delicacies compare with a yellow-pear tomato, delicately sun-warmed and sugary, right off the vine. When I send the kids out to pick berries or fruit, I have to specify that at least *some* are supposed to go in the bucket. My younger daughter adores eating small, raw green beans straight off the garden trellis; I thought she was nuts till I tried them myself.

The soreness in my hamstrings at the end of a hard day of planting or hoeing feels good in a way that I can hardly explain—except to another gardener, who will know exactly the sweet ache I mean. My children seem to know it, too, and sleep best on those nights. I've found the deepest kind of physical satisfaction in giving my body's muscles, senses, and attentiveness over to the purpose for which they were originally designed: the industry of feeding that body and keeping it alive. I suspect that most human bodies have fallen into such remove from that original effort, we've precipitated an existential crisis that requires things like shopping, overeating, and adrenaline-rush movies to sate that particular body hunger.

And so I hope our family's efforts at self-provision will not just 40 improve the health and habitat of my children but also offer a life that's good for them, and knowledge they need. I wish all children could be taught the basics of agriculture in school along with math and English literature, because it's surely as important a subject as these. Most adults my age couldn't pass a simple test on what foods are grown in their home counties and what month they come into maturity. In just two generations we've passed from a time when people almost never ate a fruit out of season to a near-universal ignorance of what seasons mean. One icy winter I visited a friend in Manhattan who described the sumptuous meal she was making for us, including fresh raspberries. "Raspberries won't grow in the tropics," I mused. "And they sure don't keep. So where would they come from in the dead of winter?" Without blinking she answered, "Zabar's!"[2]

[2]Specialty grocery store on Manhattan's Upper West Side.

Apparently the guys running the show don't know much about agriculture, either, because the strategy of our nation is to run on a collision course with the possibility of being able to feed ourselves decently (or at all) in twenty years' time. I can't see how any animal could be this stupid; surely it's happening only because humans no longer believe food comes from dirt. Well, it does. Farmers are not just guys in overalls, part of the charming scenery of yesteryear; they are the technicians who know how to get teensy little seeds to turn into the stuff that comprises everything, and I mean *everything*, we eat. Is anybody paying attention? For every farm that's turned over to lawns and housing developments, a farmer is sent to work at the Nissan plant or the Kmart checkout line. What's lost with that career move is specific knowledge of how to gain food from a particular soil type, in a particular climate—wisdom that took generations to grow.

I want to protect my kids against a dangerous ignorance of what sustains them. When they help me dig and hoe the garden, plant corn and beans, later on pick them, and later still preserve the harvest's end, compost our scraps, and then turn that compost back into the garden plot the following spring, they are learning important skills for living and maintaining life. I have also observed that they appreciate feeling useful. In fact, nearly all the kids I've ever worked with on gardening projects get passionate about putting seeds in the ground, to the point of earnest territoriality.

"Now," I ask them when we're finished, "what will you do if you see somebody over here tromping around or riding a bike over your seedbeds?"

"*We'll tell them to get outta our vegables!*" shouted my most recent batch of five-year-old recruits to this plot of mine for improving the world one *vegable* at a time.

Maria Montessori[3] was one of the first child advocates to preach the wisdom of allowing children to help themselves and others, thereby learning to feel competent and self-assured. Most of the teachers and parents I know agree, and they organize classrooms and homes that

[3]Italian physician, educator, and humanitarian (1870–1952), best known for her revolutionary philosophy of education, especially for very young children.

promote this. But in modern times it's not easy to construct opportunities for kids to feel very useful. They can pick up their toys or take out the trash or walk the dog, but all of these things have an abstract utility. How useful is it to help take care of a dog whose main purpose, as far as they can see, is to be taken care of?

Growing food for the family's table is concretely useful. Nobody needs to explain how a potato helps the family. Bringing in a basket of eggs and announcing, "Attention, everybody: FREE BREAKFAST" is a taste of breadwinning that most kids can attain only in make-believe. I'm lucky I could help make my daughter's dream come true. My own wish is for world enough and time that every child might have this: the chance to count some chickens before they hatch.

STUDY QUESTIONS

1. Kingsolver's essay contains both NARRATIVE and ARGUMENT. Mark the sections that are primarily narrative and those that are primarily argument. How do these sections work together to create the case for eating locally and organically?

2. Do you find Kingsolver's argument about the benefits of self-provisioning effective? Why or why not?

3. When writing about Lily's chickens, Kingsolver often puts words in the chickens' mouths, imagining what they might be thinking or wish to say. Do you find this form of anthropomorphism effective? Why?

4. *For Writing.* Write a five- to seven-page essay in which you make an argument somehow related to the production and consumption of food. Like Kingsolver, include narrative to support your argument.

TERESA LUST { *The Same Old Stuffing*

TERESA LUST (b. 1964) grew up in Washington State, where she learned to cook from her mother. After earning a degree in biology, she took up cooking as a profession and has worked in restaurants in Washington State, California, and New England. Lust says that she draws from her heritage—her mother's Italian family and her father's German background—in writing about food and cooking.

In "The Same Old Stuffing," from her essay collection *Pass the Polenta* (1998), Lust discusses her mother's practice of stuffing the Thanksgiving turkey with two kinds of stuffing: one made from Lust's paternal grandmother's recipe, the other based on a recipe from her Italian maternal grandmother. In describing this process, she shows the ways traditions begin, are sometimes broken, then become "time honored." Such traditions, she observes, "need not concern themselves with balance, or daily nutritional requirements, or even historical accuracy." As you read, observe how the author uses family anecdotes, history, and descriptive recipes to weave her own experiences into a much broader history of an American holiday.

BEFORE YOU SET OUT TO revamp your Thanksgiving meal, it pays to consider all the repercussions. Just because the editors of the glossy food magazines have grown weary of the same old turkey and fixings, and even though they are absolutely giddy with excitement over the smoked quail, the spicy black bean stuffing, and the sun-dried tomato and arugula gratin they have in store for this year's feast, it does not mean that everyone will welcome innovation at the Thanksgiving table. Quite the contrary. All some people really want is the tried and true. Some people have grown quite fond of their annual mix of turkey and trimmings, each and every dish, and they do not consider it an onerous task to repeat the meal from one year to the next. They gain comfort from the familiarity and the ritual of it all; any tampering with the menu, no matter how minor or well intentioned, only serves to make them feel shortchanged.

This fact my mother discovered to her dismay when she tried out a little something at our own Thanksgiving meal. For years before anyone realized it had become a tradition, she roasted our holiday turkey with two types of stuffing inside it. She filled the bird's main cavity with my paternal grandmother's sage-and-onion dressing. This quintessential American farmhouse preparation was a genuine family heirloom, as Nana had learned to make it at her own mother's side. And for the bird's neck cavity, my mom fixed what you could call an Italian-American hybrid stuffing. Although this filling was not authentically Italian, it was a recipe from my mother's family, and it bespoke her immigrant heritage with its classic Mediterranean combination of sausage, spinach, raisins, and nuts.

Then one autumn as the holiday loomed near, my mom found herself contemplating our annual Thanksgiving spread. She saw it suddenly in a new and somewhat bothersome light. What had seemed a skillful act of diplomacy all these years, this bringing together of two family traditions inside one bird, why, it now smacked to her of excess. How the fact had escaped her for so long, she did not know, for she did not go for over-indulgence when it came to family meals. My mother was accommodating, don't misunderstand me. She was a mom who once finished up a marathon session of Dr. Seuss books with a breakfast of green eggs and ham at the behest of her four daughters. Still, she made us eat our peas, and she said things like, "The day your papa starts raising cows that don't come with livers is the day I'll quit serving liver and onions for dinner. Now eat up." Yes, she knew where to draw the line.

What suddenly struck my mother as disturbing was not a matter of gluttony or expense or grams of fat, but of balance. What with the mashed potatoes, the baked yams, the penny rolls, and two types of stuffing, there was altogether too much starch on the plate. Starch, starch, starch. The redundancy of it became an offense that the English teacher in her could no longer abide. Of an instant, the solution became clear: two stuffings were one stuffing too many. One of them would have to go.

So she said to my father, "Jim, which stuffing do you prefer at 5 Thanksgiving?"

He replied, "My mother's sage-and-onion dressing, of course. It's the stuffing of my youth. It's the heart of the Thanksgiving meal. By God, it's a national tradition, that stuffing, and I can't even imagine the holiday without it."

This was not the response my mother had in mind. Nana's sage-and-onion dressing had been her candidate for dismissal, because naturally, she preferred her family's stuffing, the one with the Italian touch of sausage, spinach, and raisins. She saw my father's point, though. We celebrated the holiday with his side of the family, and she had them to bear in mind. The children would be too preoccupied with the mashed potatoes to care a whit one way or the other about the stuffing, but her in-laws would feel deprived, no doubt, if Nana's dish didn't grace the table. And she had to admit that the sage-and-onion version was more in keeping with the all-American spirit of the holiday. It was more faithful, she assumed, to history. Good heavens, even school-children knew that sage-and-onion dressing appeared on the Pilgrims' rough-hewn banquet table, right alongside the spit-roasted wild turkey, the hearth-braised sweet potatoes, the cranberry sauce, and the pumpkin pie.

I must admit I envisioned such a meal, just as I pictured Miles Standish brandishing a kitchen knife and gallantly carving the turkey roast while he gazed deep into the limpid eyes of Priscilla Mullens.[1] But there is no record of stuffing—sage-and-onion or otherwise—bedecking the table at the Pilgrims' first thanksgiving, which it turns

---

[1] Priscilla Alden Mullins (ca. 1602–85) arrived in America on the *Mayflower*. Her relationship with Myles Standish (ca. 1584–1656) may have been a legend but was immortalized in the poem "The Courtship of Miles Standish," by one of her descendants, Henry Wadsworth Longfellow (1807–82).

out was not a somber meal, but a frolicsome affair of hunting, games, and wine which lasted three days. For that matter, there isn't even any specific mention of turkeys having been served, though one colonist wrote of an abundance of fowl at the event, and most scholars feel safe in assuming this bounty included a few turkeys. All anyone knows for certain is that the Mayflower folks cooked up five deer, oysters, cod, eel, corn bread, goose, watercress, leeks, berries, and plums. Pumpkins made an appearance, too, but no one bothered to record just how they were cooked. They certainly were not baked in a pie crust, though, for the wheat crop had failed and the ship's supply of flour had long since run out.

The traditional meal as we know it dates back not to the solemn, high-collared Pilgrims, nor even to Colonial times, but to home cooks of the nineteenth century. Not until this era did the idea of an annual day of thanksgiving first take hold. The driving force behind the holiday was New Englander Sarah Josepha Hale (whose legacy also includes the nursery rhyme "Mary Had a Little Lamb"). As editor of the popular magazine *Godey's Lady's Book*, she promoted the holiday for nearly twenty years within the periodical's pages. She wrote letters annually to the state governors and to the president, and one by one the states gradually took up the idea. Finally, Abraham Lincoln, desperate for any means to promote unity in the war-ravaged country, declared the first national Thanksgiving in 1863.

And what did the mistress of the house serve up at this new holiday meal? Her standard company fare for autumn, of course: roast turkey with cranberry sauce, scalloped and mashed potatoes, candied sweet potatoes, braised turnips, creamed onions, cranberry sauce, mince pie, pumpkin pie—the menu has endured remarkably unchanged. And yes, it was standard procedure then to roast the turkey with a stuffing.

The actual practice of filling up a bird's cavity dates back to antiquity; the space made a handy cooking vessel for families who all too often owned only one pot. Recipes have varied over the millennia. The cookbook attributed to the Roman gastronome Apicius gives a formula that includes ground meat, chopped brains, couscous, pine nuts, lovage, and ginger; other than the brains, it sounds like something right out of a trendy contemporary cookbook. English cooks during the Middle Ages favored heavily spiced and honeyed productions based on pieces of offal that today would make our rarefied stomachs churn. Nineteenth-century American cooks went on stuffing birds, no matter how many pots and pans they had on hand in the kitchen, and recipes much like Nana's sage-and-onion dressing were a beloved part of many an early Thanksgiving repast.

No less dear, though, or popular, or traditional, were a number of other variations. Homemakers in the corn-growing South who went to stuff a turkey favored cornbread in their recipes. Along the eastern seaboard, they tucked in dozens of nectar-sweet shucked oysters, while across the country as far north as the chestnut tree once grew, they featured loads of tender chestnuts in their fillings. And many cooks treasured recipes that called for ground meat, dried fruits, autumn greens, and shelled nuts—the very products of the fall harvest upon which my mother's family recipe was based, so she need not have dismissed her version as unconventional so hastily.

The genteel ladies of the last century would have viewed my mother's dilemma not as a surplus of starch at the meal, but as a paucity of meats. They were impassioned carnivores, these American predecessors of ours, and one meager turkey would have seemed woefully inadequate at a meal showcasing the prodigious bounty of the land. Pull out the stops, Darlene, I can all but hear them tell her. Along with the requisite turkey, they decorated their tables with a chicken pie, a joint of beef, a roast goose, if the budget would allow. Certainly these additional viands would serve to put my mother's menu back on kilter.

I'm sure, too, that at least one of these women would have felt bound by duty to draw my mother aside and whisper that she really ought to call her preparation *dressing* and not *stuffing.* The word "stuffing" has been in use for centuries. Sir Thomas Elyot's *Dictionary* of 1538 uses it as a synonym for "forcemeat," defined as "that wherewith any foule is crammed." Sir Thomas obviously wasn't much of a cook, or he would have known that cramming a fowl isn't such a great idea, for the filling expands during the roasting, and it can burst out at the seams if it is packed too tightly. At any rate, all this stuffing and forcing and cramming proved simply too much for the delicate sensibilities of the

Victorian age, and the more discreet term "dressing" came into fashion. Today, schoolmarmish cookbooks often wag a finger and insist that when it is on the inside of the bird it is stuffing, and when it is baked in a separate dish, it's dressing. In reality, this does not play out. If Grandma calls her dish stuffing, then stuffing it is, regardless of its location inside or alongside the bird. Same goes for Aunt Pearl's dressing, no matter where she puts it.

Had my mother sought the counsel of Mrs. Sarah Josepha Hale or her contemporaries, then, she might have spared herself some anxiety. For although she had resolved herself to her decision, the idea of forgoing her family recipe did not rest easy with her. The days wore on and she grew positively disgruntled. Then one brisk, gray morning with two weeks yet to go before Thanksgiving, she found herself pushing her cart down the butcher's aisle at the supermarket when inspiration struck. Who ever said holiday recipes were for holidays, and holidays only? Who? She need not go without her annual dose of her family's stuffing after all. So she hoisted a fresh turkey into the cart, made a few other spur-of-the-moment additions to her shopping list, and went home and set to work.

She pulled her big frying pan out of the cupboard, set it over a low flame on the stove-top, melted half a stick of butter in it, then crumbled in three-quarters of a pound of bulk pork sausage. After the meat began to brown, she stirred in a diced onion, a couple of cloves of pressed garlic, a few stalks of cut-up celery, and a cup or so of sliced button mushrooms. These she let simmer gently until the onions were translucent. She added a large container of the chopped garden spinach she had blanched and frozen last spring, heated it through, then scraped the contents of the pan into a large ceramic bowl. When the mixture cooled to room temperature she sliced a stale loaf of French bread into cubes—enough to make about four cups—then added the bread to the bowl along with a couple of ample handfuls of raisins, sliced almonds, and freshly grated Parmesan cheese—a good half cup of each. She seasoned the stuffing with salt, black pepper, and generous pinches of oregano and rosemary, then drizzled in a glass of white wine. Using her hands, she combined all the ingredients thoroughly, then put a finger to her tongue. A pinch more salt and that would do it. Finally, she spooned the stuffing into the bird, trussed it up, and put it in the oven to roast for the rest of the afternoon.

Incidentally, my mother is quite an accomplished seamstress. She could sew bound buttonholes on a turkey if she wanted to. But she agrees with me that trussing need not be the intricate knit-one-purl-two operation that many cookbooks describe. Such elaborate needlework lingers from the days of the kitchen hearth-fire, when trussing was done to keep the drumsticks and wings from dangling in the flames as the bird turned on a spit. It now functions as a stuffy, old guard test of a cook's dexterity—yes, but can she truss a turkey? By the turn of this century, the massive iron kitchen range had become a standard feature in the American home, and oven roasting rendered unnecessary all the knotting and stitching and battening down. Trussing now primarily serves to keep the stuffing in place, and to give the bird a demure appearance, its ankles politely crossed, when it arrives at the table. Folding back the wings and tying the drumsticks together with kitchen twine usually make for ample treatment.

As my mom put the neck and giblets into a stock-pot on the stove for gravy, she decided a side dish of mashed potatoes would be just the accompaniment to round out the meal. Then she discovered she had a few sweet potatoes in the bin under the kitchen sink, and she thought, now wouldn't those be nice, too, roasted with a little butter, ginger, and brown sugar? And when she remembered the tiny boiling onions that had been rolling around in the refrigerator's bottom drawer, she decided she might as well bake them up au gratin with some bread crumbs and cream.

The turkey spittered and spattered away in the oven, filling every nook in the house with its buttery, winter-holiday scent, and the next thing my mom knew, she was rolling out the crust for a pumpkin pie. My father arrived home from work, draped his overcoat across the banister, and walked into the kitchen just in time to see her plopping the cranberry sauce out of the can. She placed it on the table in a sterling silver dish, its ridged imprints still intact and its jellied body quivering gloriously—God bless those folks at Ocean Spray, they were always a part of our turkey dinners, too. She turned to my father and said, "Dinner's almost ready."

My mom watched as her family gathered around the table and 20
enjoyed a complete turkey feast on that evening in early November.
After the meal, my father stretched back in his chair and folded his
hands behind his head. He'd always thought it a shame, he said, a
needless deprivation, that Americans ate roast turkey only once a year
at Thanksgiving. This fine dinner just proved his point. What a treat,
yes, what a treat. But the family's pleasure that night was merely an
added perk for my mother, as she had prepared the meal for herself,
only for herself, and she was feeling deeply satisfied.

When the official holiday finally arrived, my mother made good on
her vow and let Nana's sage-and-onion dressing preside at the evening
meal. Out came the frying pan, and she started to sauté two chopped
onions and four thinly sliced stalks of celery, including the leaves, in a
stick of butter. After a moment's thought, she added two plump cloves
of minced garlic to the simmering pan. She couldn't resist. She knew
Nana thought her a bit heavy-handed in the garlic department, but so
what, it was her kitchen.

When the vegetables were limp and fragrant, she pulled the pan
from the heat and set it aside to cool. She put the mixture into a bowl
along with eight cups of firm, stale bread cubes, a generous spoonful
of dried sage, a healthy handful of chopped fresh parsley, some salt
and pepper, and a pinch of nutmeg. She gave these ingredients a light
mixing, drizzled in enough broth to make the filling hold together
when she squeezed a handful of it between her fingers—three-quarters
of a cup, maybe a bit more—then tossed the dressing together again
lightly before she spooned it into the Thanksgiving bird.

That evening Nana arrived with her sweet pickles and her three
pies—apple, pumpkin, mincemeat. Cousins poured into the house
toting covered casserole dishes, an uncle walked through the door,
then an aunt. We soon sat down around two tables to dine, our plates
heaped to the angle of repose. Amid the clanking of cutlery and the
giggling and guffawing, and the festive bustle, my father paused. His
fork pierced a juicy slice of dark thigh meat and his knife was poised
in midstroke. He looked down intently and his eyes circled clock-
wise, studying the contents of his plate. He craned his neck and took
an inventory of the platters and bowls laid out on the buffet counter

across the room. "Darlene," he said, "this is some spread we have here, don't get me wrong. But you know what's missing is that other stuffing you make. The one we had the other day with the cornucopia of raisins and nuts and such."

My mom nearly dropped her fork. "But you told me you preferred your mother's dressing."

He looked back down at the turkey and trimmings before him. "Well, 25 yes, but that doesn't mean I don't prefer yours, too. It just doesn't seem like a proper Thanksgiving without that second stuffing on the table. Don't you agree?"

What he meant, of course, was that my mom's dish had to turn up missing before he understood just what a part of the celebration it had become. So the year the turkey had only one stuffing was the year that both recipes became permanent fixtures on my mother's Thanksgiving menu. When time-honored traditions get their start while you're not looking, it seems, they need not concern themselves with balance, or daily nutritional requirements, or even historical accuracy. For such rituals rise up out of memories, and memories are not subject to hard facts. They are not interested in making room for change.

STUDY QUESTIONS

1. How did the traditional Thanksgiving meal many Americans eat each year develop?

2. Lust's PERSONAL ESSAY includes MEMOIR, PROCESS ANALYSIS, and references to history. Which parts do you find most effective? Why?

3. How does she tie these forms of writing together in one essay? Look closely at her use of TRANSITIONS. Which ones work best? Why?

4. What words does Lust use to DESCRIBE the foods she mentions? What synonyms for the word *food*? What is the effect of these word choices on you as a reader?

5. *For Writing.* Think about a tradition in your family—perhaps a particular dish a relative prepares for a certain holiday meal each year, or some other way of celebrating that seems unique to your family. Research the origins of that tradition by interviewing members of your family. Then write a personal essay that shows how that tradition came to be.

MARCUS SAMUELSSON { *My African Mother*

Marcus Samuelsson (b. 1970) is a chef, restaurant owner, and writer of nonfiction—cookbooks and a memoir. When Samuelsson was a toddler in Ethiopia, where he was born, his mother died of tuberculosis; he was adopted by a family in Sweden. He now lives in New York. Samuelsson has appeared as a judge on television cooking shows such as *Top Chef*, *Iron Chef America*, and *Chopped*; he has also appeared as a contestant on cooking shows.

"My African Mother" is the first chapter of Samuelsson's 2012 memoir *Yes, Chef*. In this selection, he acknowledges that he has never seen a photograph of his mother and that when he asks his Ethiopian relatives about her, they speak in generalities. What he does know about his mother is what she ate and what she fed him. He pieces together what he "knows" of his mother not through memory (for he was only three when she died) but through what he sees when he looks in the mirror and what he knows of other African women from the village where he was born. As you read this excerpt, notice the way Samuelsson structures it using the known and the unknown.

I HAVE NEVER SEEN A picture of my mother.

I have traveled to her homeland, dozens of times. I have met her brothers and sisters. I have found my birth father and eight half brothers and sisters I didn't know I had. I have met my mother's relatives in Ethiopia, but when I ask them to describe my mother, they throw out generalities. "She was nice," they tell me. "She was pretty." "She was smart." *Nice, pretty, smart.* The words seem meaningless, except the last is a clue because even today, in rural Ethiopia, girls are not encouraged to go to school. That my mother was intelligent rings true because I know she had to be shrewd to save the lives of myself and my sister, which is what she did, in the most mysterious and miraculous of ways.

My mother's family never owned a photograph of her, which tells you everything you need to know about where I'm from and what the world was like for the people who gave me life. In 1972, in the United States, Polaroid introduced its most popular instant camera. In 1972, the year my mother died, an Ethiopian woman could go her whole life without having her picture taken—especially if, as was the case with my mother, her life was not long.

I have never seen a picture of my mother, but I know how she cooked. For me, my mother is *berbere*, an Ethiopian spice mixture. You use it on everything, from lamb to chicken to roasted peanuts. It's our salt and pepper. I know she cooked with it because it's in the DNA of every Ethiopian mother. Right now, if I could, I would lead you to the red tin in my kitchen, one of dozens I keep by the stove in my apartment in Harlem, filled with my own blend and marked with blue electrical tape and my own illegible scrawl. I would reach into this tin and grab a handful of the red-orange powder, and hold it up to your nose so you could smell the garlic, the ginger, the sundried chili.

My mother didn't have a lot of money so she fed us *shiro.* It's a chick- 5 pea flour you boil, kind of like polenta. You pour it into hot water and add butter, onions, and *berbere.* You simmer it for about forty-five minutes, until it's the consistency of hummus, and then you eat it with injera, a sour, rich bread made from a grain called teff. I know this is what she fed us because this is what poor people eat in Ethiopia. My mother carried the chickpea powder in her pocket or bag. That way, all she needed to make dinner was water and fire. Injera is also por- table, so it is never wasted. If you don't finish it, you leave it outside and let it dry in the sun. Then you eat it like chips.

In Meki, the small farming village where I'm from, there are no roads. We are actually from an even smaller village than Meki, called Abrugandana, that does not exist on most maps. You go to Meki, take a right in the middle of nowhere, walk about five miles, and that is where we are from.

I know my mother was not taller than five feet, two inches, but I also know she was not delicate. Those country women in Ethiopia are strong because they walk everywhere. I know her body because I know those women. When I go there now, I stare at the young mothers to the point of being impolite. I stare at those young women and their children and it's like watching a home movie that does not exist of my childhood. Each woman has a kid, who might well be me, on her back, and the fingers of her right hand are interlocked with another slightly older kid, and that kid is like my sister. The woman has her food and wares in her bag, which is slung across her chest and rests on her hip. The older kid is holding a bucket of water on her shoulders, a bucket that's almost as heavy as she is. That's how strong that child is.

Women like my mother don't wear shoes. They don't have shoes. My mother, sister, and I would walk the Sidama savannah for four hours a day, to and from her job selling crafts in the market. Before three p.m. it would be too hot to walk, so we would rest under a tree and gather our strength and wait for the sun to set. After eight p.m. it was dark and there were new threats—animals that would see a baby like me as supper and dangerous men who might see my mother as another kind of victim.

I have never seen a picture of my mother, but I know her features because I have seen them staring back at me in the mirror my entire life. I know she had a cross somewhere near her face. It was a henna tattoo of a cross, henna taking the place of the jewelry she could not afford or even dream of having. There was also an Orthodox cross somewhere on the upper part of my mother's body, maybe on her neck, maybe on her chest, near her heart. She had put it there to show that she was a woman of faith. She was an Orthodox Ethiopian Christian, which is very similar to being Catholic.

I don't remember my mother's voice, but I know she spoke two languages. In *The Souls of Black Folk*, W. E. B. DuBois spoke of the double consciousness that African Americans are born into, the need to be able to live in both the black world and the white world. But that double consciousness is not limited to African Americans. My mother was born into it, too. Her tribe was a minority in that section of Ethiopia and it was essential to her survival that she spoke both the language of her village, Amhara, and the language of the greater outside community, which is Oromo. She was cautious and when she left the Amharic village, she flipped that switch. She not only spoke Oromo, she spoke it with a native accent.

I don't know my mother's face, but I sometimes think I remember the sound of her breath. I was two when a tuberculosis epidemic hit Ethiopia. My mother was sick, I was sick, and my sister Fantaye was doing only slightly better than the two of us. We were all coughing up blood and my mother had seen enough in her young life to measure the ravages of that disease. She knew she had to do something. She put me on her back. It was all coming at her now: the fatigue and the fever; pieces of her lung splintering and mixing with her throw-up; the calcifications on her bones, where the disease had already spread. She and Fantaye walked more than seventy-five miles, my mother carrying me the whole way, under a hot sun, from our village to the hospital in Addis Ababa to get help. I don't know how many days they walked, or how sick my mother was by the time she got there. But I do know that when we arrived, there were thousands of people standing in the street, sick and dying, awaiting care. I do not know how my mother managed to get us through those lines and into that hospital. I do know that she never left that hospital and that perhaps it was only by the miracle of that henna cross that Fantaye and I got out alive.

●　○　●

Today, in the dead of night when I should be sleeping, I sometimes imagine the breath of the woman who not only gave me life, but delivered me from death. I sometimes reach into that tin by my stove and take a handful of *berbere,* sift it through my fingers, and toss it into the pan. I watch my wife cook and I imagine that I can see my mother's hands. I have taught myself the recipes of my mother's people because those foods are for me, as a chef, the easiest connection to the mysteries of who my mother was. Her identity remains stubbornly shrouded in the past, so I feed myself and the people I love the food that she made. But I cannot see her face.

STUDY QUESTIONS

1. In this MEMOIR, Samuelsson reflects on what he knows and does not know about his mother. Make two lists: What does he know? What does he not know?

2. Samuelsson uses a METAPHOR, writing, "For me, my mother is *berbere*, an Ethiopian spice mixture" (paragraph 4). He develops this metaphor into a SYMBOL. Why do you think Samuelsson sees his mother as a spice mixture? Why is this significant?

3. Why does Samuelsson use the food of his native Ethiopia as a vehicle for trying to remember his mother? In what other ways might someone structure a memoir about someone or something he or she knows little about?

4. *For Writing.* Brainstorm a list of things you know about someone important in your life. Brainstorm another list of things you do not know about that person. Write a four- to five-page memoir structured by what you know and do not know.

MARK STRAND { *Pot Roast*

MARK STRAND (b. 1934) was born in Canada and has lived many places
in the United States, as well as in South America and Central America.
Currently, he teaches English and comparative literature at Columbia
University. A poet, translator, art critic, and writer of nonfiction, Strand
earned his BA from Antioch College, a BFA in art from Yale, and an MA
from the University of Iowa, where he attended the Iowa Writers'
Workshop. A prolific writer, Strand has written more than twenty
books, edited several anthologies, and published a number of
translations.

"Pot Roast" appeared in Strand's volume of poetry *The Late Hour*
in 1978. In this poem, the speaker eats pot roast while staring out a
window. The poem at first appears gloomy, since the speaker mentions seeing "no living thing" and observes that 'there is little / to love
or to praise," yet the memories of the pleasure of eating pot roast as a
child lighten the tone as the poem progresses. Notice the way the
speaker meditates on the sensory power of food and its link to
memory.

I gaze upon the roast,
that is sliced and laid out
on my plate,
and over it

I spoon the juices 5
of carrot and onion.
And for once I do not regret
the passage of time.

I sit by a window
that looks 10
on the soot-stained brick of buildings
and do not care that I see
no living thing—not a bird,
not a branch in bloom,
not a soul moving 15
in the rooms
behind the dark panes.
These days when there is little
to love or to praise
one could do worse 20
than yield
to the power of food.
So I bend

to inhale
the steam that rises 25
from my plate, and I think
of the first time
I tasted a roast
like this.
It was years ago 30
in Seabright,
Nova Scotia;
my mother leaned
over my dish and filled it
and when I finished 35
filled it again.
I remember the gravy,
its odor of garlic and celery,

and sopping it up
with pieces of bread.   40

And now
I taste it again.
The meat of memory.
The meat of no change.
I raise my fork in praise,   45
and I eat.

STUDY QUESTIONS

1. Strand uses the word "praise" twice in this poem. In the last stanza, what is the speaker praising? Why do you think he finds little to praise earlier in the poem?

2. Most poets try to use strong, active verbs in their poetry. Make a list of verbs Strand uses. Which ones are most effective in showing the TONE of the poem? Why?

3. *For Writing.* Is there a scent or taste that brings you back to your childhood? Make a list of sensory images or experiences you link to particular memories, then write a poem or an essay that shows the link between that image/experience and a memory. Use strong verbs, just as Strand does.

FRANCINE WEINBERG

RICHARD BULLOCK　　{　*Glossary*

W. W. NORTON

ABSTRACT A genre of writing that summarizes a book, an article, or a paper, usually in 100–200 words. Authors in some academic fields must provide, at the top of a report submitted for publication, an abstract of its content. The abstract may then appear in a journal of abstracts, such as *Psychological Abstracts*. An *informative abstract* summarizes a complete report; a briefer *descriptive abstract* works more as a teaser; a stand-alone *proposal abstract* (also called a **topic proposal**) requests permission to conduct research, write on a topic, or present a report at a scholarly conference. Key Features: **summary** of basic information • objective description • brevity.

ACTION VERB A **verb** that expresses a physical or mental action (*jump, consider*).

ACTIVE VOICE A grammatical construction in which the subject or agent of the action is also its grammatical subject: *The boy hit the baseball. See also* **passive voice**.

AD HOMINEM **ARGUMENT** A logical **fallacy** that attacks someone's character rather than addressing the issues.

ADJECTIVE A **modifier** that describes a **noun** or **pronoun** (*a challenging task, a cloudless blue sky*).

ADVERB A **modifier** that tells more about a **verb** (*speak loudly*), an **adjective** (*extremely loud*), another adverb (*very loudly*), or a whole **clause** (*Sometimes you need to speak loudly*).

ALLEGORY An extended **metaphor**, in which one thing (usually nonrational, abstract, religious) is implicitly spoken of in terms of something concrete. In an allegory, the comparison is expressed in an entire work or large portion of a work.

ANALYSIS A **genre** of writing that methodically examines a topic or text by breaking it into its parts and noting how they work in relation to one another.

ANECDOTES Brief **narratives** used to illustrate a point.

ANNOTATED BIBLIOGRAPHY A **genre** of writing that gives an overview of the published research and scholarship on a topic. Each entry includes complete publication information and a **summary** or an **abstract** for each source. A *descriptive annotation* summarizes the content of a source without commenting on its value; an *evaluative annotation* gives an opinion about the source along with a description of it. Key Features: statement of the scope • complete bibliographic information • relevant commentary • consistent presentation.

APA STYLE A system of documenting sources used in the social sciences. APA stands for the American Psychological Association. *See also* **documentation**.

APPENDIX A section at the end of a written work for supplementary material that would be distracting in the main part of the text.

APPLICATION LETTERS Letters written to apply for jobs or other opportunities. *See also* **résumés**. Key Features: succinct indication of qualifications • reasonable and pleasing **tone** • conventional, businesslike form.

ARGUING A **strategy** that can be used in any kind of writing to support a **claim** with **reasons** and **evidence**.

ARGUMENT, ARGUMENTATIVE ESSAY A **genre** of writing that uses **reasons** and **evidence** to support a **claim** or **position** and, sometimes, to persuade an **audience** to accept that position.

Key Features: clear and arguable position • necessary background • good reasons • convincing support for each reason • appeal to readers' values • trustworthy **tone** • careful consideration of other positions.

ARTICLE The word *a, an,* or *the,* used to indicate that a **noun** is indefinite (*a, an*) or definite (*the*).

AUDIENCE Those to whom a text is directed—the people who read, listen to, or view the text. Audience is a key part of every text's **rhetorical situation**.

AUTHORITIES People or texts that are cited as support for a writer's **argument**. A structural engineer may be quoted as an authority on bridge construction, for example. *Authority* also refers to a quality conveyed by a writer who is knowledgeable about his or her subject.

BANDWAGON APPEAL A logical **fallacy** that argues for a thought or an action solely because others support it.

BEGGING THE QUESTION A logical **fallacy** that goes in a circle, assuming as a given what the writer is trying to prove.

BILDUNGSROMAN A novel that depicts the growth and development of a **character** and the character's self-understanding.

BLOCK QUOTATION In a written work, long **quotations** are set off indented and without quotation marks. In **MLA style:** set off text more than four typed lines, indented ten spaces (or one inch) from the left margin. In **APA style:** set off quotes of forty or more words, indented five spaces (or half an inch) from the left margin. *See also* **quotation.**

BLOG From *Web log*, a Web site with frequent postings by its authors, links to other sites, and comments posted by readers. Blogs present personal opinion and so should not be considered authoritative sources.

CAUSE AND EFFECT A **strategy** for analyzing why something occurred and/or what its consequences are. Sometimes cause and effect serves as the **organizing** principle for a whole text.

CBE STYLE A system of documenting sources in the sciences. CBE stands for the Council of Biology Editors. *See also* **documentation.**

CHARACTER (1) A fictional person who acts, appears, or is referred to in a work; (2) a combination of a person's qualities, especially moral qualities, so that such terms as "good" and "bad," "strong" and "weak," often apply.

CHARACTERIZATION The artistic presentation of a person in fiction or nonfiction. A term like "a good character" can, then, be ambiguous—it may mean that the character is virtuous or that he or she is well presented by the writer

regardless of his or her characteristics or moral qualities.

CHRONOLOGICAL ORDER A way of organizing text that proceeds from the beginning of an event to the end. Reverse chronological order proceeds in the other direction, from the end to the beginning. *See also* **in medias res.**

CITATION In a text, the act of crediting information from a source. A citation and its corresponding parenthetical **documentation** or footnote or endnote provide minimal information about the source, and complete bibliographic information appears in a list of **works cited** or **references** at the end of the text.

CLAIM A statement that asserts a belief or position. In an **argument,** a claim needs to be stated in a **thesis** or clearly implied, and requires support with **reasons** and **evidence.**

CLASSIFY AND DIVIDE, CLASSIFICATION AND DIVISION A **strategy** that either groups (classifies) numerous individual items by their similarities (for example, classifying cereal, bread, butter, chicken, cheese, ice cream, eggs, and oil as carbohydrates, proteins, and fats) or breaks (divides) one large category into smaller categories (for example, dividing food into carbohydrates, proteins, and fats). Sometimes classification and/or division serves as the **organizing** principle for a whole text.

CLAUSE A group of words that consists of at least a subject and a predicate; a clause may be either independent or subordinate.

CLIMAX The point at which the action stops rising and begins falling or reversing.

CLUSTERING A process for generating ideas and text, in which a writer visually connects thoughts by jotting them down and drawing lines between related items.

COHERENCE The quality that allows an audience to follow a text's meaning and to *see* the connections among ideas, sentences, and paragraphs. Elements that can help to achieve coherence include the title, a clearly stated or implied thesis, topic sentences, an easy-to-follow organization with clear transitions, and parallelism among comparable ideas.

COLLABORATION The process of working with others.

COMMA SPLICE Two or more independent clauses joined by only a comma: *I live free, I love life.*

COMMON GROUND Shared values. Writers build common ground with audiences by acknowledging others' points of view, seeking areas of compromise, and using language that includes, rather than excludes, those they aim to reach.

COMPARE AND CONTRAST, COMPARISON AND CONTRAST A strategy that highlights the similarities and differences between items. Using the *block method* of comparison and contrast, a writer discusses all the points about one item and then all the same points about the next item; using the *point-by-point method*, a writer discusses one point for both items before going on to discuss the next point for both items, and so on. Sometimes comparison and/or contrast serves as the organizing principle for a whole text.

COMPLEMENT A noun, noun phrase, pronoun, or adjective that modifies either the subject or the direct object of a sentence. A subject complement follows a linking verb and tells more about the subject: *She is a good speaker. She is eloquent.* An object complement describes or renames the direct object: *Critics called the movie a masterpiece. We found the movie enjoyable.*

CONFLICT A struggle between opposing forces, such as between two people, between a person and something in nature or society, or even between two drives, impulses, or parts of the self.

CONVINCE, CONVINCING In argument, to present evidence, usually in the form of facts and figures, in support of the writer's opinion. Convincing may differ from persuading in that convincing is designed to get the reader to agree while persuading is designed to get the reader to act.

COUNTERARGUMENT In **argument**, an alternative **position** or objections to the writer's position. The writer of an argument should not only acknowledge counterarguments but also, if at all possible, accept, accommodate, or refute each counterargument.

CREDIBILITY The sense of trustworthiness that a writer conveys through his or her text.

CRITERIA In an **evaluation**, the standards against which something is judged.

CUBING A **process** for generating ideas and text in which a writer looks at a topic in six ways—to **describe** it, to **compare** it to something else, to associate it with other things or **classify** it, to analyze it (*see* **analysis**), to apply it, and to argue for or against it (*see* **argument**).

DEDUCTION, DEDUCTIVE REASONING In **argument**, a method of drawing a conclusion in which the writer asserts that a thing is true based on general or universal premises (moving from the general to the specific): *Every virtue is laudable; kindness is a virtue; therefore kindness is laudable.*

DEFINE, DEFINITION A **strategy** that gets at the meaning of something. Three main kinds of definitions are the *formal definition*, which may iden-

tify the category that something belongs to and tell what distinguishes it from other things in that category: for example, defining a worm as an invertebrate (a category) with a long, rounded body and no appendages (distinguishing features); the *extended definition*, which, as its name suggests is longer: for example, a paragraph explaining where a worm fits in the animal kingdom and what its closest relatives are; and the *stipulative definition*, which gives the writer's particular use of a term: for example, using the term *worm* to refer to a kind of gummy candy. Sometimes definition serves as the **organizing** principle for a whole text.

DÉNOUEMENT The final part of a **plot**, in which the action is resolved.

DESCRIBE, DESCRIPTION A **strategy** that tells how something looks, sounds, smells, feels, or tastes. Effective description creates a clear **dominant impression** built from specific details. Description can be *objective, subjective,* or both. Sometimes description serves as the **organizing** principle for a whole text.

DESIGN The way a text is arranged and presented visually. Elements of design include typeface, color, illustration, layout, and white space. One component of a **rhetorical situation**, design plays an important part in reaching a text's **audience** and achieving its **purpose.**

DIALOGUE A strategy of adding people's own words to a text. A writer often uses dialogue to add detail and interest.

DICTION A writer's choice of words, particularly with regard to clarity, correctness, and/or effectiveness in writing.

DISCOVERY DRAFTING A process of drafting something quickly, mostly for the purpose of discovering what one wants to say.

DIVIDE, DIVISION *See* **classify and divide.**

DOCUMENTATION Publication information about the sources cited in a text. The documentation usually appears in an abbreviated form in parentheses at the point of **citation** or in an endnote or a footnote. Complete documentation usually appears as a list of **works cited** or **references** at the end of the text. Documentation styles vary by discipline. For example, Modern Language Association (**MLA**) style requires the author's complete first name if it appears in a source, whereas American Psychological Association (**APA**) and the Council of Biology Editors (**CBE**) style requires only the initial of the author's first name.

DOCUMENTED ESSAY A genre of writing in which the writer cites information drawn from other sources. Key Features: use of **primary** and/or **secondary** **sources** • **analysis** or **interpretation** • **documentation.**

DOMINANT IMPRESSION The overall effect created through specific details when a writer **describes** something.

DOMINO THEORY The theory that if one event is allowed to take place, a series of similar events will follow, as when a line of dominoes is placed on end close together, toppling one will cause the entire line to fall.

DRAFTING The **process** of putting words on paper or screen. Writers often write several drafts, **revising** each until they achieve their goal or reach a deadline. At that point, they submit a finished final draft.

EDITING The **process** of fine-tuning a text—examining each word, phrase, sentence, and paragraph—to be sure that the text is correct and precise and says exactly what the writer intends. *See also* **proofreading** and **revising.**

EITHER-OR ARGUMENT A logical **fallacy** that oversimplifies to suggest that only two possible **positions** exist on a complex issue. The fallacy is also known as a **false dilemma.**

ETHNOGRAPHY A **genre** of writing that uses **fieldwork**—interviewing and observing—to present a picture of a group of people. Key Features: focus on members of a specific group • observation over time in group's natural setting • close analysis of a few members.

ETHOS A mode of **persuasion** that appeals to the character, feelings, moral nature, or guiding beliefs of a person, group, or institution; in writing, ethos can refer to the attempt by the writer or speaker to demonstrate his or her credibility.

EVALUATION A **genre** of writing that makes a judgment about something— a source, poem, film, restaurant, whatever—based on certain **criteria**. Key Features: **description** of the subject • clearly defined criteria • knowledgeable discussion of the subject • balanced and fair assessment.

EVIDENCE The data you present to support your **reasons**. Such data may include statistics, calculations, **examples**, **anecdotes**, **quotations**, case studies, or anything else that will **convince** your reader that your reasons are compelling. Evidence should be sufficient (enough to show that the reasons have merit) and relevant (appropriate to the argument you're making).

EXAMPLE, EXEMPLIFICATION A **strategy** that uses examples to clarify or support a point.

EXPLAINING A PROCESS *See* **process analysis**.

EXPLETIVE A word such as *it* or *there* that stands in for information provided later in the sentence: *It was difficult to drive on the icy road. There is plenty of food in the refrigerator.*

EXPOSITION, EXPOSITORY (1) In literature, the first part of a plot, where background information is established; (2) in composition and rhetoric, a rhetorical **strategy** whose main purpose is to inform the reader about a subject through explanation, interpretation, clarification, or other means.

FABLE A **genre** of writing that employs a typically legendary story with a lesson to be learned by its **audience**. Key Features: animal characters or personified natural forces • an instructive **purpose** • ends with a moral (a short, easily remembered lesson).

FALLACY, LOGICAL Faulty reasoning that can mislead an **audience**. Fallacies include *ad hominem*, bandwagon appeal, begging the question, either-or argument (also called **false dilemma**), false analogy, faulty causality (also called *post hoc, ergo propter hoc*), hasty generalization, and slippery slope.

FALLING ACTION the fourth part of action in a classical **plot**, during which the **audience** sees the effects of the **conflict**.

FALSE ANALOGY A **fallacy** comparing things that do resemble each other but that are not alike in the most important respects.

FALSE DILEMMA *See* **either-or argument**.

FAULTY CAUSALITY *See* *post hoc, ergo propter hoc*.

FIELD RESEARCH, FIELDWORK The collection of firsthand data through observation, interviews, and questionnaires or surveys.

FLASHBACK In narrative (*see* narrate), an interruption of the main story in order to show an incident that occurred at an earlier time.

FORMAL WRITING Writing intended to be evaluated by someone such as an instructor or read by an audience expecting academic or businesslike argument and presentation. Formal writing should be carefully revised, edited, and proofread. *See also* informal writing.

FRAGMENT, SENTENCE A group of words that is capitalized and punctuated as a sentence but is not one, either because it lacks a subject, a verb, or both, or because it begins with a word that makes it a subordinate clause.

FRAME STORY A story that surrounds another story, often used as an introductory device or organizing principle.

FREEWRITING A process for generating ideas and text by writing continuously for several minutes without pausing to read what has been written.

FUSED SENTENCE Two or more independent clauses with no punctuation between them: *I live free I love life.*

GENERATING IDEAS AND TEXT A set of processes, such as freewriting, clus-

tering, and looping, that helps writers think of topics, examples, reasons, evidence, and other parts of a text.

GENRE A classification of text marked by and expected to have certain key features and to follow certain conventions of style and presentation. In the literary world, readers recognize such genres as the short story and novel (which are expected to have plots) and the poem (which may not have a plot but has other characteristics, such as rhythm); in academic and workplace settings, readers and writers focus on other genres, which also meet expectations in content, style, and appearance. Genres include abstracts, annotated bibliographies, application letters, arguments, ethnographies, evaluations, lab reports, literacy narratives, literary analyses, profiles, proposals, reflections, résumés, reports, and textual analyses.

HASTY GENERALIZATION A fallacy that reaches a conclusion based on insufficient or inappropriately qualified evidence.

HOME PAGE The introductory page of a Web site.

HYPERBOLE An over-the-top exaggeration: *I'll bet you a million bucks I'll get an A on my paper.*

IMAGERY Broadly defined, any sensory detail or evocation in a work; more narrowly, the use of figurative language to evoke a feeling, to call to mind an idea, or to describe an object.

IN MEDIAS RES In the middle of things (Latin); a device for introducing a subject in the middle of the action, rather than at the chronological beginning.

INDEFINITE PRONOUN A **pronoun**, such as *all, anyone, anything, everyone, everything, few, many, some,* and *something,* that functions like a **noun** but does not refer to or take the place of a specific noun.

INDEPENDENT CLAUSE A **clause**, containing a **subject** and a **verb,** that can stand alone as a sentence: *She sang. The world-famous soprano sang several popular arias.*

INDUCTION, INDUCTIVE REASONING In **argument,** a method of drawing a conclusion in which the writer asserts that a thing is true by generalizing from a particular observation (moving from the specific to the general): *All the squirrels I have seen are brown; therefore all squirrels are brown.* Note that this particular observation can be proved wrong, since others have observed white and black squirrels.

INFORMAL WRITING Writing not intended to be evaluated—sometimes not even read—by others. Informal writing is produced primarily to explore ideas or to communicate casually with friends and acquaintances. *See also* formal writing.

INQUIRY, WRITING AS A process for investigating a topic by posing questions, searching for multiple answers, and keeping an open mind.

INTERPRETATION The act of making sense of something or explaining what one thinks it means. Interpretation is the goal of writing a literary analysis or textual analysis.

IRONY A situation or statement characterized by a significant difference between what is expected or understood and what actually happens or is meant.

JOURNALISTIC NARRATIVE A genre of writing that prizes accuracy, objectivity, and balance, telling a story in the most impartial and efficient way possible. Key Features: answers the questions *who, what, where, when, why,* and *how,* usually in the first paragraph • simple writing style • most important facts placed first, details filled in later • includes quotations from people involved.

KEYWORD A term that a researcher inputs when searching databases and online search engines for information.

LAB REPORT A genre of writing that covers the process of conducting an experiment in a controlled setting. Key Features: explicit title • abstract • statement of purpose • methods •

results and discussion • **references** • **appendix** • appropriate format.

LAYOUT The way text is arranged on a page or screen—for example, in paragraphs, in lists, on charts, and with headings.

LETTER WRITING A process of generating ideas and text by going through the motions of writing a letter to someone to explain a topic.

LINK On a Web page, a URL, word, or image that, when clicked, opens a different page.

LINKING VERB A verb that expresses a state of being (*appear, be, feel, seem*).

LISTING A process for generating ideas and text by making lists while thinking about a topic, finding relationships among the notes, and arranging the notes as an outline (*see* **outlining**).

LITERACY NARRATIVE A genre of writing that tells about a writer's experience learning to read or write, or about the role of literacy or knowledge in the writer's life. Key Features: well-told story • vivid detail • indication of the narrative's significance.

LITERACY PORTFOLIO An organized collection of materials showing examples of one writer's progress as a reader and/or writer.

LITERARY ANALYSIS A genre of writing that argues for a particular interpretation of a literary text—most often fiction, poetry, or drama. *See also* analysis and **textual analysis**. Key Features: arguable thesis • careful attention to the language of the text • attention to patterns or themes • clear interpretation • MLA style.

LITERATURE (1) Literary works, including fiction, poetry, drama, and some nonfiction; (2) the body of written work produced in given field.

LOGICAL FALLACY *See* fallacy, logical.

LOGOS A mode of persuasion that appeals to logic; that is, an attempt by the writer or speaker to prove a point through logical reasoning. *See also* deduction and induction.

LOOPING A process for generating ideas and text in which a writer writes about a topic quickly for several minutes and then summarizes the most important or interesting idea in a sentence, which becomes the beginning of another round of writing and summarizing. The process continues until the writer finds an angle for a paper.

MEDIUM (PL. MEDIA) A means for communicating—for example, in print, with speech, or online. Texts consisting of words are said to use *verbal media* (or oral/aural), whereas photographs, films, and sculptures are examples of *visual media* (though some verbal texts include visual images, and some visual texts include words).

MEMOIR A **genre** of writing that focuses on something significant from the writer's past. Key Features: good story • vivid details • clear significance.

METAPHOR A figure of speech that makes a comparison without using the word *like* or *as*: *"All the world's a stage /And all the men and women merely players"* (William Shakespeare, *As You Like It* 2.7.138–39).

MLA STYLE A system of documenting sources used in the humanities and fine arts. MLA stands for the Modern Language Association. *See also* **documentation.**

MODAL A helping **verb** such as *can, could, may, might, must, should, will,* or *would* that indicates probability or necessity.

MODIFIER A word, **phrase**, or **clause** that describes or specifies something about another word, phrase, or clause (*a long, informative speech; an intellectually demanding presentation; the actors spoke in union*).

NARRATE, NARRATION, NARRATIVE A **strategy** for presenting information as a story, for telling what happened. It is a pattern most often associated with fiction, but it shows up in all kinds of writing. When used in an essay, a **report,** or another academic **genre,** a narrative must support a point, not merely tell an interesting story for its own sake. It must also present events in some kind of sequence and include only pertinent detail. Sometimes narrative serves as the **organizing** principle for a whole text. *See also* **literacy narrative.**

NARRATOR/SPEAKER The character or person who tells the story.

NOUN A word that refers to a person, place, animal, thing, or idea (*director, Stephen King, forest, Amazon River, tree frog, notebook, democracy*).

OBJECT A word or phrase that follows a **preposition** or receives the action of a **verb.** In the sentence *I handed him the mail that was on the table, him* is the indirect object and *mail* is the direct object of the verb *handed; table* is the object of the preposition *on.*

ORGANIZING Arranging parts of a text so that the text as a whole has **coherence.** The text may use one **strategy** throughout or may combine several strategies to create a suitable organization.

OUTLINING A **process** for generating ideas and text or for examining a text. An *informal outline* simply lists ideas and then numbers them in the order that they will appear; a *working outline* distinguishes support from main ideas by indenting the former; a *formal outline* is arranged as a series of headings and indented subheadings, each on a separate line, with letters and numerals indicating relative levels of importance.

PARAPHRASING Rewording a text in about the same number of words but without using the word order or sentence structure of the original. A paraphrase is generally used when you want to include the details of a passage but do not need to quote it word for word. Like a **quotation**, a paraphrase requires **documentation**.

PASSIVE VOICE A grammatical construction in which the object of an action becomes the grammatical subject: *The baseball was hit by the boy. See also* active voice.

PATHOS A mode of **persuasion** that appeals to the **audience's** emotions.

PERSONAL ESSAY A **genre** of writing that tells about a personal experience. Key Features: well-told story • vivid detail • indication of the narrative's significance.

PERSUADE, PERSUASION, PERSUASIVE In **argument**, to attempt to motivate your reader to behave in a specific way. Persuading may differ from **convincing** in that convincing is designed to get the reader to agree, while persuading is designed to get the reader to act.

PERSUASIVE ESSAY A **genre** of writing in which the writer presents an **argument** and attempts to **convince** the reader to agree and then **persuade** the reader to act upon its conclusions. Key Features: logical reasoning • necessary background • convincing **evidence**.

PHRASE A group of words that lacks a subject, a verb, or both.

PLAGIARISM Using another person's words, syntax, or ideas without giving appropriate credit and **documentation**. Plagiarism is a serious breach of ethics.

PLOT/STRUCTURE The arrangement of the action. Traditionally, a plot has five parts: exposition, rising action, climax, falling action, and dénouement.

POINT OF VIEW A position from which something is considered.

PORTFOLIO A collection of writing selected by a writer to show his or her work, sometimes including a statement assessing the work and explaining what it demonstrates.

POSITION A statement that asserts a belief or **claim**. In an **argument**, a position needs to be stated in a **thesis** or clearly implied, and requires support with **reasons** and **evidence**.

POST HOC, ERGO PROPTER HOC After this, therefore because of this (Latin); also called **faulty causality**. A fallacy of assuming that the first of two events causes the second.

PREDICATE In a sentence or **clause,** the verb and the words that tell more about the verb—its **complements, modifiers,** and **objects.** In the sentence *Mario forcefully stated his opinion,* the predicate is *forcefully stated his opinion.*

PREPOSITION A word or group of words that tells about the relationship of a **noun** or **pronoun** to another part of the sentence. Some common prepositions are *after, at, because of, before, in, on, on top of, under, until, with,* and *without.*

PRIMARY SOURCE A source such as a literary work, historical document, work of art, or performance that a researcher examines firsthand. Primary sources also include experiments and **field research.** In writing about the Revolutionary War, a researcher would likely consider the Declaration of Independence a primary source and a textbook's description of the writing of the document a **secondary source.**

PROCESS In writing, a series of actions that may include **generating ideas and text, drafting, revising, editing,** and **proofreading** a text. *See also* **process analysis.**

PROCESS ANALYSIS A **strategy** for telling how something is done or how to do something. Sometimes an analysis of a process serves as the **organizing** principle for a whole text.

PROFILE A **genre** of writing that presents an engaging portrait of a person, place, or event based on firsthand **field research.** Key Features: interesting subject • necessary background • distinctive angle • firsthand account • engaging details.

PRONOUN A word that takes the place of a **noun** or functions the way a noun does.

PROOFREADING The final **process** in writing, when a writer checks for correct spelling and punctuation as well as for page order, any missing copy, and the consistent use of typefaces and fonts. *See also* **editing, revising,** and **rewriting.**

PROPOSAL A **genre** of writing that argues for a solution to a problem or suggests some action. *See also* **topic proposal.** Key Features: well-defined problem • recommended solution • answers to anticipated questions • call to action • appropriate **tone.**

PURPOSE A writer's goal: for example, to explore, to express oneself, to entertain, to demonstrate learning, to inform, or to persuade. Purpose is one element of the **rhetorical situation.**

QUESTIONING A **process** of generating **ideas and text** about a topic—asking, for example, *what, who, when, where, how,* and *why,* or other questions.

Glossary

QUOTATION Someone's words repeated exactly as they were spoken or written. Quotation is most effective when the wording is worth repeating or makes a point so well that no rewording will do it justice, or when a writer wants to cite someone's exact words or quote someone whose opinions disagree with others. Quotations need to be acknowledged with **documentation**.

REASON A statement supporting a **claim** or **position**. A reason, in turn, requires its own support.

REFERENCES (APA) The list of sources at the end of a text prepared **APA style**.

REFLECTION A **genre** of writing that presents a writer's thoughtful, personal exploration of a subject. Key Features: topic intriguing to the writer • some kind of structure • specific details • speculative **tone**.

RELATIVE PRONOUN A **pronoun** such as *that, which, who, whoever, whom,* and *whomever* that connects a **subordinate clause** to a sentence: *The professor who gave the lecture is my adviser.*

REPORTING A **genre** of writing that presents information as objectively as possible to inform readers about a subject. *See also* **lab report, journalistic narrative**. Key Features: tightly focused topic • accurate, well-researched information • various writing strategies • clear **definitions** • appropriate **design**.

RESEARCH The practice of investigating sources, whether written, oral, or visual, to advance knowledge and to provide support for a writer's **claim**. *See also* **documented essay**.

RESPOND, RESPONDING (TO WRITING), RESPONSE A process of writing in which a reader responds to a writer's work by giving his or her thoughts about the writer's title, beginning, clarity of **thesis**, support and **documentation, organization, stance,** treatment of the **audience,** achievement of **purpose,** handling of the **genre,** ending, and other matters.

RÉSUMÉ A **genre** of writing that summarizes someone's academic and employment history, generally written to submit to potential employers. **Design** and word choice depend on whether a résumé is submitted as a print document or in an electronic or scannable form. Key Features: organization that suits goals and experience • succinctness • design that highlights key information (print) or that uses only one typeface (scannable).

REVISE, REVISION The **process** of making substantive changes, including additions and cuts, to a draft so that it contains all the necessary information in an appropriate organization. During revision, a writer generally moves from whole-text issues to details with the goals of sharpening the focus and strengthening the argument.

REWRITING A process of composing a new draft from another perspective—from a different **point of view**, **audience**, **stance**, **genre**, **medium**, sequence, and so on.

RHETORIC The "art, practice, and study of (ethical) human communication" (Andrea Lunsford). Rhetoric can but doesn't necessarily incorporate the art of **persuasion**; in the field of composition, the term is not typically used in the sense of insincere or inflated language.

RHETORICAL QUESTION A question asked merely for effect with no answer expected: *What were you thinking?*

RHETORICAL SITUATION The context within which writing or other communication takes place, including **purpose**, **audience**, **genre**, **stance**, and **media/design**.

RISING ACTION The second of the five parts of **plot** structure, in which events complicate the situation that existed at the beginning of a work, intensifying the **conflict** or introducing new conflict.

ROGERIAN ARGUMENT A method of argument, introduced by psychologist Carl Rogers, based on finding common ground on all sides of an issue before stating one's own **position**.

SATIRE A **genre** of writing in which the writer holds up human failings to ridicule and censure. Key Features: **irony** • sarcasm • **purpose** of improving the reader.

SECONDARY SOURCE An **analysis** or interpretation of a **primary source**. In writing about the Revolutionary War, a researcher would likely consider the Declaration of Independence a **primary source** and a textbook's description of writing of the document a secondary source.

SETTING The time and place of the action in a piece of writing.

SIGNAL PHRASE A phrase used to attribute **quoted, paraphrased,** or **summarized** material to a source, as in *she said* or *he claimed.*

SIMILE A figure of speech that compares two items using *like* or *as*: *"Still we live meanly, like ants"* (Henry David Thoreau, *Walden*), *"The Wind begun to knead the Grass—/As Women do a Dough—"* (Emily Dickinson).

SLIPPERY SLOPE A **fallacy** that asserts, without **evidence**, that one event will lead to a series of other events that will culminate in a cataclysm.

SPEAKER The person, not necessarily the author, who is the **voice** of a piece of writing.

STANCE A writer's or speaker's attitude toward his or her subject as conveyed through the **tone** and word choice.

STRATEGY A pattern for organizing text to analyze cause and effect, classify and divide, compare and contrast, define, describe, explain a process, narrate, and so on.

STEREOTYPE A characterization based on the conscious or unconscious assumption that a particular aspect—such as gender, age, ethnic or national identity, religion, occupation, and marital status—is predictably accompanied by certain character traits, actions, even values.

STREAM OF CONSCIOUSNESS A method of writing in which the writer conveys the thoughts and feelings of the speaker or a character through a continuous flow of conscious experience; an interior monologue.

STYLE (1) In writing, the arrangement of sentences, phrases, words, and punctuation to achieve a desired effect; (2) the rules of capitalization, punctuation, and so on recommended for the documentation of a source.

SUBJECT A word or word group, usually including at least one noun or pronoun plus its modifiers, that tells who or what a sentence or clause is about. In the sentence *An increasingly frustrated group of commuters waited for the late bus*, the subject is *An increasingly frustrated group of commuters*.

SUBORDINATE CLAUSE A clause, containing a subject and a verb, that contains a subordinating word and therefore cannot stand alone as a sentence: *He wheezes when he exercises. My roommate, who was a physics major, tutors high school students in science.*

SUMMARY A condensation of a text into a briefer but still faithful version in lieu of a paraphrase or a quotation.

SUMMARY-RESPONSE A genre of writing in which the writer or speaker presents both a summary of a text or texts and responds to the text. Key Features: brief summary of the text • highlights of major points of the text • evaluation of the text.

SYMBOL A person, place, thing, event, or pattern in a literary work that designates itself and at the same time figuratively represents or "stands for" something else. Often the thing or idea represented is more abstract or general; the symbol, more concrete and particular.

SYNTHESIZING IDEAS A way of generating new information or supporting a new perspective by bringing together ideas and information from two or more sources.

TEXTUAL ANALYSIS A genre of writing in which a writer looks at what a text says and how it says it. *See also* analysis and literary analysis. Key Features:

summary of the text • attention to context • clear **interpretation** • reasonable support for your conclusions.

THEME (1) The central or dominant idea or concern of a work; (2) the statement a poem makes about its subject.

THESIS A **claim** or statement of a writer's **position** or main point.

TONE A writer's or speaker's attitude toward his or her readers and subject. A writer's tone reflects his or her **stance** and may be formal or informal, optimistic or pessimistic, playful, ironic, and so on.

TOPIC The subject of a piece of writing; what a text is about.

TOPIC PROPOSAL A statement of intent to examine a topic; also called a proposal **abstract.** Some instructors require a topic proposal in order to assess the feasibility of the writing project that a student has in mind. Key Features: concise discussion of the subject • clear statement of the intended focus • rationale for choosing the subject • mention of resources.

TOPIC SENTENCE A sentence, usually the first in a paragraph, that encapsulates what that paragraph is about. The topic sentence often includes a **claim** that will be supported in the paragraph.

TOULMIN ARGUMENT A six-part method of analyzing the structure of **arguments** formulated by British philosopher Stephen Toulmin. The elements of this model include the **claim,** the grounds, the warrant, the backing, the qualifier, and the rebuttal.

TRANSITIONS Words or **phrases** used to make clear the connection between ideas and text.

VANTAGE POINT The position or standpoint from which a writer **describes** something.

VERB A word or a group of words that conveys an action (*dance, determine, observe*) or a state of being (*be, seem*) and is an essential element of a sentence or **clause.**

VOICE The acknowledged or unacknowledged source of a piece of writing's words; the speaker; the "person" telling the story.

WORKS-CITED LIST (MLA) At the end of a researched text prepared **MLA style,** the list of all the sources cited in the text, with full bibliographic information.

STUDY QUESTIONS

1. Why was this study of media undertaken? Explain why Niven chose unemployment as his test case. What were Niven's conclusions?

2. At some point in your life, a teacher probably has instructed you to avoid passive VOICE (for example, "papers were chosen"). Locate some instances of passive voice in this selection. Why do you think Niven chose to use it? Do you find it effective?

3. EVALUATE the sources Niven cites. What kinds does he use, and how effective are they? How do they contribute to Niven's study?

4. Using the subheadings in the essay as your guide, evaluate the structure of this essay. What pattern does it follow? What other kinds of essays or RESEARCH follow this pattern?

5. *For Writing.* Consider how Niven's hypothesis relates to his results and conclusion sections. Then, using either the same test case that Niven uses or an equally applicable one, such as health care, create a hypothesis about how both liberal and conservative media represent it. Follow the media on TV, in print, and online for two weeks to test your hypothesis. Then, in an essay, ANALYZE your findings.